THE BODY

SUNY Series in Buddhist Studies
Kenneth K. Inada, Editor

THE BODY

Toward an Eastern Mind-Body Theory

YUASA Yasuo

edited by
Thomas P. Kasulis

translated by
NAGATOMO Shigenori
Thomas P. Kasulis

STATE UNIVERSITY OF NEW YORK PRESS

PUBLISHED BY
STATE UNIVERSITY OF NEW YORK PRESS, ALBANY

© 1987 STATE UNIVERSITY OF NEW YORK

ALL RIGHTS RESERVED

PRINTED IN THE UNITED STATES OF AMERICA

FOR INFORMATION, ADDRESS STATE UNIVERSITY OF NEW YORK
PRESS, STATE UNIVERSITY PLAZA, ALBANY, N.Y., 12246

Library of Congress Cataloging-in-Publication Data

Yuasa, Yasuo.
    The body: toward an Eastern mind-body theory.

    (SUNY series in Buddhist studies)
    Translation of: Shintai.
    Includes index.
    1. Mind and body.   2. Body, Human (Philosophy)
3. Philosophy, Japanese.   I. Kasulis, T. P.,
1948–   . II. Title. III. Series. [DNLM:
1. Philosophy. 2. Psychophysiology.   BF 168 Y94s]
BD450.Y8213   1987   128'.2   86-22994
ISBN 0-88706-469-8
ISBN 0-88706-468-X (pbk.)

10 9 8 7 6 5 4 3 2 1

CONTENTS

EDITOR'S INTRODUCTION

Human understanding uses categories and analysis. To understand a phenomenon, we superimpose a conceptual grid by which we relate it to the known and define what must be investigated further. But the grid itself always conceals a bit of reality. When the study's focal point is not hidden by the lines of the grid, there is generally no problem, but when that obfuscation does occur, there is a critical blindspot. The more intently we look for the answer in terms of the grid, the more impossible the task becomes. In such instances the only solution is to readjust the grid, to alter the categories through which we understand the world and our experience. Such an alteration may eventually involve a full-scale reorientation in our ways of knowing.

In this book, Professor Yuasa suggests such a reorientation in our understanding of the body. Yuasa is fully at home with Western methodologies. Yet, as an astute scholar of Japanese philosophy, he discovered a locus of ideas in modern Japanese thought that cannot be readily plotted within the ordinary Western parameters. He finally isolated the factor: modern Japanese thinkers held a view of the body incommensurate with Western philosophical categories. But what exactly was this view and why could the Western concepts not articulate it? These questions took Yuasa deeper into the Japanese, and eventually other Asian, traditions.

His studies revealed that Asian traditions typically do not sharply separate the mind from the body. Although the mind and body may be conceptually distinguishable from some perspectives, they are not assumed to be ontologically distinct. This is an interesting, but not in itself remarkable, claim. One could argue, for example, that even Spinoza, with his theory about the two modes of a single substance, would be sympathetic to such a thesis.

Yuasa's next discovery, however, is not so easily ingested into the Western tradition: Eastern philosophies generally treat mind-body unity as an *achievement*, rather than an essential relation. This insight relates a number of formerly disconnected observations about Asian culture. First, it is clearer why meditation and philosophical insight are inseparable in the Eastern traditions: wisdom must be physically as well as intellectually developed. Truth is not only a way of thinking about the world; it is a mode of being in the world, part of which includes one's own bodily existence. Thus, meditation and thinking are not to be separated.

Second, if the unity of mind and body (or "body-mind" in the Japanese idiom) is achieved, insights can be tested by deeds. This point explains why *satori* in Zen Buddhism is verified by action rather than by asserted propositions. Furthermore, this achieved unity accounts for the immediacy and physicality in Zen descriptions of enlightenment: the Zen Buddhist's goal is said to be knowing the truth as one knows the water to be cold when one drinks it. That is, knowledge of the truth is a psychophysical awareness beyond mere intellection.

Third, through Yuasa's discovery, we can better grasp the nondualism central to so many Asian traditions. In conceiving an integration of body and mind, the various Eastern philosophies undercut such Western dichotomies as spirit-matter, subjectivity–objectivity, and theory–praxis. The Asian philosophers are not merely posing an alternative metaphysics. In fact, they are not doing metaphysics at all in the traditional Western sense. Instead, their task is what Yuasa, following C. G. Jung, calls *metapsychics,* an approach examined in detail by this book.

Before evaluating the philosophical significance of the Eastern claims for achieving mind-body unity, we must clarify its nature. After all, the Western tradition, especially since Descartes, has generally denied the unity of body and mind. Where such a unity is envisioned, it has typically been thought to occur via an essential, substantial, unchanging link (such as the pineal gland, the soul, or even the brain), not via the evolution of the mind-body system itself. It is natural, therefore, to demand a more explicit account of this phenomenon than we find in classical Japanese texts.

Yuasa accepts this challenge and poses a description in terms of three major Western systems: existential phenomenology, psychoanalysis, and neurophysiology. In each case, he demonstrates that the Western disciplines have approached the threshold of recognizing the body-mind unity found in Eastern thought. They always stop short, however, because their respective methodologies limit them to investigating only the universal or normal state of affairs. They assume, that is, that the connection between the mind and body must be constant (not developed) and universal (not variable among different people). Since they do not consider exceptional personal achievements, the body-mind unity remains for them a theoretical possibility rather than a state actualized by exemplary individuals such as religious and artistic masters.

It is as if the grid of Western thought has a place for the concept of an achieved body-mind unity, but that place is hidden behind the crosshatching of the Western concepts. The Western tradition can recognize the possibility, but its concepts intersect so that a blindspot occurs precisely where the body-mind unity can be found—in the enlightened state achieved through years of spiritual and physical cultivation. Therefore, at present at least, we cannot focus sharply on the phenomenon itself within our Western frameworks; we can only approach it. To see it clearly, we have to reorient the grids by which we have traditionally understood the world. In this attempt, we encounter the problematics, daring, and profundity of Yuasa's book.

Let us briefly restate the significance of this situation in terms of comparative philosophy. In Japanese thought, Yuasa has discovered a concept, what we are calling "achieved body-mind unity," for which he has found no exact Western correlate. Still, Yuasa's careful study of Western phenomenology, psychoanalysis, and neurophysiology reveals no inherent logical objection to such an idea. In fact, these three disciplines hint that such a unity is theoretically possible. Why, then, has the Western tradition not formally recognized this possibility?

The main thrust of Western intellectual history has avoided the discussion of the perfected human being. The focus has been rather on the universal, not the exceptional. Yuasa finds today's Western thinkers more open to discussing the exceptional than were their predecessors, but, oddly, they examine mainly the negative side, that of the abnormal or diseased. Modern Western neurophysiology and psychoanalysis have opened the door to the extraordinary in human life, but only, as it were, the back door of the subnormal instead of the front door of the supernormal.

A similar situation applies to Western philosophical investigations. In contemporary existentialism's recognition of embodiment, authenticity, the unity of thought and action, and the ideal of freedom, one finds at least the theoretical framework for such a phenomenon as achieved body-mind unity, but still the emphasis falls on the universal human condition instead of on the perfected state. Existentialism emphasizes, for example, two choices: we may either be authentic to our situation, recognizing our inherent freedom, or we may be immersed in bad faith, denying what we are. Little discussion is offered, however, of the process by which we can gradually change what we existentially are by opening new options previously unavailable to us. (Yuasa does not discuss the speech act and performative theories of contemporary language philosophy, but these theories have a similar slant. They recognize the incarnate, practical aspect of language, but their focus is predominantly and self-consciously on *ordinary* language, those everyday speech acts we all use, instead of on the exceptional uses achieved by poets and religious figures.)

Yuasa's treatment of comparative philosophy is one of his greatest contributions. His analysis respects the fundamental divergence between traditional Eastern and Western thought, yet simultaneously points the way to meaningful dialogue. In brief, what most distinguishes Eastern from Western mind-body theories is a methodological decision as to which phenomena should be analyzed. For the modern Western tradition, a mind-body theory is primarily concerned with the empirically observable correlations between mental and somatic phenomena. In the Japanese tradition, however, the mind-body theories generally focus on how a disciplined practice allows one to attain body-mind unity. So in studying the Western mind-body problem, it is appropriate to investigate the act of raising one's arm, for example. What is the relation between mental intention and the somatic movement? In the Japanese theories, however, learning to hit a baseball would be a more appropriate example. What are the relationships among the intellectual *theory* of the swing, the somatic *practice* of the swing, and the integrated *achievement* of the skill? In this contrast, we again see the difference between concentrating on an intrinsic mind-body connection versus an acquired mind-body unity.

Given this difference in perspective, it is not surprising that Western mind-body theories typically discuss the will, for example, asking whether it is free or determined, mental or somatic. In Eastern thought, on the other hand, the will is seldom analyzed. Conversely, Eastern mind-body theories frequently discuss how creativity is expressed within a standardized style or form, whereas Western philosophers believe such issues fall outside the domain of the mind-body problem. So aesthetics is seldom part of the West's approach to mind-body issues.

This difference does not imply that Western and Eastern mind-body theories are unrelated, however. It is tempting for Western philosophers to ignore the Eastern traditions on the grounds that they are interested in different issues. But from a more balanced standpoint, these presuppositional and methodological disparities raise the question of complementarity. To have an adequate mind-body theory, should one not take into account *all* the phenomena, those of traditional interest in either East or West? If we seek the full philosophical significance of the mind and body, should we not investigate both the relation between intention and movement as well as the connections among the theory, practice, and achievement of a skill? If there is complementarity, of course, there must be some continuity between the Eastern and Western concerns. Yuasa's most controversial and thought-provoking hypothesis is that the connection might be understood through his distinction between the "bright" and "dark" consciousnesses.

Yuasa suggests consciousness is double-layered. The surface is called *"bright"* because it is capable of self-conscious awareness. It is, in fact, the layer identified by Descartes' *cogito*, the "I think." This is the realm of thought and, in itself, can be abstractly imagined (as Descartes did) to be disembodied. This bright consciousness has been the object of most modern Western philosophy of mind. Concretely, however, it does not stand on its own. It is only the surface of something deeper, something not itself capable of bright self-consciousness. Yuasa calls this layer the *"dark"* consciousness. Psychoanaltically, it resembles the unconscious in some ways. Neurophysiologically, it parallels, in part, the functions of the autonomic nervous system. Phenomenologically, it approximates the lived body examined by Merleau-Ponty and Bergson in their discussions of the sensory-motor circuits. In Buddhist terms, it is related to what is called "no-mind." In a more precise sense, however, it is none of these. It is rather their common ground, a single aspect of consciousness viewed from various perspectives.

To appreciate the point of Yuasa's distinction, we may consider the case of a motorist whose car goes into an unanticipated but controlled swerve to avoid hitting a dog. If asked later how she managed to avoid running over the animal, the driver might reply that she "simply reacted." How did she know when and how to get out of the way, to undertake the complicated maneuver involving steering, braking, and timing? In a sense, the act was an *impulse*, the triggering of a conditioned response. That is, the specific rationale of what had to be done and how to do it was dark; it was not something of which the driver was self-conscious.

This interpretation resembles a depth psychological account, but only to a certain extent. The discussion of impulse and dark rationale is reminiscent of the psychoanalytic discussions of the unconscious, yet the impulse to steer out of the dog's path is not an abnormal, libidinous compulsion to behave in an irrational manner. Rather, the motorist's impulse is a *learned* response, the result of months of disciplined training and years of practical experience. The driver's response is conditioned, but not passively by external social factors. Rather, years ago the driver self-consciously decided to condition herself. At some earlier point in her life, the driver had to filter through the bright consciousness all the knowledge used spontaneously by the dark consciousness: knowing how animals might behave along country roads, how to find the brake, how much pressure to use in stopping, and how to steer the car in a skid so as not to lose control. In other words, knowledge in the bright consciousness had to be internalized through praxis into the dark consciousness. The bright consciousness is reflective; it takes time to deliberate. The dark consciousness, on the other hand, is spontaneous and impulsive. In the split second when the evasive maneuver was executed, there was no time to think of alternatives. There was only the purely responsive act. In a significant sense, the *body*, not the mind, decided the action.

But how does one train the dark consciousness to make the right "decisions?" The mechanism is complex, and Yuasa would be the first to admit the issue requires further study. In this book, he limits himself to a discussion of (mainly Japanese) Buddhist cultivation techniques, Indian yogic disciplines, and the training of artists in Japanese poetry and drama. These investigations give us promising leads, however. The initial step in all these disciplines is that the mind (the bright consciousness) deliberately places the body into a special form or posture. Whether learning a golf swing or learning to sit in meditation, the beginning phase is awkward. The body is uncooperative or inert and one feels, we say, "self-conscious." The self-conscious bright consciousness is imposing its form on the dark consciousness. Gradually, though, the posture becomes natural or second nature. It is *second* nature because the mind has entered into the dark consciousness and given it a form; it is an acquired naturalness. Once the transformation takes place, however, there is no further need for the self-reflective bright consciousness and one can act creatively and responsively without deliberation.

Western philosophers have taken account of this connection between the bright and dark consciousness. Even a philosopher as classically Western as Aristotle recognized the philosophical importance of habit. Aristotle maintained that the mere study of moral principles would never produce a moral person. True mortality is achieved only through praxis, the incarnate practice of moral decision making in order to establish proper habits. In effect, one consciously fits one's behavior into a form until that form becomes second nature. By such a means we develop moral character. The key difference between Aristotle and the Eastern traditions discussed by Yuasa is that Aristotle restricted the importance of habit to "practical" sciences like ethics. The Eastern traditions, on the other hand, generally consider psychophysical habits to be elements not only in moral action but also in cognitive wisdom. In other words, for those Eastern philosophies, all instances of knowing are both practical and theoretical.

In short, enlightenment involves the free movement between the bright and dark consciousness. Such a movement also occurs in the psychotic, but the polarity is, as it were, reversed; in the subnormal state, the dark consciousness rises up to direct the bright consciousness. In the enlightened master or consummate artist, however, the bright consciousness has put the dark consciousness into a form or posture, preparing it to respond in an approved, yet autonomous, manner.

For the bright consciounsess to enter the dark, a psychophysical path is needed. The explanation of this mechanism must itself have a psychophysical perspective. There is something futile in the Western philosopher's attempt to unravel the relationship between the mind and body in a strictly conceptual, that is, mental fashion. Conversely, it is equally futile to try to analyze the relationship on simply physiological grounds as if the mind-body connection were the same in both a living person and a corpse. Such unilateral approaches can only produce overly simplified reductionisms. In this book, meditation is examined as a traditional Eastern technique for integrating the physiological and intellectual. As Yuasa insightfully observes, most contemplative traditions begin with a mindfulness, or even control, of breathing. Respiration is one physiological function that can be controlled willfully or allowed to function through the autonomic nervous system. Hence, the meditation on breathing is a direct route by which the bright consciounsess can contact the dark consciousness. Once the route has been opened, further possibilities of interaction develop. According to Yuasa's analysis, this is the core of Eastern mind-body theories.

This Introduction began with the suggestion that Yuasa hopes to reorient the conceptual categories within which we usually understand the body. The specific reorientation will probably vary with the reader's training, interests, and experience. Still, as a cue to help readers think through the implications of Yuasa's thesis, I can list a few points found to be most thought-provoking from my own perspective.

THE ROLE OF THE BODY IN RELIGIOUS PRACTICE

Much recent philosphical discussion about religion has focused upon religious belief as a disposition to act or think in certain ways under specified circumstances. This interpretation is highly illuminating. There is no doubt that a religious person often views the world and behaves differently from one who is nonreligious. An intriguing question arises from this discussion, however, that is often ignored. Namely, how does the religious person come to have those distinctive dispositions? Perhaps this issue has been so little studied because it seems to take us out of philosophy into mysticism (religious beliefs as based in ineffable encounters with the sacred), or pietistic devotion (religious beliefs as originating in revealed scriptures), or behavioral conditioning (religious beliefs as transmitted from one's parents). Yuasa's analysis opens a more complex and philosophically interesting alternative, however.

Religious beliefs are embodied through religious practices. In fact, the practices may be said to precede the belief. That is, one becomes a religious Jew, for example, by participating in Jewish religious life. It is not that one practices Judaism only after becoming religious. Philosophers and theologians sometimes overlook this basic phenomenological fact. With all their emphasis on belief and knowledge, it is easy for them to forget that practice precedes, or at least accompanies, them both. It may seem that this position leads to behaviorism: one believes in God, for instance, because one is conditioned to do so. There is some truth in this, but the key point is that the conditioning comes from *oneself*. It is more a sensitivity than a conditioning in any usual sense of the word.

Religious sensitivity, like the appreciation of music or art, for example, is a *cultivated* mode of relating to the world. Thus, the behaviorist is not wrong in saying that if one is raised in a nonreligious environment, one is less likely to be religious as an adult. But the same would hold true for an aesthetic appreciation, as in the love of ballet; continued and prolonged exposure deepens one's awareness and appreciation. Religiousness is not merely a cerebral, intellectual function; it also involves a foundation in the dark consciousness. Again, this dark consciousness is not the Freudian unconscious. For Yuasa, religiousness is not the sublimation of instinctual, libidinous drives, but a creative expression achieved through the disciplined internalizing of specific forms and postures of the religious tradition. In other words, the conviction behind religious belief is a psychophysical achievement attained through performing the proper religious forms. A person with little exposure to music—one who has not listened to it, played it, become involved with it—cannot insightfully evaluate a performance of Beethoven's Fifth Symphony. Analogously, religiousness is acquired through years of psychophysical exposure and practice. One must be an insider to the religious life in order to grasp its meaning. Religious sensitivity, like artistic sensitivity, is rooted in an acquired expert knowledge.

PSYCHOSOMATIC HEALING

Folk medicine generally recognizes but cannot explain the complex of relationships between the mind and body. Modern Western medicine, on the other hand, is grounded in physiology, knowledge originally arising from the dissection of corpses, the vivisection of animals, and surgery on anesthetized human beings. In these three contexts, there is no functional human consciousness, so traditional physiology teaches little about the living mind-body relationship. In the past few decades, however, Western science has developed the means to observe physiological changes correlated with unimpaired mental activity. We can for the first time study the living mind-body via scientific instrumentation. Even in this research, though, the Western methodological prejudice toward the normal and universal has often prevented any consideration of *achieved* mind-body relationships. Most recently, however, researchers have begun to take seriously the claims of yogins, Zen Masters, and other spiritually developed individuals. The preliminary evidence indicates these individuals can indeed consciously control physiological functions formerly thought to be strictly autonomic: pulse rate, blood pressure, and the frequency of brain waves, for example.

This discovery has not yet fully penetrated the working assumptions of medical researchers, however. There are still many scientists (and philosophers) who are undertaking the Cartesian project of trying to locate the mind in specific physiological processes. It has not yet occurred to these scientists that, if the preliminary studies of the spiritual masters are valid, one must accept the fact that the physical functions of the mind differ among the average person, the mentally disturbed, and the master of spiritual discipline. In other words, the mind-body relation is not a simple given. It is a complex, changing connection that must always be understood in terms of a specific psychophysical context. If this assumption is correct, then any illness, any disruption in the normal psychophysical state, may be treated through a variety of avenues.

Actually, our contemporary situation reflects this pluralism. On television, we may watch a faith healer cure physical ailment · right after seeing a "Nova" program about the biochemical treatment of psychological disorders. Other treatments, like biofeedback, relaxation response, and yogic breathing, combine psychological and physiological factors.

What is Yuasa's contribution to our understanding of these phenomena? He argues that the integration of mind and body is only partial in the average human being. Full integration is the result of prolonged, assiduous cultivation. This implies that there are degrees of mind-body integration attainable by each person in his or her particular context. Hence, some patients may be able to cure their ulcers with daily meditation exercises, whereas others may need drugs or an operation, for example. Healing and prognosis must be viewed within the broadest psychosomatic horizon: physicians must ask what healing processes are available to each patient in his or her own context.

More practicing physicians are at least peripherally aware of these aspects of disease and prognosis, but as an institution, medical science is more conservative. The American Heart Association, for example, endorses daily exercise and abstention from smoking. Why does it not also endorse daily meditation, relaxation exercises, or even prayer? Perhaps it does not want to advocate any "religious" practice and to be accused of spiritual proselytizing. By avoiding such endorsements, however, health organizations may be discouraging the use of viable techniques for prophylaxis and cure. Yuasa advocates the empirical scrutiny of spiritual disciplines. Some research has begun, of course; if it is carried out in a more comprehensive manner, the gap between Eastern and Western forms of healing may be narrowed, perhaps so much that such institutional fears of criticism will no longer obstruct the study and utilization of all possible forms of psychosomatic healing.

FREEDOM AND CONDITIONING

As noted already, the Western philosophical issue of free will and determinism is seldom discussed by Japanese philosophers, and Yuasa's book is no exception. Yet, by the very fact that Yuasa is concerned with self-cultivation, the nature of conditioning is examined from a distinctively Asian perspective. Specifically, Yuasa is interested in the process by which one conditions onself to achieve spiritual freedom and aesthetic creativity. Again, we find the Japanese emphasis on *achieving* freedom, rather than the Western focus on the universal *presence* of freedom or determinism. That is, Yuasa's question is not about whether human beings are intrinsically free, but about how freedom can be psychophysically attained.

A fact of human behavior is that the best route to overcoming a conditioned response is through reconditioning. Thus, if I wish to cut down on smoking and habitually smoke after breakfast, I can break the habit by establishing a new habit, perhaps sucking on a lollipop every day immediately after the morning meal. At first, this may seem strictly behavioristic and outside the domain of human freedom, but actually the point is that one is free to change habits. Our spontaneous, everyday habits are generally not self-consciously executed. They are, in the sense of the term used above, impulsive; that is, they arise from the dark consciousness. Yet, the actions, once completed, can become the object of the bright consciousness's reflection. Furthermore, the bright consciousness can deliberately establish a behavioral form or mode that can eventually become second nature. At this point, the actions will no longer be self-conscious, but they will fit the pattern originally established by self-consciousness (the bright consciousness).

Extrapolating from Yuasa's description, we may say that there are actions that are not premeditated, but still part of a self-consciously chosen behavioral pattern. By this interpretation, we are responsible for those spontaneous actions that typify our standard mode of being in the world. Consider, for example, the case of a drunk driver who accidentally kills a pedestrian. Certainly, the motorist is responsible for the death, although the act does not qualify technically as murder because the driver was partially incapacitated. It was an act of negligence, not premeditation.

The line of thought we have just been developing requires further analysis of this case, however. Did the motorist often drive while intoxicated? Was he or she ever ticketed for the offense and brought to court? In other words, it is relevant to know whether the motorist had established a habit of drunk driving, had had the opportunity to reflect on that pattern of behavior with its possible consequences, and had made no (bright) conscious attempt to alter that (dark conscious) habit. Thus, the habitual, reflectively self-conscious drunk driver must be distinguished from the light drinker who, perhaps for the first time in his or her life, celebrated overzealously and drove home while intoxicated. The first driver would be more responsible for the consequences of the accident insofar as he or she recognized, yet made no efforts to change, a pattern of drunken driving.

This view of responsibility is similar to the scholastic notion of the near occasion of sin. According to this doctrine, one is morally responsible not only for sins, but also for allowing oneself to enter situations in which one has habitually fallen into sin in the past. Like many of the other notions arising from the medieval monastic traditions, this concept is rich in psychological insight. Consider, for example, a rapist who consciously knows that acts of voyeurism lead him to a point of excitement in which he loses self-conscious control of his behavior. The bright consciousness can, let us suppose, choose whether to perform the act of voyeurism, however. Often we might think that at the moment of the actual rape, the psychologically disturbed person may not be fully responsible for his actions since he cannot at that point distinguish right from wrong. Our new interpretation, however, would argue that he is still responsible for his actions insofar as he consciously chose, and was morally responsible for, the preceding act of voyeurism, knowing (in the bright consciousness) that in the past such activity had led him to perform uncontrollable (dark conscious) acts of rape. Such an interpretation of moral, and perhaps legal, responsibility could be extended to adjudicate cases of temporary insanity as well. One may not be fully responsible for those actions driven by uncontrollable, morally disorienting rage, but certainly one *is* responsible for knowing one's quick temper and for not working on eliminating that weakness of character.

Yuasa's analysis implies that many, perhaps most, of our actions are not self-consciously willed at the time performed. Certainly, Hank Aaron's swinging at a baseball is not a self-conscious activity at the moment of the swing. Still, we hold him responsible for his performance, whether he strikes out or hits a home run. Why? Because he has devoted years of conscious cultivation to developing his swing. In a similar way, it can be argued, we are responsible for actions arising out of patterns of behavior we have self-consciously recognized and either cultivated or did not countercondition.

CROSS-CULTURAL PHILOSOPHICAL DIALOGUE

Truth knows neither geographical nor national boundaries. So the pursuit of wisdom cannot afford to be provincial. In some ways, the Japanese are the epitome of comparative philosophers. Modern Japanese intellectuals generally know more about the full range of Asian philosophies than do their colleagues on the Asian mainland. For example, Indian philosophers rarely discuss Chinese thought; the Chinese seldom discuss Indian, especially non-Buddhist, thought. But the Japanese deeply appreciate the mainland traditions so influential in their own intellectual history, and study all great Asian traditions in an attempt to know their own philosophical roots. Similarly, many Japanese intellectuals know quite well the major works of Western philosophy, especially those of the modern Continental tradition. Some Japanese philosophy departments are so thoroughly Western in orientation, in fact, that they seem to be branches of European departments. Furthermore, living in one of the most advanced technological nations of the world, the Japanese philosopher is generally as knowledgeable about scientific developments as are European or American philosophers. In short, Japan is at the crossroads of many great intellectual traditions and movements.

It is not surprising, then, that Yuasa refers to a broad range of disciplines: modern Japanese philosophy, Buddhist history and doctrine, Hindu meditation, traditional Japanese aesthetics, neurophysiology, and phenomenology. In fact, the superficial reader might accuse Yuasa of simple eclecticism. A more careful reading reveals, however, that Yuasa's focus is not only on what these various disciplines have said about the body, but also on how they approach the topic. That is, Yuasa is at least as much interested in methodology as in content. Thus, even if one disagrees with some point in Yuasa's interpretation of Bergson, or if one finds that some of Yuasa's neurological information is outdated, the book's main thesis may still stand. That is, the thrust of Yuasa's argument depends not so much on the individual facts he accumulates, as it does on the interrelations and contrasts of the various intellectual traditions and disciplines. To make this clearer, we now attempt to state the main thesis of the book in a few sentences.

Different academic disciplines and cultural traditions have recognized, under various names, the underlying interaction between mind and body. The distinct methodological perspectives have isolated different aspects of this phenomenon. One aspect that traditionally has been emphasized in several Eastern traditions, although often overlooked in the West, is that the degree of integration between mind and body is variable and can be developed through various methods of personal cultivation. Although such a possibility is not explicitly denied in most modern scholarly disciplines, the explicit recognition of this fact would have a positive effect on future research.

An attractive feature of Yuasa's enterprise is its respect of both Eastern and Western thought, as well as its interdisciplinary understanding. It does not insist that one tradition or discipline is simply right and another wrong. Where there is apparent disagreement, Yuasa often points out that it is only a case of misunderstanding—a common term is being used to refer to different phenomena or the same phenomenon is being viewed from a different perspective. As a general principle, this approach is not easily validated, yet Yuasa has made a good case in this book for one such instance: acquired body-mind unity. In this study, Yuasa has shown that there is at least one point of contact between the world of the Zen Buddhist and the physiologist, the world of the Nō actor and the psychoanalyst, the world of the acupuncturist and the phenomenologist. In short, Yuasa has given us a starting place for an East–West dialogue and the promise of finding further connections in the future. As the crossroads of the world's great intellectual traditions, Japan foreshadows the future of all societies. Through the boldness of his project, Yuasa has found a vantage point from which one can see, in some preliminary way, the underlying pattern in an apparently chaotic confrontation of modes of thought.

Although short, this book is not easy. The thoughtful reader will be challenged at every turn in the argument. Much of the material will necessarily be outside the reader's expertise, but the best advice is to press on. The key to the book is the overall framework; the details can be mulled over later. In the final analysis, the reader will most appreciate not what Yuasa specifically said, but how Yuasa's provoking analysis has opened new vistas within one's own thinking. In the metaphor used at the opening of this Introduction, one will especially appreciate the way Yuasa subtly leads us to reorient our understanding of the body.

Finally, a brief comment on the translation and editing is in order. The translators regret that the clarity and smoothness of the original Japanese text may not always be perfectly conveyed in our English. Our goal, of course, was integration of readability and accuracy. Since Japanese syntax, semantics, and style differ so much from English, however, some compromises were inevitable. In making these compromises, two criteria were followed. Where the original passage is philosophically central to the argument, the translation tends to be more literal. Where the passage concerns factual background for the main thesis, the translation is often freer. In addition, the editor used his prerogative to modify or abridge a small number of technical passages related to Asian studies that would be of interest to only a very few Western readers and might seem unnecessarily cumbersome to others in following the flow of Yuasa's argument.

Another difficulty in translating a Japanese philosophical text into English is less easily handled. The problem is one of comparative rhetoric. Quite simply, there are stylistic differences in how philosophical arguments tend to be presented in Japan and in the West. In both cases, of course, an argument stands or falls on its logical validity and strength of supporting evidence. The presentation, however, can be quite different, so much so that the Western reader may find the Japanese argument disconcerting. In the West, we tend to present our philosophical arguments so that the logical skeleton is as explicit as possible: an initial statement of thesis, the precise enumeration of the key premises, the marshalling of supporting evidence for each premise, and finally the statement of conclusions. We know, of course, that cogitation is initially never this clear-cut, but we expect the results of philosophical thought to be presented in this way when it is finally made public. We may note, for example, that although our philosophical tradition may have started with the dialogue as model, that format has become increasing rare. We find it too indefinite and ambiguous. We are suspicious of the argument that does not lay all its cards on the table right from the outset.

To those with Japanese sensitivity, on the other hand, something like the geometric presentation in Spinoza or the logically nested statements in Wittgenstein's *Tractatus* seems bizarre and equally suspicious. For the Japanese, it seems the conclusions are foregone, that the cards are laid out but the deck is stacked. The Japanese want to see more of the process of thinking along with its product. Thought does not go straight to its goal; it circumambulates a bit, takes detours, runs into dead-ends. And the Japanese are uneasy with philosophical presentations that distill out these "impurities." This difference in preference for philosophical style between the Japanese and the West may lead to misunderstanding. The Western reader should be cautioned that what at first may seem like ambiguity might actually be subtlety, what seems like unclarity may be nuance.

This is no place to go into the complexity of Japanese philosophical rhetoric, but perhaps this crude analogy may help the Western reader unfamiliar with this style of philosophical writing. Japanese philosphers often show a resemblance to the mystery writer. Observations are not simply facts, but clues; a bit of evidence, seemingly insignificant now, may suddenly become crucial much later. The presentation will not, therefore, have the linearity of a Western philosophical piece. One point does not necessarily take us smoothly into the next. Rather, like a mystery novel, the parts of the argument accumulate and only completely come together at the conclusion. In fact, the conclusion makes the previously disjointed pieces fit into a whole. In the more typical Western model, on the other hand, the conclusion is always there in the background and the argument is a set of trail markers getting us there safely with a minimum of detours and an assurance of firm ground beneath us.

I belabor this difference only as a warning to the unwary: do not confuse form with content and thereby perceive Japanese thought as "not really philosophical." Bertrand Russell is no more logical or rational than Sherlock Holmes, but we learn of their conclusions, their reasoning, their supporting evidence in radically different ways. Aware of the rhetorical differences between Japanese and Western philosophical presentation, Yuasa has written a special introduction for this English edition. In addition, I have opened each part of the book with a brief synopsis of the chapters following. For many readers my synopses may be unnecessary and can be skipped. For the apprehensive or disoriented, however, they may be reassuring markers.

On the more technical level, the following conventions have been followed. Yuasa's notes appear as end notes, and explanatory footnotes are the editor's unless indicated otherwise. Japanese personal names typically follow their East Asian form, that is, family names first. As a visual reminder, when full names are given and the family name is first, the family name is written in upper-case letters.

The translators also wish to express our gratitude to Professor Yuasa for his assistance, patience, and encouragement throughout this project. The most critical sections of the translation were usually checked by him personally, and he made many valuable corrections and modifications. We were also encouraged in this translation project by several American colleagues, especially Professors Taitetsu Unno (Smith College), William LaFleur (UCLA), and James Sanford (University of North Carolina). Each made helpful suggestions concerning an earlier version. Remaining errors or misrepresentations, if any, are the sole responsibility of the translators and editor. Finally, we would like to thank the Series editor, Kenneth Inada, and the staff of SUNY Press, especially Michele Martin, Nancy Sharlet, and Malcolm W'illison, for their kind assistance in making this publication possible.

Thomas P. Kasulis

Northland College
Ashland, Wisconsin
June 1986

Author's Preface and Acknowledgements
(Japanese Edition)

It has already been five years since I published the book *Kindai Nihon no tetsugaku to jitsuzon shisō* [Modern Japanese philosophy and existential thought]. Mr. SHIMIZU Yoshiharu, a representative from the publisher and an old friend, having taken the trouble to bring out that book, asked if I had a theme to suggest for another volume in a projected series on Japanese thought. At the time, I simple proposed "the body," since I had become aware of the unique view of the body in the Japanese philosophers studied in my previous book. As I see it, their view is not derived from Western philosophy, but rather from Japanese intellectual history. More broadly, it seems connected to a rich ancient tradition in Eastern thought. The body is not only interesting for philosophy; it is also clearly relevant to various other intellectual and cultural concerns, such as artistic expression and a theory of labor. Consequently, I wondered if I might not be able to deal with various topics under the single pivotal theme of the body. This project was eventually realized through the help of Mr. AIKAWA Yōzō. For several years, then, I have been pondering what the body is, and I would like to express my gratitude to the publisher, Sōbunsha, and to these two men for their encouragement.

I had two concerns. One was to discover the historical origin for the unique view of the body found in modern Japanese philosophy. What I especially wanted to consider was the role of personal cultivation in Eastern religions like Buddhism. How is this cultivation related to Buddhist theory? Furthermore, the philosophy of cultivation has had no small influence on Japanese intellectual history, not only in religion, but also in the arts, culture, and labor theory. Religious cultivation is related to artistic cultivation, for example. I wanted to delve into such theoretical connections.

Second, I wanted to reevaluate the traditional Eastern body–mind theories from a contemporary perspective. I have long been interested in the relationships among Eastern thought, depth psychology, and psychiatry—an interest generated through my study of existentialism. Consequently, I wondered if I might not be able to shed new light on Eastern theories of the body by utilizing contemporary theories on the mind-body relation. After a rough survey of intellectual history, I decided to study mainly contemporary philosophical theories of the mind-body, as well as physiology, psychosomatic medicine, and Eastern medicine.

Owing to my lack of expertise in the medical fields, progress was slow. Moreover, as I entered into new areas, I was at a loss how to organize my initial ideas. More than once I considered abandoning this project, but Mr. Aikawa urged me to press on. Because of that encouragement, this book has taken its present shape.

One of the characteristics of Eastern body-mind theories is the priority given to the questions, "How does the relationship between the mind and the body *come to be* (through cultivation)?" or "What does it *become?*" The traditional issue in Western philosophy, on the other hand is, "What *is* the relationship between the mind-body?" In other words, in the East one starts from the experiential assumption that the mind-body modality changes through the training of the mind and body by means of cultivation (*shugyō*) or training (*keiko*). Only after assuming this experiential ground does one ask what the mind-body relation is. That is, the mind-body issue is not simply a theoretical speculation but it is originally a practical, lived experience (*taiken**), involving the mustering of one's whole mind and body. The theoretical is only a reflection on this lived experience.

So we must maintain that this theoretical investigation presupposes practical experience. The content at the base of this theoretical investigation does not derive simply from intellectual speculation; it includes experiential verification. This is evident, for example, when we think about Yoga or Zen. This is why Western psychiatrists and clinical psychologists are sometimes interested in the Eastern philosophies of Yoga and Zen, and why an exchange between psychosomatic medicine and Eastern thought has also occurred in recent years.

Rarely does an ancient Western philosophical theory immediately connect with contemporary positivistic and empirical research. Herein lies another unique characteristic of Eastern thought: there is a difference in the intellectual histories of East and West regarding the relationship between theory and practice, or philosophy and the empirical sciences. At any rate, the central theme, the fundamental concern of this book, is to

---

*See footnote, p. 49, for translation of *taiken* as "lived experience."

question as a contemporary Japanese what I think of the Eastern intellectual heritage.

Part I, in which I deal with modern Japanese philosophies of the body, is a revision of a report first submitted to a study group, *Bukkyō shishō no hikakuronteki kenkyū* [Comparative research into Buddhist thought], in which I participated through the cordial invitation of Professor TAMAKI Kōshirō, a specialist in Indian philosophy. He has given me warm, sincere encouragement on many occasions. MOTOYAMA Hiroshi, President of the Institute of Religion and Psychology, has freely shared his knowledge of actual cultivation practice and medical problems. Through his generosity I have contacted psychologists and physicians. I would like to take this opportunity, then, to thank Drs. Motoyama and Tamaki for their constant interest in my work.

YUASA Yasuo

Spring, Fifty-second year of Showa (1977)

Author's Introduction
(English Edition)

In the splendid development of Western culture in which form is regarded as being, and giving form as good, there is much to be respected and learned. But at the bottom of the Eastern culture that has nurtured our ancestors for thousands of years, isn't there something such that we see the form in the formless and hear the sound of the soundless? Our hearts long for these.

NISHIDA Kitarō

The direct motive behind my taking an interest in the theory of the body lies in my research into modern Japanese philosophy. The first part of this book investigates the views of the body expounded by WATSUJI Tetsurō (1889–1960) and NISHIDA Kitarō (1870–1945). These two are the best known and most influential modern Japanese philosophers, but we shall give here a brief introduction for those readers who have little background in Japanese philosophy.

If we compare their dates with European philosophers, we see that Watsuji was contemporary with Martin Heidegger, and Nishida was slightly younger than Edmund Husserl. Nishida's philosophy is usually said to be influenced by Zen Buddhism. D.T. Suzuki, who introduced Zen to the West, was his friend from boyhood and, as a youth, Nishida became familiar with the Rinzai Zen school with which Suzuki was affiliated. Nishida's philosophy developed under the influence of European philosophy, however, and we might say that it is an Eastern philosophy in a modern form.

The Western philosophers most influential for Nishida were William James and Henri Bergson. James's theory of "pure experience" is especially influential in Nishida's maiden work, *Study of Good,* for example, In his meditative Zen experience, Nishida tried to discover the stream of pure experience prior to the separation between subject and object. Moreover, he recognized the great value of Bergson's intuitionism, believing intuition to be a higher consciousness beyond reflective self-consciousness. (The reader might think it strange that Nishida did not pay much attention to Husserl's phenomenology, but it was only in Nishida's later years that Husserl came to be known in Japan.)

Most influential in the Japanese philosophical world at the beginning of this century was Neo-Kantianism, so Nishida naturally studied Kant and started his own theoretical system by utilizing Kantian terminology. This terminological borrowing was probably a misfortune for modern Japanese philosophy, because the essence of Nishida's philosophy is not an idealistic rationalism, but rather a strongly religious tendency towards recognizing the value of nonrational intuition. One of his major works is entitled *The Determination of Nothingness toward Self-Consciousness.* "Nothing" or "nothingness" is a term indicating the Buddhist *satori,* that is, the experience of emptiness (*śūnyatā*) in Mahāyāna Buddhism. Nishida calls the ultimate experience of nothingness, "absolute nothing." The "determination toward self-consciousness" refers to the various categories of experience vis-à-vis self-consciousness. In other words, he interprets these experiences to be determined by a mystical intuition correlated with a transcendental dimension. We could also say that his philosophy is an emanative metaphysics, but expressed in Kantian terminology, he maintained that his concept of "nothing" is Kant's transcendental "consciousness-in-general"; that is, since Kant's transcendental subjectivity is that which transcends empirical consciousness, it must be, Nishida argues, a *nothing.*

Because of this tendency to force his terminology, Nishida's writings are recondite and have been understood by only a few readers having knowledge of both Eastern and Western philosophy. In focusing on Nishida's theory of the body, I simply analyze its Eastern characteristics in comparison with Western philosophy.

Now let us turn to WATSUJI Tetsurō. In his youth Watsuji intended to become a literary figure. Inf act, the famous writer, TANIZAKI Junichirō, was a close friend. He was also influenced by OKAKURA Tenshin, who was instrumental in introducing Eastern art into the Boston Museum. Watsuji thereby became very interested in Eastern art himself. His maiden work, *A Pilgrimage to Ancient Temples,* is an aesthetic essay of admiration for the Buddhist images in the old temples of Nara and Kyoto.

In philosophy he is well known for introducing into Japan the ideas of Nietzsche and Kierkegaard. Once he became a philosopher and abanadoned his literary career, Watsuji launched himself into a wide range of studies, including ancient Greek philosophy and literature, Christianity, modern Western philosophy, and Japanese intellectual history. His purpose was to elucidate the characteristics of Japanese thought and culture by comparing them with various other cultural traditions.

Watsuji went to Germany in 1927 and, while at the University of Berlin, studied European history and climate. At that time, the trip from Japan to Europe was a long one, passing through the Indian Ocean and the Mediterranean Sea. He later wrote a book entitled *Climates*[1] based on his impressions of the journey. A motive for writing this book was his reading Heidegger's *Being and Time (Sein und Zeit)*. Heidegger sought the essence of *Dasein* (personal existence) in temporality, but to Watsuji's Eastern sensibility, human being as a "being-in-the-world" must take root in the earth, which has been spatially shaped, specifically, under natural climatic conditions. Although the various peoples in the world have established their unique patterns of life and thought through their own cultural traditions, might these patterns not reflect the various characteristics of their own geography? Human history is embodied in climate. In this respect, Watsuji saw that Heidegger's work ignored nature and the human body.

As the holder of a chair in ethics at Tokyo University after returning from Europe, Watsuji entitled his major work *Ethics*. Gino K. Piovesana comments on Wawtsuji's philosophy as follows:

> Watsuji's ethic was designed as a Japanese system based upon the essential relationships of man to man, man to family, and man to society. In contrast with the private, individual ethics of the West, his ethic sees man as involved in community and society. . . . His achievement was that he systematized—although in Western categories—a traditional ethics which is a substantial part of the ethos of Japan and also of China.[2]

Methodologically, Watsuji relies more on Dilthey's hermeneutics than on phenomenology. He starts with the interpretation of the Japanese term, *ningen* (human being), a term literally meaning "between person and person." The word derives from Chinese Buddhism, indicating the world in which people live. This word characterizes a unique view of humanity nurtured in Eastern traditions. Is it not the case that what is foremost to human life is the fact that man lives in the field of human relationships rather than as individuals? Accordingly, we must abandon the modern European idea of seeing the world from the standpoint of self-consciousness. Instead, we must grasp the individual from the totality of human relationships. This is Watsuji's fundamental contention.

Watsuji does not specifically discuss the mind-body theory, but he does cite one exemplary instance: his view of marriage.[3] In opposition to the modern commonsensical view, Watsuji contends that marriage is not essentially a contractual relationship, for a contract is made with the assumption that it might be breached. According to Watsuji, the marriage contract is simply a means to stabilize the husband-wife relationship, and the essence of marriage is not really contractual. Moreover, marriage is a conjunctive relation between two individuals sharing the same essence.

Watsuji calls the husband-wife relationship a "two-person community." This means that a new whole is created by virtue of the fact that two heterogeneous beings are conjoined. Furthermore, Watsuji argues that since we cannot separate the human mind from the body, it is impossible in marriage to think of sex as being distinct from love. Love must be that which is directed towards the partner's whole personality, that is, towards a being in which mind and body are inseparable. Moreover, Watsuji maintains that a man's love and a woman's love are originally heterogeneous: man's love is an active love—a love that loves—and the woman's love is a passive love—a love that is loved. The essence of marriage as a two-person community is that a new whole is born because such heterogeneous loves are conjoined.

To Watsuji, the field of human relationships is superior to the individual, that is, the whole is higher than the individual. In conjunction with this, the human mind and body are taken to be inseparable. In Chapter One we will clarify the Eastern position by comparing Watsuji's grasp of the mind-body relationship with Western philosophy's view.

(2)

In broadest terms, what might be the distinguishing features of an Eastern theory of the body? In the East, there is an ancient term, "the oneness of body-mind" (*shinjin ichinyo*). This phrase was first used by the famous medieval Japanese Zen master, Eisai, to express the elevated inner experience of Zen meditation. This phrase is also often used in Japanese theatrical arts (the Nō drama, for example) as well as in martial arts (Jūdō and Kendō, for instance). To put it differently, the oneness of the body-mind is an ideal for inward meditation as well as for outward activities.

How can the essence of meditation and activity be the same? This unity of mind and body as a goal is probably understandable, to a degree, to the modern Westerner. For example, well-trained athletes can move the various parts of their bodies as their minds command. Ordinarily, though, one cannot do this; usually, the mind and body function separately. We can gradually approach the inseparability of the body-mind only by a long, accumulative training. According to the view held in modern sports, however, the training and enhancement of the body's capacity has nothing to do with the enhancement of one's moral personality, that is, the training of one's mind. In contrast, in the East, physical training that is not accompanied by the training of the mind as well is regarded an aberration, for the mind and body cannot be essentially separated. Consequently, the Eastern martial arts have been regarded since ancient times as an outward-moving form of meditation.

In the traditional Western views of the body, there is a strong tendency to distinguish analytically the mental from the somatic mode. The Cartesian mind–body dualism, the starting point for modern philosophy, typifies this. If the historical source of this conceptual attitude can be traced back to the Christian spirit–flesh dualism, we have found a long-standing divergence between the intellectual histories of East and West.

Obviously, it is self-evident and common sense that the mind and body are inseparable, and Western thinkers do not lack such common sense. Modern philosophy since Descartes has taken up the question of how to overcome this dualism. For example, the philosophy of Merleau-Ponty attempts to elucidate the ambiguous mode of being a body—the oneness of the body, shall we say, embracing a dual tension. So it is incorrect to assert baldly that the oneness of mind and body has been grasped only in the Eastern traditions. Going one step further, we must ask in what sense, or according to what kind of thinking, the inseparability between mind and body can be maintained. Our inquiry starts here.

In my opinion, it would seem that the theory of body not only pertains to the philosophical investigation of the mind-body relationship; it also opens the way to a wider set of problems. Inquiring what the body is, or what the relationship between the mind and body is, relates to the nature of being human. In this respect, we might say that the theory of body takes us into metaphysics. As is evident by the fact that the Cartesian dualism served as a starting point for modern epistemology, and that Merleau-Ponty's theory of body is closely interrelated with problems in ontology, the theory of body leads into a broader realm of philosophical problems.

At this point in our comparison between the intellectual East and West, we discover a fundamental difference in their philosophies and metaphysics. In other words, there is a marked difference in the methodological foundations of the theoretical organization of Eastern and Western philosophy. Unless we examine this point, we cannot grasp the uniqueness of the Eastern theory of body. At the end of Part I, we will examine this point briefly.

(3)

What might we discover to be the philosophical uniqueness of Eastern thought? One revealing characteristic is that personal "cultivation" (*shugyō*) is presupposed in the philosophical foundation of the Eastern theories. To put it simply, true knowledge cannot be obtained simply by means of theoretical thinking, but only through "bodily recognition or realization" (*tainin* or *taitoku*), that is, through the utilization of one's total mind and body. Simply stated, this is to "learn with the body," not the brain. Cultivation is a practice that attempts, so to speak, to achieve true knowledge by means of one's total mind and body.

Of course, there are various Eastern philosophies. Roughly speaking, we find personal cultivation to be stressed in the schools of Buddhism and Hinduism, both of which originated in India, as well as in Chinese Taoism. A similar tendency can be found, to a certain degree, in the Confucianism of the Sung, Yüan, and Ming dynasties. Buddhist and Hindu cultivation methods originate in what is called yoga. Yoga's source can probably be traced to the Indus civilization prior to the Aryan invasion. It spread throughout India and developed various forms independent of the differences among the religious schools. Although Zen meditation is the best known form of Buddhist cultivation, each Buddhist school originally had its own cultivation methods. Zen is merely one stream. In fact, since there is a great difference between India and China in their intellectual traditions, Indian cultivation forms could not really take hold in China.

Indian yoga is most essentially a system of practical, technical methods for training the mind and body and maintaining health. Its training and meditation methods are very realistic, numerous, and complicated. Yet if we approach Indian philosophy with a purely philosophical interest, it is overwhelmingly metaphysical and theoretical. For this reason, we tend to think that Indian meditation must be separate from reality, but in actuality it is not. We must not fail to recognize that at the foundation of Indian meditation is a very practical and technical view of the mind and body supported and verified by radical experience. Consequently, there is a realistic view of humanity hidden within it.

The Chinese intellectual tradition, on the other hand, does not emphasize such Indian metaphysical speculation and complicated theoretical analysis. The Chinese emphasis is the moral orientation represented by Confucianism and the spiritual attitude that attempts to grasp the essence of things straightforwardly and simply. Zen is a typical form of Buddhism influenced by the Chinese intellectual climate. Although Zen cultivation has not lost the realistic significance of training the mind and body, its goal is not technical but is the human pursuit of the true way to live, a strongly ethical sense of personal perfection. Even though there is this difference between Indian and Chinese philosophy, at the foundation of the Chinese systems like Zen the experience of cultivation is certainly presupposed. Taoism is another case; the system of personal cultivation developed during the T'ang Dynasty was established through the Buddhist influence. Although we know little of ancient Taoism, it is conceivable that it included cultivation methods, since we can find in Lao Tzu and Chuang Tzu scattered references to what seem to be meditative experiences.

But what, then, is cultivation? From the Buddhist standpoint, it is the search for *satori,* but enlightenment cannot be attained simply by intellectual speculation or theoretical thinking. To attain it, cultivation is necessary for the discipline of mind and body. Put differently, cultivation is a *method* to reach the wisdom of *satori,* a passage to it. Here, we have a serious methodological issue for Eastern metaphysics.

For example, the philosophy of emptiness in Mahāyāna Buddhism is one aspect of enlightenment. Seen from the theoretical, philosophical point of view, it is metaphysical. But the philosophy of emptiness also clarifies the true profile of Being in various beings (the *dharmas*). So we can say it is also an ontology. If we focus on this philosophical, logical viewpoint, it probably lacks the methodological reflection we associate with Western metaphysics. Generally speaking, we cannot find in the Western tradition the idea that cultivation is a passage to the realm of metaphysical concern. For example, Aristotle's metaphysics is understood through purely logical thinking or intellectual speculation. This is not so for the philosophy of emptiness, however.

In the Buddhist tradition, cultivation is a passage to reach the metaphysical insight of *satori*. Cultivation specifically means the discipline of the body-mind. Thus, we must examine theoretically and historically the problems concerning cultivation in order to clarify the character of Eastern thought as a philosophy. To do this, it is necessary to trace the historical changes from India to China to Japan in the theories of the body as both an ideal and an actuality. Part II undertakes this investigation.

Our next task will be to trace the evolution in Japanese theories of the body. Cultivation obviously belongs to the world of religion, but it has had a broad influence on various cultural realms outside religion in Japanese intellectual history. One example that catches our attention is the arts. For instance, there is a tradition in poetic criticism, Nō dramatic theory, and the theory of the tea ceremony to suggest that artistic "discipline" (*keiko*) is a form of cultivation. As a group, we may call these "theories of artistry." This is not only an interesting subject when seen from the theory of the body; it contains many points that are intuitively easier to understand than theoretical speculations on religion. We shall first deal with the theory of artistry, then.

The notion of cultivation in artistry (*geidō*) is derived from Buddhism. Among Japanese Buddhists, Kūkai and Dōgen took cultivation to be critical, making it the central issue in their thinking and the foundation of their theoretical systems. In their writings we can glimpse the role of the body as a philosophical subject in Japanese intellectual history. Both Kūkai and Dōgen were of course Japanese, but Dōgen was strongly influenced spiritually by Chinese Zen. In contrast, Kūkai's philosophical temperament is extremely Indian as well as Japanese. We shall also deal with these issues in Part II.

(4)

In Part III we inquire into the significance of the Eastern theories of the body for our contemporary context.

If a characteristic in Eastern thought is that a lived experience of cultivation is the methodological route to enlightenment, the first problem is how the relationship between the mind and body is grasped within cultivation. As already noted, there is a strong tendency in the Eastern theories of the body to grasp the mind and body as an inseparable unity, but this does not mean that the mind and body are simply inseparable. At the same time, it implies that they *ought* to be inseparable as an ideal. The expression, "the oneness of body-mind," means that when the dualistic and ambiguous tension in the relationship between the mind and body is dissolved, and the ambiguity overcome, a new perspective—what may be called the disclosed horizon (*Offenheit*)—will come into view. The "oneness of body-mind" describes that free state of minimal distance between movement of the mind and of the body, as for example in the dynamic performance of a master actor on a stage.

Dōgen, moreover, said that *satori* culminates within cultivation as "the molting of body-mind." This probably means that the dualistic distinction between the mind and the body is dissolved, and the mind is no longer a subject opposed to the body as an object—the body losing its "heaviness" as an inert object opposed to the movement of the mind. This state can be attained, however, only through the process of cultivation as disciplining mind and body. In this sense, the mind and body are inseparable within cultivation theory, but they are still grasped as a unity betraying a dualistic tension in their relationship, that is, as that which ought to become one.

Restated, this means that the very character of the dualistic mode in the relationship between the mind and body will gradually change through the process of cultivation. This change is encountered in the lived experience of the cultivators themselves. In cultivation, we should be able to clarify the meaning of such a lived experience. We can then question the meaning of Eastern theories of the body not only from the philosophical viewpoint, but also in light of the concrete, factual recognition of the correlative mechanism between the mind and body. In Part III, we shall use this perspective to investigate what the Eastern theories of the body mean, and what they imply for us today.

A glimmer is cast here on the difference in character between Eastern and Western thought. Western thought, at least in the modern period, has maintained a logical difference between philosophy and the empirical sciences. Modern epistemology insists that philosophy clarifies the presuppositions, methods, and logic by which positivistic, empirical, scientific knowledge is established. Contemporary ontology also insists that philosophy is the science elucidating the modes of human conduct and that it is operative on the groundwork of scientific research. In the terminology of Heideggerian ontology, science is an "ontical" (*ontisch*) endeavor, unreflective of the ground upon which it exists. In contrast, philosophy is an "ontological" (*ontologisch*) endeavor which questions reflectively its own ground. (This philosophical contention has become prominent since Kant but, as I will show later, it is an inheritance in a secularized form of a premodern tradition in Western intellectual history.)

In contrast to this Western tradition, Eastern philosophical speculation and empirical verification must essentially be one. The wisdom of *satori* is empirically verified in the process of cultivation by means of the body-mind. Based on this experience, one then expresses enlightenment in the form of theoretical speculation. From the traditional standpoint of Eastern thought, philosophical speculation and empirical research are not two distinct dimensions. The two stand, as it were, in a cooperative relation that subtly merges them. Consequently, the Eastern philosophical theory of the body does not present any objection whatsoever to the attempt to clarify its meaning from the positivistic or empirical, scientific standpoint.

We shall deal with Bergson's and Merleau-Ponty's philosophical theories of the mind-body as having taken into consideration the positivistic knowledge about the correlative mechanism of the mind-body. We shall examine their problematic issues in light of our own body-mind issues. We shall also delve into what an Eastern theory of the body means, by considering the knowledge derived from physiological psychology and other fields that have positivistically articulated the body-mind mechanism.

Not only are there many unsolved problems remaining in this field, but my own knowledge is inadequate for making a fully satisfactory clarification. Thus my endeavor still awaits future studies. My intention, as indicated in the subtitle, is to move us toward an Eastern theory of the body.

Finally, a word of gratitude to the translators. This book was first published in 1977, and Drs. NAGATOMO Shigenori and Thomas P. Kasulis began translating parts of it in 1980. Without their continued interest and dedication, the English translation would never have materialized. I would like to express to them my deepest appreciation.

YUASA Yasuo

Ibaraki prefecture
Japan

EDITOR'S SUMMARY

PART ONE

In these first three chapters, Yuasa explores examples of how twentieth-century Japanese philosophers approach the issue of the body differently from their colleagues in the West. This divergence ultimately results in a divergence in their philosophical anthropology, that is, in the way the nature of being human is analyzed and understood. Briefly, Western philosophy (especially since the early modern period) has tended to think of the mind and body as two separate entities related in some still controversially defined manner. The thrust of modern Western thought has been to isolate and define that essential relationship between the two entities.

In Eastern thought, on the other hand, the mind-body has generally been viewed from the start as a single system, and the emphasis has been on articulating the evolution of that system from ordinary human life to the highly integrated, exemplary mode: the accomplished artist, theoretical genius, enlightened religious master. In Chapters One and Two, Yuasa examines the thought of two twentieth-century Japanese philosophers, showing how their ideas exemplify this general distinction between East and West.

Since Western philosophers seldom discuss the development of the extraordinary human being, focusing instead on the universally experienced elements of human existence, we would expect a divergence between them and the Japanese philosophers who discuss the nature of enlightened existence. But what about Japanese philosophers' analysis of everday, ordinary experience? Certainly, insofar as both the East and West would be examining the same phenomena, their analyses should be quite close. After all, the universal characteristics of ordinary human existence should be just that—universal. In his discussion of WATSUJI Tetsurō in Chapter One, Yuasa shows that not to be the case. Rather, even in the analysis of the character of ordinary human being, East and West diverge. Yuasa sees the significance of this divergence in terms of the respective theories of the (mind-)body.

Watsuji's central critique of Western philosophical anthropology is that it emphasizes the mind or consciousness (and, therefore, temporality) to the virtual exclusion of the body (and spatiality). Deeply influenced by Heidegger, Watsuji was nonetheless critical of *Being and Time* for its weak treatment of the spatial character in human existence. In both *Climates* and *Ethics* Watsuji argued that the human being is always within a life-space that includes the physical environment, social community, and somatic physiology. It is not that the individual moves from individual existence (*Dasein* in Heidegger's terminology) to the communal (*Mitsein*); rather, right from the start, the individual and the social are intermeshed, just as are the mind and body. Extrapolating on Watsuji's criticisms, Yuasa sees in the modern Western philosophical tradition a bias toward understanding the human being as primarily an individual, self-conscious subject located in temporality. Missing is Watsuji's emphasis on human being as located in "betweenness" (*aidagara*). Yuasa believes this Western prejudice is also based on the classical religious preference of the spirit over the flesh.

In the discussion of NISHIDA Kitarō in Chapter Two, Yuasa shows how the divergence between East and West becomes even more pronounced when we consider the nature of extraordinary, evolved human existence in which the mind-body is a single, integrated system. Yuasa focuses on Nishida's later philosophy of "acting intuition." Yuasa points out that Nishida sees a different function for acting intuition in everyday experience in contrast to its function in the highly integrated, creative experience of the accomplished individual. On the everyday level, what Nishida calls the "*basho* (place or field) vis-à-vis being," the intuition is passive and the acting is active. This part of the analysis parallels the way the two are typically viewed in Western philosophy: through the intuition, the mind-body receives data about the outside world and internalizes it; this forms the basis for the will to determine the mind-body's behavior or activity in the world. According to Nishida, the situation changes when the person achieves a more integrated self. On this deeper level, what Nishida calls the "*basho* vis-à-vis nothing" (or the self as *basho*), the intuition becomes active and the acting (paradoxically) passive. On this level, the intuition is the creative or intellectual intuition that integrates experience in such a way that the mind-body spontaneously ("passively") acts. The person simply enacts the active, creative thrust of the intuition.

In distinguishing these two *basho*, Yuasa develops a distinction central to the argument of the book, namely, that between the bright and the dark consciousness. The bright consciousness is the self-aware, articulate, clear thinking found, for example, in Descartes' *cogito*. The bright consciousness has been the primary focus of Western philosophy, especially in modern times, since it is the refinement or ideal of the everyday, universal experience of the mind. In the bright consciousness, we are self-aware of ourselves as the acting-intuition vis-à-vis being. We know what is, why it is, and how we want to act toward it.

The dark consciousness, corresponding more to Nishida's acting intuition in the *basho* vis-à-vis nothing, is seldom discussed in the West, however. In the dark consciousness, the bright glance of Descartes' (or Husserl's) *cogito* disappears. The mind-body acts of itself, creatively and spontaneously without explicit awareness of the what, why, and how. The dark consciousness is not to be confused with the unconscious in Freudian psychoanalysis, although there are important similarities. (Generally speaking, as the function of repressed traumatic memories and instinctual drives, the Freudian unconscious is an abnormal, diseased function of the dark consciousness, below rather than above the functioning of the everyday.) The dark consciousness is a positive source of creativity, inspiration, and intellectual insight. When Goethe wrote a poem in his sleep, when Newton had his insight into the laws of gravitation, when a masterful musician has performed, they were not self-consciously aware of the whats, whys, and hows. The acting intuition as the dark consciousness was simply operating.

Chapter Three is a brief discussion of where these observations lead in developing a methodology for research into Eastern mind-body theories. Most importantly, we must recognize that the Eastern theories cannot be separated from the issue of personal development. For the East, the mind-body is an evolving system that can be further developed, integrated, and enhanced. (From such a perspective, the abstract, generalized methodological perspective in modern Western philosophy may often seem disembodied and impersonal.) It is not surprising, for example, that Eastern thought has tended to be of more interest to contemporary Western psychoanalysts and psychologists than it has to Western philosophers. Personal development has not, in the modern West, been a major philosophical theme. To appreciate the significance of the Eastern perspective, therefore, we must temporarily suspend some of our Western philosophical methodological assumptions in order to see how the project of body-mind enhancement actually functions in Eastern traditions. This will be the focus of Part II.

Part I

Views of the Body in Modern Japanese Thought

We should not rise above the earth with the aid of "spiritual" intuitions and run away from hard reality. . . . Man may have lost his ancient saurian's tail, but in its stead he has a chain hanging on to his psyche which binds him to the earth—an anything-but-Homeric chain of given conditions which weigh so heavily that it is better to remain bound to them.

C.G. Jung

Chapter One

WATSUJI Tetsurō's View of the Body

Space and body in intersubjectivity

WATSUJI Tetsurō (1889–1960) calls his ethics "the science of the person."* "Person" (*ningen*†) here is not simply the "individual person" (*hito*), but really means *between* man and man. The Japanese word *ningen* was originally a Buddhist term signifying the human world as contrasted with the worlds of beasts and of heavenly beings. Recognizing this point, Watsuji maintains that to clarify the idea of the human being, we must first take note of the "betweenness" (*aidagara*) in which people are located. This betweenness consists of the various human relationships of our life-world. To put it simply, it is the network which provides humanity with a social meaning, for example, one's being an inhabitant of this or that town or a member of a certain business firm. To live as a person means, in this instance, to exist in such betweenness.

Critics have pointed out that Watsuji's philosophy of the person captures well the characteristically Japanese patterns of behavior and thinking. For example, a popular theme in premodern Japanese literature is "the snare of human emotions and obligations," and modern psychopathologists have remarked that the psychologies of dependence (*amae*) and androphobia are uniquely Japanese symptoms.[1] Both exam-

---

*"Science" translates *gaku,* a term with denotations spanning "science" (in the German sense of *Wissenschaft*), "study," and "imitation." In his book *Rinrigaku* [Ethics], Watsuji deftly plays on all these meanings. The first, very brief section of this earlier work has been translated by David Dilworth as "The Significance of Ethics as the Study of Man" in *Monumenta Nipponica,* 26:3–4 (1971).—Ed.

†The common Japanese word for person, *ningen,* is composed of two characters, the first meaning "person" or "man" and the second "space" or "between." Like Heidegger, Watsuji uses etymological discussions as part of his phenomenological method.—Ed.

ples, we may say, symbolize a specifically Japanese mode of thought that we vividly feel in actual life: we live our lives within a network of betweenness.

But what does it mean to exist in betweenness (aidagara)? The Japanese term "between" (aida) signifies, in its physical sense, a spatial distance separating thing and thing. So our betweenness implies that we exist in a definite, spatial basho* [place, topos, field]. Naturally, this basho is not a position in the neutralized, physical space that obliterates any human significance; rather, it is the life-basho in which we find the interconnected meanings of the life-world. Behind Watsuji's project of attempting to grasp the fundamental human mode of being in the light of betweenness, however, is the view that to exist in space is the primordial fact, the primary significance, of being human. Watsuji often speaks of betweenness as "the extension of [embodied] subjective* (shutaiteki) space," his equivalent of the Intersubjektiver Raum [the intersubjective space] or the intersubjective basho.

Let us take the relation between the self as subject and the space serving as its basho of existence. In taking a concrete content and elaborating on it, the relation is transformed into the connection between the human being and the nature embracing it. Before undertaking his study of ethics, Watsuji wrote a book called Climates † in which he said that to live in nature as the space of the life-world—in other words, to live in a "climate"—is the most fundamental mode of being human. According to the Preface of that book, Watsuji undertook the project of grasping the fundamental human being from the standpoint of spatiality only after he had

---

*Basho is a common Japanese word indicating a physical place. Primarily through the influence of Nishida, however, the word has become a technical term in modern Japanese thought. Roughly speaking, it designates the conceptual field within which an experience takes place. Nishida's use is influenced by the notions of topos in Aristotle and field (Feld) in physics as well as in Neo-Kantianism. Since no single word captures well all these nuances, the translators have left the word in romanized Japanese.

A Japanese reader might well read this chapter without considering basho to be a technical term, but since the next chapter discusses Nishida's theory of basho in detail, Yuasa is subtly utilizing the ambiguity between the word's common and technical usages.—Ed.

*There are two Japanese philosophical terms for the subject as distinguished from the object: shukan and shutai. The former, consisting of the characters for "subject" and "seeing," is more psychological, whereas the latter, consisting of the characters "subject" and "body," is more incarnate in nuance. Thus, the former is more likely to occur in discussions of the subject as the seat of feelings, desires, and knowledge, but the latter in connection with the somatic, historical, and social actions of the subject. Obviously, given the theme of this book, Yuasa generally favors the use of shutai and its adjectival form shutaiteki. When the distinction is critical, we make it explicit by saying "(embodied) subject."—Ed.

†This work has been translated into English as A Climate by Geoffrey Bownas (Tokyo: Japanese Government Printing Office, 1961) and later reprinted as Climate and Cultures (Tokyo: Hokuseidō Press, 1971).—Ed.

been puzzled by the fact that Heidegger's *Being and Time* sought that fundamental being in *temporality*. Watsuji writes:

> I started thinking about the nature of climates in the early summer of 1927 when I read Heidegger's *Being and Time* in Berlin. His attempt to grasp the structure of man's existence as temporality was extremely interesting, but my concern was this: while temporality is presented as the subject's (*shutaiteki*) structure of being, why isn't spatiality equally well presented as a fundamental structure of being? Needless to say, it is not that [the notion of] spatiality does not come up in Heidegger: it seemed as though the "living Nature" of German Romanticism was resurrected afresh in his very scrutiny of the concrete space within man's existence. Still, it is almost obliterated by the glare of temporality. There I saw the limitation of Heidegger's work.
>
> Temporality cannot be a true temporality unless it is in conjunction with spatiality. The reason that Heidegger stopped there is that his *Dasein* is limited to the individual. He simply grasped human (*ningen*) existence as the Being of the individual person (*hito*). This is only an abstracted aspect when we considered persons under the double structure of being both individual and social. When persons are seen in this concrete double structure, temporality can proceed together with spatiality. . . . The reason that questions like these arose could be due to the fact that while I was immersing myself in the detailed analysis of temporality, I was being filled with impressions of various climates.[2]

In short, to exist in a climate, to exist in the concrete aspect of space, is to exist in "living Nature." This is as significant for the human mode of being as is its existence in history qua temporality. In fact, for Watsuji, spatiality is thought of as being more primary than temporality. It is clear that betweenness in our life-world must, in some sense, have a spatial, *basho*-like determination for its foundation. This is the case irrespective of how we may think of the relationship between the interconnection of natural space and the human (or intersubjective) meanings of the life-world. We shall call such an intersubjective space our "life-space," that which we experience and discover everyday within the life-world in its interconnected meanings.

To exist in betweenness is to exist within the life-space. Furthermore, to exist in a spatial *basho* means nothing other than to exist as a human being by virtue of one's body; I exist in my body, occupying the spatial *basho* of here and now: This is what it means for me to exist within the world. This is evident in our everyday, natural understanding and requires no further explanation here. We should bear in mind, of course, that in explaining his concept of betweenness Watsuji does not offer any explicit account of the body. But when we delve into the implicit

assumptions behind Watsuji's insight, the spatial existence of the body
has a decisive relevance to his understanding of the nature of humanity.

In clarifying the fundamental human being, we must first comprehend persons in their state of betweenness. In taking this position,
Watsuji criticizes the Western notion of self-consciousness in the modern
philosophical tradition beginning with Descartes. The opening line of
Watsuji's *Ethics* reads: "The primary significance of this attempt to define
ethics in terms of the science of the person (*ningen*) is to rid modern
philosophy of the erroneous view that ethics is simply concerned with individual consciousness."[3] For Descartes, the most fundamental mode of
the human being is the conscious subject, or empirically speaking, the
subject with psychological functions. For Descartes, the body is an extended thing (*res extensa*) occupying spatial volume. Thus, we have the story
of the Cartesianist, Arnold Geulincx, who upon kicking a cat, said of it,
"It is nothing but an intricate machine." In other words, upon this view,
the body's mode of being is equivalent to that of a physical object occupying space. For the conscious subject, moreover, space appears as the spatial experience of a perspectively observed self. By this definition, the
body is merely a part of the human subject's spatial experience, that is,
the body is understood to be the spatial experience closest to the self.
When we generalize abstractly from this line of thought about the
relationship between the self as an empirical subject and the spatial experience appearing to the self, we arrive at that modern epistemology
which opposes subject and object.

This way of thinking develops in modern Western philosophy out of
our everyday, natural experience. Insofar as I am living as a person, I cannot help but exist here and now through my body; the world appears with
the *here* as its pivotal point in the spatial experience of a perspectively observed self. This, too, is self-evident in our ordinary experiences and requires no further elaboration. But what, then, is the real difference between this Western approach and Watsuji's? Let us imagine a dialogue
between the two.

For a philosophy of self-consciousness, the human space is, more
than anything else, that which appears *to a self as spatial experience*. Isn't this
the most immediately experienced spatial mode of being? A follower of
Watsuji might respond as follows. That a subject can have such a spatial
experience is actually due to the fact that an (embodied) subject is placed
in space. Space, prior to a particular subject's spatial experience, exists
first (even historically) as the life-space, endowed with various human
meanings. This life-space enables the human subject to have that very
spatial experience of the self.

The philosopher of self-consciousness would probably make the
following counter-rebuttal. Watsuji's way of thinking is really just a naive

realism. To think that the life-space exists prior to a particular subject's spatial experience is analogous to a physicist's attempting to locate particular objects in physical space by presupposing the existence of that space beforehand. Such being the case, the objective or nonsubjective space Watsuji thinks to be primary is, from the standpoint of critical epistemology, nothing but a secondary constituent established by abstraction from the life-space immediately experienced by the human subject.

Continuing this dialogue still further, the Watsuji advocate must respond as follows: We may grant that from the standpoint of a critical epistemology, the so-called objective space can be said to be an abstraction from our immediate experiences or from the experience of our life-space. What is at issue here, however, is not the procedure of human cognition but rather the human mode of being. It would be impossible for a human subject to exist with the body in the midst of the life-space unless the person had first received a life-in-the-world, that is, his or her existence. What is at issue is this *a priori* restriction in the subject's everyday experiences, in its very mode of being.

The starting point which makes it possible for a human subject in the life-space to have a spatial experience is the fact that one's existence is bestowed upon one in this world, bestowed by *something unknown,* without any dependence on the will of the human self. There is, in other words, the fundamental passivity of life itself and it is this passivity which indicates the existence of a particular subject. By virtue of the fact that one receives one's life in such a life-world, the human being incorporates various meanings and embodies them. Based on these meanings, the human subject comes to have the experience of its own life-space. One is born in the life-space under various structural interconnections of meanings, and by growing up in them, one can then, so to speak, *become* a human subject.

Of course, even against this defense of Watsuji, our dialogue might continue with a new objection arising from the standpoint that regards the immediate experience of consciousness as primordial. Such a discussion may go on endlessly without any definite conclusion, so let us now take another tack.

Differences between East and West in understanding spatial-temporal experience

Although Watsuji's view is greatly influenced by contemporary Western philosophy, it is undeniable that at the ground of Watsuji's interpretation of the human being is a radically different way of thinking from what we find in traditional expressions of Western philosophy. In explaining the life-world's interconnected meanings found in betweenness, Watsuji adopts from Heidegger's *Dasein* analysis the idea of "understanding our everyday being" (*alltägliche Seinsverstandnis*). He also utilizes the method of "understanding" (*Verstehen*) found in Dilthey's hermeneutics of life. Hence, Watsuji directly criticizes only the early modern philosophy of self-consciousness represented by Descartes and Kant, and not contemporary Western theories. As generally recognized, the mode of thinking that opposes the subject and object, the mode started by Descartes, is today basically superseded, having been rejected by both the life-philosophies and phenomenology. Although Watsuji himself also considers these early twentieth-century movements, utilizing them in his own work, he does not take much into account the modes of Western thought prior to the modern period. Nonetheless, when he does raise questions, taking the philosophy of Cartesian self-consciousness for his target, he distinctive approach to the human being makes possible a direct collision with certain Western philosophical modes of thought ranging from ancient to modern times.

Of course, when we restrict ourselves to surveying just the development of Western philosophy, there are indeed great differences between Cartesian and medieval thought. There is, similarly, a major transformation from earlier modern epistemology to contemporary ontology or existentialism. If we broaden our perspective, however, and contrast Western with Eastern thought, the divergences there are much greater than those we find within the Western tradition itself. Our emphasis is on outstanding the heterogeneity between the East and West in their traditional modes of thinking. Now we must try to articulate this heterogeneity with respect to the standpoint of the mind-body problem.

As already stated, we may recognize in Watsuji's view of the person an emphasis on space as the *basho* of human existence, thereby stressing the spatial existence of the body. In the traditional Western view of humanity on the other hand, time (or historicity) is generally considered to be more important than space, the mind to be more important than the body. This trend in Western philosophy seems most developed in the Christian views of humanity and the world. It has been the established Christian view since Augustine to think the mind is more important than the body and that time is more important than space. Augustine's exposition of time appears in chapter eleven of the *Confessions* and in *On the Trinity,* the details of which have been carefully examined in various technical works. For our purposes, we need only consider a few summary remarks.[4]

In the human psyche (*anima*), there dwells the spiritual essence of the image of God (*imago Dei*), but man's love (*amor*) is a desire (*cupiditas*), that is, it remains a love for created things, because the soul is really conjoined to his carnal body (*corpus*). Faith involves the transformation of the love that is directed toward external, created things (that is, toward the spatial world as the *basho* of their existence) into the love directed toward God, who is found deep inside one's soul. In *On the Trinity* the functions of the mind (*mens*)—memory (*memoria*), intelligence (*intelligentia*), and will (*voluntas*)—are correlated with the three persons (*persona*) of God: the Father, the Son, and the Holy Spirit. Memory recollects the existence of God, the cause of all things; intelligence knows the basic nature of the self as being linked with God; and will loves this nature of the self. In the *Confessions,* these three functions are explained in terms of time: they are grasped as the taking hold of the past (memory), the taking hold of the present (intuition), and the taking hold of the future (expectation). The original meaning of "mind" (*mens*) is a "consciousness which takes hold of time" within the self.

Underlying Augustine's views are, of course, the Christian dualism of flesh and spirit as well as the cosmology of the creation out of nothing (*creatio ex nihilo*). According to the Christian tradition, God and the spatial universe that is God's creation (including the self's corporeal body) are placed in the relationship between eternity and time. While God exists on the external other shore transcending time, the spatial world and the corporeal person within it exist in the stream of time, bounded by the creation through God's free will and by the Last Days. By grasping the available total stream of time, the mind is directed toward God inside the soul, free of space and body. The body indicates the principle of the flesh, carrying original sin with it. From this arise the traditional views of humanity and value in Western intellectual history. From the essential mode of being human, this history excludes both corporeality and the spatiality that is the *basho* for it.

Now then, how should we view Descartes? Speaking in most general terms, for Descartes the most essential fact in the human being is the *cogito* subject. That is, to have a mind is primary; to have a body that occupies a *basho* in space is of secondary importance. This view of human existence, which makes consciousness (broadly speaking, the mind) primary and the body secondary, may actually be a secularized form of the Christian flesh–spirit dualism. Naturally, there are important differences between the views of humanity in medieval Christianity and in Descartes, especially in terms of whether one should seek the essence of the mind in the intellectual, cognitive function, as well as in terms of how the body's mode should be viewed. Nevertheless, in grasping the general relationship between mind and body, we may say that there is a basic continuity here: axiologically speaking, the mind (spirit or consciousness) is regarded as having greater importance than the body (flesh or corporeal things). Gilson's interpretation, which sees the scholastic tradition behind Descartes' *cogito,* is possible for just this reason.

Descartes' philosophy does not deal directly with the problem of time, but since Augustine, Western philosophy has traditionally considered time to be essentially relevant only to the subject's acts of consciousness. Kant's epistemology may be typical in this respect. Although he does treat time and space equally as *a priori* forms of sense intuition in a knowing subject, this initial impression is deceiving. Upon closer examination, we find that for Kant, time-consciousness is more fundamental and important than space-consciousness: self-consciousness (*Selbstbewusstsein*) is only the consciousness of the self's identity, its continuing to be the self through the passage of time. Kant understood this "thoroughgoing identity of self-consciousness" (*durchgängige Identität des Selbstbewusstseins*) to be the fundamental way of defining "consciousness in general" as the knowing subject.[5] In this respect, self-consciousness is, in truth, the *consciousness of the temporal self.*

If, on the other hand, space-consciousness had been regarded as more primary, the fundamental state of consciousness would have been the juxtaposition of momentary space-experiences, temporally cut off from before and after. If that view had been taken, time-consciousness—as that mode of self-consciousness in which the self continues always to be the self, much as a movie is constituted from the consecutive projectings of the frames of a film—would become a secondary constitutent. Thus, if like Kant we take our most fundamental fact to be the consciousness of the human subject's self-identity, that is, the experience of life in which the self always continues to be the self, then we would have no alternative but to regard time-consciousness as more fundamental than space-consciousness.

Let us shift our focus to more recent developments in Western thought. At first, we might assume that contemporary Western philosophy has moved far from the traditional Christian view of humanity. Yet, when we restrict our interest only to the relationships between mind and body and between time and space, we find that the traditional ideas live on. For example, Bergson regarded the most immediate experience of consciousness to be that of *lived time* in the sense of "sheer duration" (*durée pure*). For him, spatial experience is the familiar form into which intellectual thinking is liable to fall by force of habit; the essence of life cannot be sought therein. For Bergson, at the extreme limit wherein the fluidity of such lived time stops, one may conceive of a state of so-called "sheer perception" (*perception pure*). It is only through such a limited conception that we have the world of spatial, mechanistic cause and effect, a world governing lifeless objects. The way Bergson grasps pure consciousness may, of course, be radically different from the way consciousness is grasped by the early modern rationalists like Descartes and Kant, but insofar as Bergson seeks the essence of human life primarily in consciousness and temporality rather than spatiality, he is really within the traditional patterns of Western philosophy after all.

Heidegger's *Dasein*-analysis, as noted already, regards temporarlity as the most fundamental human mode of being. Instead of using the term "consciousness" (*Bewusstsein*), Heidegger prefers to use "being-there" (*Dasein*). He calls "being-in-the-world" the mode of being in which *Dasein* as subject relates to the world. Even though he strives to overcome modern epistemology's opposition of subject and object, Heidegger, like Bergson, considers the experience of time to be more essential than that of space. The mode in which *Dasein* exists as being-in-the-world is posed in terms of the subject's way of taking hold of time, that is, the attitude of grasping the past and future. According to Heidegger, *Dasein* is related to things in the world by "care" (from *Besorgen*), meaning that *Dasein* projects into the world (that is, it takes hold of the *future*) while being thrown into it (that is, it takes hold of the *past*). This understanding of time reminds us of Augustine. As Watsuji's criticism points out, Heidegger makes the world's spatiality into a secondary issue for understanding human existence. Consequently, Heidegger virtually disregards the spatial body. Heidegger's thought may often reject much of early modern epistemology, but in terms of the broad perspective taken here, he still remains within the traditional Western mode of thinking.

When we juxtapose Watsuji's ideas with the just-mentioned trends in Western philosophy, his view of humanity is obviously very different. In Watsuji's analysis of human existence, to be the subject in the acts of consciousness is not fundamentally important. Consequently, the emphasis on time-consciousness, or the attempt to grasp the relationship between person and world in light of temporality, is inadequate to investigating human existence; spatiality is most important. All beings exist most fundamentally as occupying a *basho* in space. If this interpretation of Watsuji is correct, to exist *with a body* in a spatial *basho* is the most fundamental mode of human being. Even though Watsuji never explicitly says this, the implication is there in what he does say. Behind Watsuji's view, we may find the backdrop of a traditionally Japanese, or more generally Eastern, mode of thinking about the relationship between humanity and nature. In the Christian tradition, nature and the spatial universe are creations inferior in status to human beings, who are endowed with the spirituality of God's image. Consequently, the human spiritual eye can objectify other creations. In the East, however, the essential destiny of human life is to be

embraced by life's rhythm in natural space; it is to be together with the
animals and plants, with all things that have life, with what the Buddhists
call "all sentient beings" or "all living beings" (*sattva*).

How should we understand Watsuji's way of thinking in terms of
mind-body theories? His line of thought maintains, for example, that to
be the subject of acts of consciousness is not essential to being human.
Does this mean then that the *physiological* functions of the body are the
most essential determinant of being human? No. The sole emphasis on
the physiological functions (as distinct from the mind) lurks behind the
Western intellectual tradition, specifically, as a potentially heterodox, rev-
olutionary way of thinking. It is a possibility arising out of the opposition
that Christians find between God and evil or between the principles of
spirit and flesh. In other words, when the human essence is traditionally
defined as lying solely in the spirit, this excludes all significant consideration of the body. Hence, there arises in compensation a heretical view that
sees the essential human mode of being exclusively in the physiological
or physical functions of the body. Out of the Cartesian dualism of mind
and body arose the parallelism of mind and matter, the latter eventually
developing into a mechanistic view of humanity (French materialism).
The completion of German idealism was its inversion, the rise of
materialism (Marxism).

Unity of body-mind

As noted above, Watsuji never dealt explicitly with the body and the
philosophical issues relevant to it, but we can see glimpses of his views in
many of his writings. In his early work, *Ancient Japanese Culture,* he
analyzed Japan's oldest songs, emphasizing that the ancient Japanese
people did not distinguish between subjectivity and objectivity. "For
them, what is known through the senses must be immediately the mind."
There is no distinction between the mind and the flesh, so there is no
clear consciousness of the distinction between the self and the modes of
external beings in one's bodily sensations. "They loved nature, becoming
one with its whirling life. . . . This intimate embrace with nature does not
allow one to make nature into an object of thinking." In this manner, as
Watsuji states, the ancient Japanese people's grasp of life is such that,
"There is in their love a subtle harmony between body and mind, and in
their appreciation of nature a peaceful embrace with nature."[6] We may
represent this by saying that mind-body-nature exists as an inseparable unity.

In *Climates,* Watsuji expands on this unity in analyzing the relationship between humanity and nature. In his *Ethics,* moreover, he often refers to the "carnal body." We find therein the following kind of example: Leaving her infant at home, a mother goes out of the house but is always drawn back to the infant. The infant, too, anxiously awaits the mother's return. Although this gravity-like attraction is not a physical gravity, there is nonetheless a very real gravity pulling them together.

> The carnal interconnection is always found wherever there is betweenness, even though the manner of conjunction may differ. We find it not only between a husband and wife, but it is also clearly visible even between friends. To feel like seeing a friend is to tend to go physically near him . . . Seen in this light, the interconnection between carnal bodies contains the moment of experience, a moment that will naturally develop into a psychological relationship. It is, therefore, clearly a mistake to regard this relationship simply as a psychological relationship without the interconnection between carnal bodies. However its psychological moment may be contained, the carnal bodies still draw themselves to each other and are interconnected. This relation is neither physical nor psychological, nor the conjunction of the two. Generally, it is not an objective relatedness but a subjective relatedness in the carnal body.[7]

Accordingly, Watsuj's concept of betweenness, the subjective interconnection of meanings, must be grasped as a *carnal* interconnection. Moreover, this interconnection must not be thought of as either a psychological or physical relatedness, nor even their conjunction.

In addition, Watsuji unfolds his theory of virtue in the study of ethics, giving it the title, "The Organization of Human Relations." Therein he indicates the various human relationships subsumed under the general term "betweenness." It starts with the two-person community (the husband and wife) and then encompasses the immediate family, relatives, the territorial community, the economic organization, the cultural community, all the way up to the state. What catches our attention concerning this point is that the two-person community, the minimum unit of the "organization of the ethical ought," is sought in the carnal interconnection between husband and wife. With this as a source, all the other human relationships are established. This contention is ventured as an objection against the traditional Japanese idea of the family that esteems so highly the relationships of offspring, but Watsuji's standpoint is still not an offshoot of the modern Western idea esteeming the individuality of the subject and the equality between the sexes. Watsuji says that the husband-wife relationship as the two-person community cannot be established until first both sex and love, the two moments of "body" and "mind," accompany each other without separation. This is the ground for the birth of human life and consequently serves as a foundation for all human relationships, that is, for the existence of the "organization of human relations." For this reason, Watsuji says human relationships are neither simply psychological nor simply physical, nor even the conjunction between the two. From the outset, we are not to think of body apart from mind. In other words, the fundamental mode of being human must be grasped as the unity of mind-body or the "oneness of body-mind" (*shinjin ichinyo**): this is Watsuji's claim. We might say his thinking is, indeed, very Eastern in that it spurns analytical thought.

Although Watsuji's way of thinking points us in a completely different direction from that of traditional Western philosophy, his analysis does not teach us much about mind-body theory in a positive way. In investigating the interconnections of meanings in the life-world, philosophers, humanists, and social scientists tend to be carried away in their analyses of psychological relationships, forgetting that the problems of body and space are related to these considerations. One of Watsuji's achievements in contemporary philosophy is that by urging us to reflect on this point, he observed that human relationships are, in truth, the relationships of our carnal interconnections in space.

Still, in the final analysis, he goes no further than to assert that human relationships are neither psychological nor physiological-carnal; he does not define positively the relationship between mind and body. He only says negatively that the way of thinking found in Western philosophy is not based on "the oneness of body-mind" (*shinjin ichinyo*). Yet, it is just self-evident common sense that the body and mind are inseparable. As long as we live, it is impossible for human existence to cut off the body from the mind. What should we do in order to clarify analytically this oneness of body-mind? This is our next concern.

Shinjin ichinyo is a Buddhist term, especially frequent in Zen Buddhist texts.—Ed.

Chapter Two

NISHIDA Kitarō's View of the Body

I t is said that the philosophy of NISHIDA Kitaro* was based on his lived experience (*taiken* †) within seated meditation (*zazen*). By investigating his philosophy, therefore, we should be able to have a still deeper insight into traditional Eastern modes of thinking. Before examining in any detail his view of the body, a few introductory remarks are in order.

Nishida's philosophy is sometimes sarcastically referred to as an "I philosophy" parallel to the Japanese "I novels." Except for a couple of works from his early period, his writings do tend to be a recondite soliloquy, lacking clear theoretical organization and method. Moreover, Nishida supposedly never touched his manuscripts once they were completed. Perhaps for these reasons there are many intuitive leaps in his process of reasoning, and he tends to change subtly the meanings of concepts as he uses them. Consequently, in attempting to evaluate his ideas from

---

*NISHIDA Kitarō (1870–1945) is generally recognized as the most influential of Japan's modern philosophers. ("Modern" in Japanese thought refers to the post-Meiji period beginning in 1868 and continuing to the present, the era in which Western philosophy has had its first significant impact.) Several of Nishida's works have been translated into English, including: *A Study of Good,* translated by Valdo Viglielmo (Tokyo: Japanese Government Printing Bureau, 1960); *Intelligibility and the Philosophy of Nothingness* translated by R. Schinzinger (Tokyo: Maruzen, 1958; subsequently reprinted by the East-West Center Press and more recently by Greenwood Press); *Fundamental Problems of Philosophy,* translated by David A. Dilworth (Tokyo: Sophia University Press, 1970); *Art and Morality,* translated by David A. Dilworth and Valdo H. Vigleilmo (Honolulu: University Press of Hawaii, 1973). The most thorough treatment of Nishida's thought in English is a dissertation by Robert J. Wargo, "The Logic of Basho and the Concept of Nothingness in the Philosophy of Nishida Kitarō," University of Michigan, 1972.—Ed.

†Japanese philosophers use two words for "experience," *keiken* and *taiken,* which correspond roughly to the German distinction between *Erfahrung* and *Erlebnis.* When the distinction seems most relevant, the translators have rendered *taiken* as "lived experience." Again, the *tai* of *taiken* is a character signifying the body.—Ed.

the standpoint of contemporary philosophy, it would be difficult to make the value of his thought sufficiently clear were we to be too literal in restating his position. I would like, therefore, to attempt a free interpretation from my own standpoint, applying to Nishida's thought the terminology and theoretical structure of contemporary philosophy.

The body's ambiguity in acting intuition

In its most fundamental outlook, Nishida's philosophy underwent little change between the earlier and later phases. As for his mind-body theory, though, we find a particularly interesting analysis in his later works where he also presents the theory of so-called "acting intuition" (*kōiteki chokkan**). It is this theory that will be our central focus. Roughly defined, acting intuition is *to act based on intuition;* Nishida's underlying contention is that the two moments of acting and intuiting are always simultaneous and inseparable. Generally speaking, since acting and intuiting are both basic modes of human being-in-the-world (to use Heidegger's phrase), we can say that acting intuition also indicates a fundamental mode of being. In investigating these modes, our present interest is the structure of the relationship between humanity and the world. Acting intuition may be interpreted as a conceptualization of this structure or, stated differently, it may be said that the self, as a human subject, exists by associating itself with the world through the relational structure of acting intuition.

Nishida's unique contribution to our study begins with his interpretation of the acting intuition's structure vis-à-vis the body. In particular, in his essay "Logic and Life" (contained in the second volume of his *Collected Philosophical Essays*), he attempts a particularly detailed investigation of this topic. This essay of his will, therefore, be our special interest.

As a being-in-the-world, a person can live only under the fundamental restriction of having a body. Consequently, the various modes of human being-in-the-world, including cognition, also exist under that restriction. To use Nishida's words, a human is a being "of which there is no self unless there is a body,"[1] and "A body is that *which is seen* as well as *that which sees;*"[2] That is to say, as a subject which sees as well as an object (*kyakutai†*) which is seen, the embodied self is ambiguous in its being.

---

*Other translators have rendered *kōiteki chokkan* as "active intuition."—Ed.

†Parallel to the treatment of "subject," Japanese philosophy recognizes two terms for "object," *kyakkan* and *kyakutai.* These are, respectively, the objects of the *shukan* and *shutai.* The *tai* of *kyakutai,* like the *tai* of *shutai,* signifies the body. See editor's note, Chapter 1, p. 000.—Ed.

There is no ego without a body. . . . Even our own bodies are seen from
the outside. Yet our body is that which sees as well as that which is seen.
There is no seeing without a body.[3]

That a body is "that which sees" indicates how the self exists in the world
as a subject, while its being "that which is seen" indicates how it exists as
an object. Consequently, human being as a being-in-the-world has an
ambiguous character: "that which is seen" and "that which sees." Obviously, a subject (that which sees) exists as a subject in acts of consciousness, that is, in a broad sense it is a *mental* dimension. Conversely, an object (that which is seen) exists as a *body's* dimension. In other words, a
person exists in the world in this unity of mind-body or, as it were, in this
bodily consciousness.

Incidentally, Merleau-Ponty also defined the body as both "the seeing" (*le voyant*) and "the visible" (*le visible*).[4] Despite this resemblance,
though, Nishida was of an earlier generation and obviously could not
have been influenced by Merleau-Ponty. In any case, according to
Merleau-Ponty, the body's objective character (the in-itself) exists with respect to the self; that is, my body is phenomenally experienced here and
now as "the visible" *for me.* However, as is evident from our preceding
quotation, according to Nishida the body's objectivity is grasped as "that
which is seen from the outside." So Nishida implicitly presupposes the
existence of *others* in the life-space.

The network of a human being's interconnected meanings, what
Watsuji calls "betweenness," governs the life-space as the field of everyday experience. Nishida believes the human body shows us to be in this
field of communal, interconnected meanings; the body is the object, the
"that which is seen" *by everybody.* In the case of Merleau-Ponty, however,
the body occupies a privileged position as the "that which is visible"
closest to oneself (one's own body) and "that which is visible" further
away from one's body (others' bodies and nonhuman objects). For
Nishida, though, such a problem cannot arise: one's own body does not
occupy a privileged position, at least in the field of ordinary experience;
the body must be treated solely as a "that which is seen," as an object in
just the same respect as other objects. This implies that Nishida, like Watsuji, regards as primary the manner in which my body exists objectively
in space.

In any case, as a being-in-the-world, the human being displays an
ambiguous character, what we might call a "subjective-objective" being;
human life is only possible as restricted by corporeality. This is the fundamental characteristic for acting intuition in the field of everyday experience. Clearly, in Nishida's acting intuition, acting is related to the *subjective* aspect of human being, whereas intuition is related to the *objective*
aspect. If our focus is on the body's spatial relation to the world, acting is

how a person *actively* approaches the world. In other words, action is the person's active relating to the things (beings) in the world through the body. In contrast, since the body exists as one spatial object among other beings, the self comprehends *passively* the state of things in the world through the intuitions of bodily sense. We noted previously that the body displays an ambiguity in being both subjective and objective in the world as life-space; now we see this implies that acting and intuiting are moments in an active-passive relational circuit between the body and things in the world-space. From these observations, we can sketch the structure of acting intuition. (See Figure 1.)

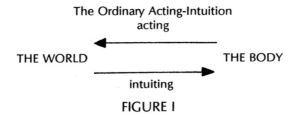

The Ordinary Acting-Intuition
acting

THE WORLD   THE BODY

intuiting

FIGURE I

Time-consciousness and space-consciousness in relation to the body

Given the body's ambiguous subjective-objective character, let us now analyze in more detail the active-passive relationship between the person and the *other* world-space. We will focus on the specific relationship between temporal experience and spatial experience in terms of the body. Nishida's position will be most clear if we contrast it with Heidegger's being-in-the-world (*In-der-Welt-Sein*). As mentioned in Chapter One, Heidegger thought of care or concern as the fundamental attitude by which *Dasein* as a human subject relates itself to the world. *Dasein* is related caringly to the various beings in the world found around the self. Given this concept of care in the light of the subject's *time-consciousness,* there emerges a unique mode of being, what is called the "thrown project" (*geworfener Entwurf*). *Thrownness* implies a caring about the fact that a human subject is thrown into its (past) relationships with the things in the world; *project* implies caring with respect to projecting something (towards a future) for the world. Accordingly, the subject's caring attitude, the taking in hand of the past and future, is called the thrown project. Although this terminology is somewhat difficult, Heidegger's explanation—when viewed psychologically or ontically—is quite understandable. For example, caring about others is simply the fact that the self projects something towards the future for the sake of others; at the same time, the self is thrown into the world, restricted by the human interconnectedness already established in the life-world with others, that is, it is restricted by past *betweenness*.

Obviously, the thrown project indicates how a subject (*Dasein*) relates itself to the world in terms of time-consciousness. But how could we understand the two structural moments of thrownness and project if we were to reinterpret these notions with an emphasis on their *spatial* relation to the world? What if we thereby introduced a consideration of the *body's* way of being in the world-space? What would happen is that Heidegger's structure of the thrown project would come quite close to that of the active-passive relationship in the life-space of man's being, the very relationship we analyzed in the last section. Let us examine more closely how this is so.

First, in human being as an object, the person bears a *passive* relation to the world through the function of the body's sense intuitions. As long as one has a body, one is always placed within relationships to beings other than oneself, namely, to other people and to physical objects. Insofar as acting intuition is a possible mode under the restrictions of corporeality, it is always, and has already been, thrown into a passive relationship with the world. From birth, a person exists as a life already thrown into various relationships with things. In short, as something essentially thrown into the world, human beingness in its bodily intuitions must be grasped in that thrownness.

What, then, is the structure of acting intuition when we consider it from the other side, the side of *acting?* Within the field of everyday experience, the person relates through his or her actions to the various beings in the world. In this case, the self cannot act until it utilizes its body. As Nishida says, if there is no body, there is no acting. How, then, should we interpret the relationship between the being of the self and that of physical objects? In "Logic and Life," Nishida notes that within acting, there is the dimension of *instrumentality*. This may be a Heideggerian influence. When Heidegger regards the fundamental attitude of *Dasein* to be care about beings in the world, what he had in mind was *Dasein*'s relation to "equipment" or *Zuhandenes* (literally, "things on hand"). Incidentally, although Nishida was not directly influenced by Heidegger's writings, Nishida did have a close disciple, MIKI Kiyoshi,* who studied Heidegger carefully.

---

*For a brief outline of Miki's thought as well as a survey of modern Japanese philosophy in general, see Gino K. Piovesana, *Contemporary Japanese Philosophical Thought* (NY: St. John's University Press, 1969). The discussion of Miki is found on pp. 177–186.— Ed.

What is distinctive about Nishida in comparison with Heidegger, though, is Nishida's attempt to understand instrumentality from its relationship to the body. In some acts, we may or may not use an instrument, but this is not the point. For, as is often said, an instrument is an extension of the body. Consequently, as long as we examine the human being from the aspect of the acting subject, the body itself can be said to be a kind of instrument. Nishida writes:

> Man has not only things, but also his body, as his instrument. Along with having a bodily existence, man possesses his body as an instrument. . . . We see our self objectively through and through and yet we always transcend the world of objects. Therein lies our human (subjective) being.[5]

An instrument is a thing and the world is the interconnection of things in their totality. Here, if we grasp the human being-in-the-world with respect to bodily action, the self is primarily inseparable from the body; the body always accompanies a human being's instrumental nature and, moreover, the instrument's being has its foundation in the being of things as objects. Ultimately, the world is the total interconnection of the being of things. Consequently, as a being-in-the-world seen from the aspect of the body's objectivity, the human being is a knot or node in the reticulate interconnection of objective beings, that is, in the network of self-body-instruments-things-world.

This only applies to the person as object, however. From the aspect of the human subject, the total interconnection of beings assumes a subjective tint as well. First of all, *acting* is purposively relating to the beings in the world. In the field of ordinary experience, as long as we are acting purposively, we are always, consciously or unconsciously, related to the world. Interconnected in a means-end relationship, the total self-world network is endowed with a meaning from the standpoint of one's own life. When viewed from the acting self, all things assume meanings as *instruments*. All that can be found in the world, even other people, can be a means or an end for the acting subject. An instrument in a means-end relationship, as Heidegger points out, is always endowed with the sense of "for the purpose of." A hammer is an instrument for the purpose of striking; a star at the end of the universe has a research purpose for an astronomer or cosmologist. Viewed from the subject's perspective, all the beings in the world appear as interconnected meanings in terms of a means-end, that is, they appear under the mode, "for the purpose of." What appears in the interconnection of human intersubjective meaning is the world as life-space. Putting forward a purpose for this world and giving meaning to one's life, one projects toward the actualization of purpose. In this sense, the human subject can be called a "project." If this interpretation is correct, the activeness of acting within the life-space is related to what Heidegger calls the project of *Dasein*.

What, then, is the difference in attitude between Heidegger and Nishida? Following our interpretation, if the structure of *Dasein's* thrown project is the relation of the self to the world as life-space, the result is a dual relation of activity-passivity toward the beings of the world-space. We might also say that the self and the world are linked together in terms of the centripetal-centrifugal circuit of intuiting and acting. In the case of Heidegger, however, the structure of the thrown project does not have this active-passive relationship with the life-space; for him, the thrown project solely takes in hand the past and future within the subject's time-consciousness; that is to say, space-consciousness is not directly considered.

For example, "thrownness" is defined, ontically (or psychologically), as "mood" or "attunement" (*Stimmung*), and ontologically (or logically), as "disposition" (*Befindlichkeit*).[6] In this case, space only exists beyond the veil of an attuned state. As the subject, *Dasein* does not have an immediate concern for space; its concerns remain within the interiority of the self. Psychologically, a mood is a state in which certain feelings in their singularity or plurality continue *temporally*, for example, such feelings as depression, sorrow, anxiety, and merriment. When a person is overtaken by a fixed mood, he or she is concerned exclusively with his or her interior state, separated from the state of the world-space. For instance, if one is fixed on sorrow, one will not be able to escape from it when physically in the bright clear days of spring. Consequently, to understand thrownness into the world in terms of mood or state of mind means to pull back one's body from the life-space, confining oneself to one's interior consciousness. The interior consciousness of the subject, then, is abstracted as the temporality of being human, as that which exists here and now while taking in hand the past and future.

That Heidegger's thrown project is here understood only as the structure of time-consciousness follows from his exclusion of the body and his consideration of spatiality as only secondary. For him, to live in time is the most primordial fact of life for being human. As already mentioned, this reflects Heidegger's heritage, the traditional modes of thinking in Western intellectual history. (It should be noted in passing, however, that our account here does not take into consideration Heidegger's thought after the so-called *Kehren* or "turning.")

If this is Heidegger's view, what is Nishida's understanding of the structural relationship between self and world, the relationship implicit in his notion of the acting intuition? First of all, acting intuition is, more that anything else, a bodily relation to that world-space. We tend to forget in our daily life, however, that the self's being is delimited by the body. Thus, even though this is commonly overlooked, we must recognize that the body's being in the life-space is a fundamental restriction on human being. One's own life, for example, is a possibility within the body, and insofar as that is true, death is inevitable; but in the field of our ordinary experience, we forget this basic restriction on life. Therefore, on the outer layer of the subject's consciousness of the world appear the various acts of consciousness—thinking, feeling, willing—which relate to the beings in the world. The consciousness of temporality, in taking in hand the past and future, is such a consciousness, caringly attentive in its association with the things in the world. At the center of temporal consciousness lies the self-consciousness of the human subject.

As we observed in the previous chapter's discussion of Kant, self-consciousness is primarily time-consciousness, not space-consciousness. That is, self-consciousness is the consciousness of self-identity in which the human self continues to be a self in spite of the passage of time. This consciousness of self-identity is primarily, however, only that which can exist between the beginning and the end, the birth and death of the self. Furthermore, it is nothing but a consciousness related to the world of ordinary experience, or, psychologically speaking, it is a consciousness during the waking state; in the state of deep sleep wherein the caring association with the world stops, the function of self-consciousness disappears. Yet, as we shall see, the ordinary, everyday self-consciousness, immersed in a caring association with the world, tends to be viewed as inauthentic in Eastern traditions like Buddhism. More specifically, they say we must note the relationship between the body and space which underlies and substantially restricts the time-consciousness appearing on the surface layer of consciousness.

The basho *vis-à-vis being and vis-à-vis nothing**

In the field of ordinary experience, the bodily (sense) intuition is the passive relation to the world, and bodily action is the active relation. Insofar as one has an embodied existence, this kind of subjective-objective (active-passive) relation to the world-space is fundamental to human life. That is, for a *bodily* life in the world, there is no primordiality to

*Others have translated *yū no basho* and *mu no basho* as the "*topos* [place] of Being" and the "*topos* [place] of Nothingness." The present translators believe the phrase "vis-à-vis" better captures the nuance of Nishida's use of the phrases and is more consistent with the interpretation developed by Yuasa.—Ed.

Heidegger's thrown project in subjective time-consciousness, that is, to the caring attitude for beings, an attitude based in the taking hold of past and future. Heidegger's view is no more than an understanding of the surface layer of the conscious subject vis-à-vis those beings within the field of ordinary experience; it does not truly overcome the view of the ego developed in modern philosophy. In order to overcome this standpoint of ego-consciousness, we must take note of the structure of the active-passive relation between the body and the world-space, the relation underlying the time-consciousness of the subject. This is the conclusion of our comparison between Heidegger and Nishida.

Our next concern is to ask how the subject's mode of ordinary experience is possible. In other words, we must ask about the *ground* for establishing the acting intuition's structure within the field of everyday experience, that is, the ground that establishes the world of ordinary, human experience. To use Nishida's terminology, it is a question about the "*basho* vis-à-vis nothing."

Our inquiry into the *basho* vis-à-vis nothing will be posed in the following terms. We shall call the acting intuition in the field of ordinary experience "the acting intuition in the *everyday self*." In contrast, the acting intuition grounded in the *basho* vis-à-vis nothing will be called "the acting intuition in the *self as basho*." The everyday self is the consciousness that one is a human subject, or it is the self's way of relating to the life-space while maintaining human ego-consciousness. Nishida suggests that by retaining the ego-consciousness as the human subject, this relation to the world must be considered an inauthentic or aberrant way of life. The authentic life must be discovered in the self as *basho*, that which transcends the everyday self's mode. In other words, the self as *basho* is the authentic self in contrast with the inauthentic everyday self. Consequently, the question concerning the *basho* vis-à-vis nothing amounts to asking how a self can go from the inauthentic to the authentic dimension.

We must first consider the theory of *basho* in Nishida's early thought. In our ordinary understanding, a *basho* (place) is the ground which supports all things existing in *space*. All beings in the world, including human being, exist in the *basho* that they occupy. The *basho* is a fundamental restriction on beings' existence; without it, no beings can exist in the world. Consequently, when we have a certain understanding of the Being of a being, as for example when we say that "there is a tree growing (by the roadside)," the understanding of the Being's *basho* (in this case, the roadside) is always included in the understanding of the being's (in this case, the tree's) Being. Why do all beings need a *basho* for their ground of Being? Needless to say, it is because all beings, even humans, have the characteristic being of the in-itself, that is, they are all "objects" or "things" occupying space.

In short, we discover in our ordinary understanding that all beings exist with their respective *basho* as their ground; this understanding is in the "mind" of the self as human subject. In other words, it is the understanding of Being based on conscious experience in its widest sense. In the experience in which a self, as the subject of ego-consciousness, is related to things in the environmental world, the *basho,* as the ground of the Being of beings, is disclosed to the everyday self, to the self as subject. We can call the experience of this everyday *basho,* "the experience with respect to the *basho* vis-à-vis *being,*" meaning the experience of a conscious subject with respect to the *basho* understood as *being* [the opposite of nothing].

Incidentally, if all beings have *basho* for their ground of Being, this should apply equally well to humans being in the world. Where, then, can we find the *basho* for being human, the ground of Being for the human being? Replacing the word "human being" (*ningen*) with "self" (*jiko*), where can we find the ground for the self's life in the world? This is our next question.

Modern thought has given two opposing answers to this question. The first is the objectivistic attitude represented by natural science. A being, in this case a human being, exists in the same manner as a rock or tree; it exists as a physical object, occupying a certain volume of space, having some weight and quality; that is, the human being exists as a body. When we speak of its existing as an object restricted by corporeality, the human being exists in the "*basho* vis-à-vis being," that which we have called the "world-space." In so doing, we grasp the human being as a physical body, as an object. The acts of the mind, or of consciousness, are here nothing but a secondary epiphenomenon accompanying bodily functions.

Nevertheless, when the self lives in the world as a human being, that is, as one instance of existence, this does not mean that it exists as a "thing" in the *basho* vis-à-vis being (the world-space) in the same way as a rock, for instance. Despite the objectivists' assertions, a human being possesses a mind together with its body. From the standpoint of the objectivists, there is no satisfactory answer to our question about the *basho* as the ground of the Being of human being. They simply do not investigate the "*basho* vis-à-vis being" in this sense. To question philosophically the ground of being human is to ask what it means for the self to live in this world as a human existence.

The other solution found in modern philosophy is that of the subjectivistic attitude represented by idealism. All beings in the world have as their respective *basho* the ground of Being: this is understood through the self-conscious experience (*keiken*) of the world-space. Consequently, the experience of *basho* is just a part of conscious experience. If this were correct, the question concerning the ground of human being would solve itself once we reflectively analyze the experience of the self, that is, the self as conscious subject. Were we to proceed in this manner, we would grasp the relationship between self and world from the aspect of consciousness or of the mind. Descartes' mind-body dualism separates the function of consciousness from the body. Kant's "consciousness in general" is a logical, transcendental subjectivity transcending not only the physiological, but also the empirical and psychological, functions. In Kant, the experience of *basho* is reduced to space-experience in general, an *a priori* form of sense intuition within transcendental subjectivity. Accordingly, for Kant, even though human beings live in the world, it does not follow that they, as instances of human existence, live in the here and now with a body in this *basho;* for Kant, it only means that the human being shares in "the One," the transcendental subjectivity that is everywhere and yet nowhere. The essence of the self as a human subject disappears in the rarefied atmosphere of a logic that disregards the body.

As we have seen, dealing with the mode of being human from the side of physiological objectivity, the objectivist attitude attempts to solve the questions about the *basho* grounding for the Being of beings by resorting to the terms of natural science. The subjectivist attitude of philosophical idealism, on the other hand, attempts to solve it philosophically or logically, dealing with human being only through self-consciousness as the subject experienced in the field of cognition and action. Husserl, in the work of his later period, *The Crisis of European Sciences and Transcendental Phenomenology,* said that the intellectual history of modern Europe has been constantly permeated with the tension between the objectivism of physics established by Galileo and the transcendental subjectivism opposed to it. He emphasized the importance of phenomenology's overcoming this opposition. Seeing himself as a successor to Kant, Husserl believed that the triumph of transcendental subjectivism was the means to overcoming the crisis of modern Europe. Although we cannot accept this conclusion, Husserl was quite right in asserting the presence of this tension in modern European intellectual history.

Following our discussions of the inadequacy in both objectivism and subjectivism, we come to realize that the experience of *basho* is an issue having a truly contemporary significance and, moreover, we realize that at the center of our question is the relationship between the mind and body. Our original question concerning "the *basho* vis-à-vis nothing" is an attempt to shed light on this problem from a new angle.

Dual-layered consciousness

Bearing in mind the logical and historical background discussed in the preceding section, we now consider Nishida's treatment of the experience of *basho*. When Nishida in his early period arrived at the theory of *basho*, he was not concerned with mind-body theories, but rather was interested in theorizing about the Zen experience by utilizing the conceptual structures and terminology of modern epistemology, especially those of Neo-Kantianism. For this reason, his arguments are posed in epistemological terms.

The *basho* vis-à-vis nothing is the *basho* which supports the totality of the epistemological subject-object relation. How is it to be discovered? In *From That Which Functions to That Which Sees*, generally considered to be the culmination of Nishida's *basho* theory, he states:

> *The transcendence of the consciousness in general* is the transcendence of the *basho* containing both form and matter. What is general transcends towards the bottom of what is general, what is immanent transcends towards the bottom of what is immanent, and the *basho* transcends towards the bottom of the *basho*. It is *to immerse the consciousness in the bottom of consciousness.*[7]

Obviously, Nishida's style is difficult and convoluted, full of abstruse expressions, but we can concentrate for now mainly on the phrases I italicized.

The expression "consciousness in general" is Kantian in origin, but Nishida uses the term in only an analogous way to refer to the *basho* vis-à-vis nothing. Kant's consciousness in general is a form of transcendental logic restricting and transcending the empirical ego-consciousness. The *basho* vis-à-vis nothing also transcends, in a sense, the empirical ego-consciousness, but its manner of transcendence is different from what we find in Kant; it is "the transcendence of the *basho containing both form and matter.*" Form and matter are the subjective and objective conditions for cognition, and the *basho* vis-à-vis nothing is the *basho* in which these two are established. That is to say, it is the ground that supports the totality of the subject-object relationship. The reason that it is called the "*basho* vis-à-vis nothing" is that it is the *invisible basho*, different in dimension from the *basho* vis-à-vis being that is the ground of everyday experience and is disclosed in the subject-object relation.

How is it possible to reach such a *basho?* To do that, it is necessary that "the *basho* transcend towards the bottom of the *basho.*" This means a transcendence from the *basho* vis-à-vis being to the *basho* vis-à-vis nothing, that is, a movement from that which the everyday self understands to be the ground of the Being of beings to the invisible *basho* grounding that *basho* vis-à-vis being. For this to be so, we must regard the modality of the everyday self as inauthentic. That is, the modality of the self as the subject of ego-consciousness is denied and it becomes necessary for "consciousness *to immerse itself in the bottom of consciousness*." Kant's consciousness in general is a logical abstraction from the empirical ego-consciousness. In contrast, Nishida's *basho* vis-à-vis nothing is the *basho* that can be reached by denying the fact that the self is such an ego-consciousness or, to be more precise, by letting it *disappear*. Stated differently, the ego-consciousness revealed in ordinary experience has an invisible bottom layer. If we classify the ego-consciousness that relates itself to the everyday life-space as "the layer of bright consciousness," there is also the layer of the concealed, dark *cogito* at its base. "To immerse consciousness in the bottom of consciousness" is to look existentially into this layer of the dark *cogito* not apparent on the surface of consciousness.

Ego-consciousness essentially means a consciousness of the *object* as well as of the *self*. For example, when looking at a tree, accompanying the perceptual function of looking at the tree (that is, being conscious of the tree) is the function of being conscious of the self as looking at the tree (the thinking, emotion, desire, and so forth). If we reflectively analyze such an ego-consciousness, we have the subject-object relation. Such a self-object consciousness is the aforementioned stream of the bright consciousness. In our previous comparison between Heidegger and Nishida, the time-consciousness of the subject in its relation to the world, or the attitude of taking hold of the past and future in caring about the beings of the world, is the understanding of Being in its surface dimension of ordinary experience. That is, Heidegger's "care" is nothing other than what we have called the layer of bright consciousness.

But at the bottom of this bright consciousness, or at the bottom of time-consciousness as the thrown project of relating to the world through care, is the passive-active structure of the body in its relation to the world-space. In other words, at the base of the ontological mode—the subject of the Being of human being (the for-itself)—is disclosed the ontological mode—the object (the in-itself) that is its substantial restriction. If this is correct, the *basho* vis-à-vis nothing is the bodily modality that substantially restricts the being of the self. To inquire into this is to face the interiority of the self itself. In other words, by regarding the ordinary understanding of the relationship between mind and body as inauthentic and insufficient, one inquires existentially into the true way of understanding this relationship. It is then that consciousness immerses itself in the bottom of consciousness.

In the previous quotation, Nishida wrote, "What is general transcends towards the bottom of what is general, what is immanent transcends towards the bottom of what is immanent. . . . '' What does this mean? Although these statements are obscure, the contrast between "general" and "immanent" suggests the aspects of form and of content in the acts of consciousness. Nishida thinks that these acts are fundamentally reducible to one. For example, he says the following in *The Study of Good.*

> The distinction between things like impulse and perception as contrasted with things like willing and thinking, is a difference in degree, not in kind. The *unconscious process* in the former *reveals itself of itself consciously* in the latter; therefore, by inference from the latter, we know that the former must have an identical structure.[8]

Here, both willing and thinking are taken to be representative acts of consciousness which differentiate, develop, and are evident on, the surface of consciousness. This is the layer of bright consciousness (the *cogito*). In contrast, both impulse and perception are unconscious processes. That is, they represent the dark layer of consciousness functioning at the bottom of the bright consciousness. Behind this dark consciousness lurks a capacity unifying all acts of consciousness, such as thinking, willing, emotion, and perception in their differentiating development. To use Nishida's phrase, it is a "unifying force at the bottom of our thinking and willing." As I interpret it, this is deeply linked with the body's being a substantial restriction on the conscious subject, but in this early work Nishida had not yet dealt directly with the body. As they enter into the layer of dark consciousness, the general forms of conscious acts, like thinking, willing and emoting, converge into, and are reduced to, the "unifying force" of the undifferentiated interiority of experience. This is probably what is meant by the immersion of "what is general at the bottom of what is general." The self in this manner advances from the various acts of consciousness toward the deeper and more general (undifferentiated) unifying force.

Next, the immersion of "what is immanent at the bottom of what is immanent" probably means that various aspects under the general rubric of the acts of consciousness—the concrete contents of conscious acts like emotion and impulse—are intertwined with each other in many layers. That is, for the same emotion, there are many contents, varying from the layer revealed on the surface to the deeply concealed layer into which it is difficult for the self to have insight. Sorting out Nishida's analysis of *basho,* KŌSAKA Masaaki distinguishes three states of *basho:* the *basho* vis-à-vis being, the *basho* vis-à-vis relatively nothing, and the *basho* vis-à-vis absolutely nothing.[9] Although Nishida makes no clear distinctions among the three *basho,* Kōsaka implies that, unlike the *basho* vis-à-vis being, with its fixed, immovable horizon, the *basho* vis-à-vis nothing is a region with infinite depth.

Incidentally, the term "function" in the title of the book, *From That Which Functions to That Which Sees,* * expresses the standpoint of the ego-consciousness. "Functioning" here means to internalize within the ego what is transcendent (external) to it. The ego, which attempts to know an object from the cognitive field, is "that which functions," but reality's configuration cannot be grasped from the standpoint of the epistemological subject, that is, from the standpoint of functioning *actively* towards the world. Nishida says, "Functioning is not knowing, for we know even that which functions. . . . We cannot come to know by constituting matter through form."[10] In order to grasp the true meaning of being, one has to deny the subsistent modality of the ego-consciousness qua functioning, and, as it were, immerse oneself retrogressively into the interiority of the self itself. Nishida goes on to say, therefore:

> The consciousness in general which truly objectifies all is not that which transcends [in Kant's sense] the acts [of consciousness] but that which embraces all objects within itself by receding as far as possible into the interiority of the self.[11]

When the self transforms itself by receding into its interiority, into the self qua *basho* grounded in the *basho* vis-à-vis nothing found deep within the layer of dark consciousness, it moves from the standpoint of "that which functions" to the standpoint of "that which sees"; the authentic self illuminates the *basho* vis-à-vis being from the perspective of the *basho* vis-à-vis nothing. In short, in what Nishida says of the experience of *basho,* we must note the distinction between the ordinary experience of the *basho* vis-à-vis being and the experience of the *basho* vis-à-vis nothing that exists at the bottom of the former. Moreover, we must recognize that the former is associated with the bright consciousness, whereas the latter indicates the region of dark consciousness, concealed at its base in the body.

Practical apodicticity of experience qua basho

The authentic self qua *basho* denies, and is reached by extinguishing, the standpoint of the ego-consciousness which functions actively toward the

---

*The title of this book, *Hataraku mono kara miru mono e,* can also be translated as *From the Acting to the Seeing.*

world. How is this new standpoint possible? Wouldn't it be nothing but a recession and immersion into the interiority of the dark consciousness? Nishida thinks not. He contends that the self transforms itself from the everyday self grounded in the *basho* vis-à-vis being to the self qua *basho* in the *basho* vis-à-vis nothing; in so doing, it comes to possess the configuration of reality, that is, to reach the correct knowledge of the Being of beings.

This *basho* theory has often been criticized as an abstruse, mysterious speculation, so we will find Nishida's maiden work, *The Study of Good,* easier to understand because of its strongly descriptive, psychologistic tendency. Nishida's contention in this book lies in his notion of pure experience. Although his theory of pure experience is influenced by James and Bergson, a closer examination reveals a subtle difference. Here, we shall contrast it with the notion of apodicticity in phenomenology. (Although Nishida apparently did not know Husserl's works all that well, according to a recent study, Husserl was influenced in his early period by James's psychology. Since the experience of consciousness in phenomenology is an experience with immediate apodicticity, it might bear some similarity to the notion of "pure experience" in James and Bergson.)

Nishida's pure experience, to put it simply, is prior to that self-awareness in which the self qua conscious subject is opposed to the world; in other words, it is experienced nonthetically, without any accompanying reflective self-awareness that the self is the subject of the ego-consciousness. It is, in this sense, an experience with *immediate apodicticity.* Prior to the self's being grasped in reflective self-awareness, we live in the midst of an immediate, apodictic, lived experience (*taiken*) from which such a self-awareness itself arises. In this sense, pure experience is the standpoint of the not yet differentiated subject and object.

It bears a similarity to Husserl's phenomenological apodicticity in that it is prior to the positing of the relation of subject and object, but Husserl requires the theoretical operation of the so-called *epoché* (the suspension of judgment) in order to attain immediate apodicticity. According to his phenomenology, the everyday self has an innate tendency to think under the command of the natural standpoint (*natürliche Einstellung*) that things in the world outside the self exist as objects and the self exists as the subject opposing them. He says that when we stop such an innate tendency by a thought experiment, suspending all judgments concerning the relationship between the being of the self and that of things, a stream of immediate, apodictic perception will be disclosed, a stream operating at the foundation of the world as experienced in the natural standpoint.

Nishida's pure experience, however, is an immediate apodicticity that is not disclosed by any such theoretical operation but rather by means of a *practical* activity. In explaining the state of the not yet differentiated subject and object, Nishida gives the following examples: "For instance, it is in such occasions as a person's scaling a cliff, holding on for dear life, or a musician's playing a composition he has mastered,"[12] or as "when our mind, forgetting both self and things, is lost in a sublime music, the entire world becomes a single melodious sound."[13] He says, "Pure experience is an animated state with maximum freedom in which there is not the least gap between the will's demand and its fulfillment."[14] Pure experience's immediate apodicticity is clearly one that emerges from practical operations directed toward the world; it actualizes the demands of the will.

Nonetheless, the practical in this case does not mean relating to the world from the standpoint of the everyday self as conscious subject, or through the so-called "that which functions." The self transforms itself into the self qua *basho* by delving below the layer of the bright consciousness on which appears the dimension of such functioning, and by immersing itself in the dimension of the dark consciousness. Then, the self will be impelled inevitably by means of the unifying force in the greatly expanded personality emerging from this concealed dimension. This *passive* (bodily) experience from within is pure experience's immediate apodicticity and resistant to doubt; it becomes immediately a practical action. That is, to recede retrogressively into the self's interior is a detour from advancing toward the world. In short, the immediate apodicticity of the conscious experience achieved in Husserl's *epoché* (the suspension of judgement) is a stream in what we have been calling the bright consciousness's functional relationship between the self and the world of ordinary experience. In contrast, Nishida's experience of immediate apodicticity is by means of a *practice* that confronts the self's interiority itself, that region of dark consciousness concealed at the bottom of the bright consciousness.

Psychologically speaking, the immediate apodicticity of Nishida's pure experience can be called an ecstatic state, and therein we find an analogy with the experience of *samādhi* in Zen meditation. Whether this is something more that a mere analogy will be discussed later. At any rate, Nishida's theory of acting intuition can be interpreted as an attempt to grasp afresh the notion of pure experience or of *basho* from the viewpoint of a mind-body theory.

The dual structure in acting intuition

The acting intuition is the synthetic unity of the two moments of action and intuition. What needs to be further explained is the meaning of this intuition. Because of Nishida's lack of terminological clarity and rigor, there is much room for misunderstanding. The term "intuition" in acting intuition is a case in point. As far as I can tell, Nishida uses this term in two different senses. The first use of the word is "sense intuition"; here the word *chokkan* corresponds to the English word "intuition" and to the German *sinnliche Anschauung,* but these Western words have historical roots different from the Japanese. Specifically, these words refer to the function of perception (*Wahrnehmung*) connected to the sensory organs as well as to the "intellectual intuition" (*intellektuelle Anschauung*). This latter concept requires some explanation.

To put it simply, intellectual intuition is related to inspiration. This word has often been used since ancient times in the West for the creative activity in a genius, whether an artist, scholar, or religious figure. Epistemologically, it is a higher cognitive faculty for attaining a correct conclusion without employing inferential judgments. In the history of Western philosophy, Plato's *nous* and Thomas Aquinas's *intellectus* have this meaning. Since intellectual intuition is a psychological function difficult to find in ordinary experience, modern experimental psychology does not clearly recognize its status. Still, in Nishida's concept of intuition, this classical sense of the term is still operative. For example, in *The Study of Good* the intellectual intuition is characterized as the state in which pure experience is greatly enlarged.

> The intellectual intuition is nothing more than a further enlargement and deepening of our state of pure experience. That is, it is a disclosure of a great unity in the process of a developing system of consciousness. That a scholar acquires a new insight, or a moralist a new motive, or an artist a new imagination, or a religious figure a new awakening, are all based upon a disclosure of this kind of unity.[15]

The concept of intuition in Nishida's second work, *Intuition and Reflection in Self-Awareness,* is also used in this sense of intellectual intuition. In fact, given its usage there, it might be more appropriately called creative, rather than intellectual, intuition. The adjective "intellectual" is appropriate insofar as the intuition functions in the field of intellectual cognition. Plato's *nous* and Saint Thomas's *intellectus* are restricted mainly to this meaning; here we can see the traditional Western view in which great value is placed on the human function of intellectual cognition. However, as is evident from Nishida's quotation, intuition appears not only in the field of intellectual cognition; it is a creative function which appears, as it were, in almost all fields of human experience, including moral practice, artistic creativity, and religious awakening.

The concept of intuition in the theory of acting intuition does not demarcate clearly these two different uses of the term, and we must keep both senses in mind so as not to misunderstand Nishida's argument. In our ordinary experience, we find various things in our environment. What exists in the world is, in Heidegger's terminology, either a "being" (*Seinde*) or a "being within the world" (*innerweltliche Seinde*). Although these are not Japanese terms, we can use them in our explanation of Nishida. As I said originally, acting intuition can be interpreted as the fundamental mode of being in which the person, as a "being-in-the-world" relates himself or herself to the world; but, concretely, to relate to the world means to have relationships with various beings, including the Other. The structure of this relation is the acting intuition. Accordingly, to grasp human being-in-the-world in the form of the acting intuition is to grasp the structural relationship between the self and the world in light of the modality of the *body*. For *acting* means to act on the world by means of or with a body; and *intuition,* as previously noted, means to understand, as well as accept, the Being of the beings found in the world and to do so through the body's perceptual functions. If we think of our ordinary experience and of acting intuition in light of the body, the human being can be tentatively defined as a being who *acts* on the world with a body, while understanding the modalities of beings through the sense intuition supplied by that body.

When we grasp being human as related to the body, the relationship between the body and space is most important. Since the body occupies a place in the everyday life-space, its spatial relationship with the world is more important than anything else for the acting intuition's mode of being. Thus, the person is a being who *passively* recognizes (through sense intuition) a situation in the space-world and (in embracing a judgment and thinking about it) directively acts on that world. Consequently, the acting-intuition's structure in the field of everyday experience is found to be, as we saw in Figure 1, a passive-active circuit relating the body to the world. In other words, the relationship between self and world is here established via the synthetic unity between the passive function (the sense intuition about the external world) and the active function (the action that acts on the external world).

This relation between self and world in everyday acting intuition is the dual relationship between passivity (intuition) and activity (action). This understanding is in modern Western epistemology as well, albeit in germinal form. For Kant, the conscious function of cognizing (or knowing) is to give a rational form to the matter, or raw material, presented by sense intuition. This, for Kant, is *judgment.* Consequently, the two functions of reason and intuition become the two moments linking subjectivity and objectivity, or consciousness and its object, or, even more broadly, self and world. In this case, we may interpret intuition as being passive and reason as being active. In Kant's language, the function of intuition is "receptivity" (*Rezeptivität*) and the function of reason is "spontaneity" (*Spontaneität*).[16] In other words, in intuition, consciousness *passively* receives the state of its object whereas in reason, consciousness acts spontaneously or *actively* on its object.

If we interpret Kantian cognition in this way, this relationship resembles the structure of acting intuition discussed above. Nevertheless, modern Western philosophy regards the problem of action, namely, that of the will, to be an issue for practical ethics, but not theoretical epistemology. That is, although the psychological characteristics of subjectivity, such as spontaneity and receptivity, are important in ethics in the problem of autonomy and heteronomy, these same psychological aspects are virtually ignored in epistemology. This is because modern Western philosophy seeks human essence in the rational, thinking subject; its epistemology excludes the problems of the body. This attitude obviously originates in the rationalistic view of the human being and from Descartes' mind-body dualism.

In contrast, Nishida's theory of acting intuition grasps human being-in-the-world as originally having the character of *action;* the essential mode is to act on the world, not to cognize it. Persons are subjects qua action before they are thinking, cognizing subjects. The former implies the latter. So it is clear why Nishida rejects both the rationalistic view of being human represented by modern epistemology as well as the mode of thinking that puts the subject and object in opposition to each other.

Now, to our surprise, we discover that as the self moves from the *basho* vis-à-vis being to the *basho* vis-à-vis nothing, as it transforms itself from the everyday self to the self qua *basho,* there is a reversal in the structural relationship between passivity and activity, between the self and the world, in acting intuition. As we have noted, in the field of ordinary experience, the sense intuition is a passive function in relation to the world and the action qua body is the active function. Going beyond this field, however, when the self enters into the underlying *basho* vis-à-vis nothing, this structure reverses; intuition becomes active and action passive. In other words, intuition is now the unifying force beyond the surface self-consciousness; it acts from the *basho* vis-à-vis nothing.

Conversely, on this deeper level, action now means that the self, receiving the power of its intuition, advances towards the world of everyday life. It might also be said that as the self enters into the *basho* vis-à-vis nothing, it acts, reflexively as it were, towards the world of everyday life. While being activated by the unifying force of the personality, the source of creative intuition springs from its invisible roots. Intuition is no longer the sense intuition of ordinary experience; it now has the second meaning discussed above, that is, it is more like a creative intuition, what

Nishida calls an intellectual intuition. Nishida insists in *The Study of Good* that intellectual intuition, unlike sense intuition, is not a passive function.

> Just as ordinary perception is thought to be only passive, so too intellectual intuition is thought to be only a passive, contemplative state. But true intellectual intuition is the unifying act itself in pure experience; it is a capturing of life. That is, it is like a skillful knack or, in a more profound sense, it is the spirit of the arts. For example, there is a unifying something operative behind the complex function wherein the artist is engrossed and the brush moves itself. . . . Here there is a state in which subject and object are not differentiated and the intellect and will are merged. It is a state in which the self and things are mutually responsive to each other; things do not move the self nor vice versa. There is only one world, one scene.[17]

Intuition is its authentic sense, or the creative intuition in the self qua *basho*, is the disclosure of the unifying force (which is undisrupted and united as well as creative) operative at the base of all conscious acts: intellectual thinking, moral practice, artistic performance, and religious revelation. Nishida contends that creative intuition is not passive like a sense intuition, but is active. The internal thrust of creative intuition moves the self while the self is filled with a great power beyond the everyday self. And the action in the self qua *basho* refers to the state in which the self, receiving such intuition, acts towards the world (in the ecstatic state) as "self without being a self," that is, with the ordinary dimension of self-consciousness extinguished. Therefore, Nishida says that its action is in that "animated state with maximum freedom in which there is not the least gap between the will's demand and its fulfillment." It is in this respect that the passive-active structure of acting intuition is reversed; intuition becomes active and action passive.

How should we comprehend the relationship between the mind and body in the acting intuition of the self qua *basho*? Because it exists through the body, the everyday self (as a being-in-the-world) has the ambiguous character of subjective-objective being (the for-itself and in-itself). Although the subjectivity of consciousness (the mind) and the objectivity of the body are inseparably conjoined, they are still distinguishable into subjectivity and objectivity (the for-itself and in-itself). This means that the respective functions of the mind and body are not completely one. In the preceding quotation, Nishida cited the example of having a skillfull knack at something. For those who have not acquired the knack, the body does not move along with the mind, no matter how hard the mind tries. In other words, the body is something inert, resisting the mind's movements; this is an objectivity substantially restricting the self's subjec-

tivity as a human being. As one trains, however, the movement of the
mind and body gradually come into agreement. To use Nishida's example, if one can act in the same way as an excellent musician plays a piece
that has been mastered, or as an artist whose brush moves itself in accord
with inspiration, the functions of the mind and the body become unified;
ideally, one will reach the stage of being a master performer in which
there is the "oneness of body and mind" (*shinjin ichinyo*).

Although the subjectivity of consciousness and the body's objectivity
are inseparable within the ordinary acting intuition, they are disin-
tegrated into being-for-itself and being-in-itself. This is because the consciousness in question is nothing but a layer of the bright, surface consciousness. In contrast, for the acting intuition of the self qua *basho,* the
self reaches the dark, basal consciousness, experiencing its *basho* apodic-
tically, which it does through *practice.* Thus, the disintegration of the distinction between consciousness as subjectivity and the body as objectivity
is overcome; the functions of mind and body become one. Nishida refers
to this as "becoming a thing and exhausting it." To "become a thing"
means that through practice, the mind extinguishes the self-consciousness as a subject opposing the body and its objectivity; the mind becomes
completely one with the body as thing. At this point, the body loses its objectivity as a thing and, as it were, is made subjective. This way of being a
subject is not the self-consciousness grounded in the *basho* vis-à-vis being,
but is the self qua *basho* in the *basho* vis-à-vis nothing, that is, "the self
without being a self."

To "exhaust the thing" means that the self acts towards the world as
"the self without being a self." Here, the mind's modality as subject is
directly the body's modality as object. Naturally, there can be various
stages in achieving this oneness. Since the layered consciousness or the
basho vis-à-vis nothing is a region containing an infinite variety and depth
(unlike the definite and fixed horizon of the *basho* vis-à-vis being), the degree of oneness between subjectivity and objectivity is proportional to the
degree to which the everyday self becomes the self qua *basho.* Thus, from
that which is ultimately at the *basho* vis-à-vis nothing, or, to use Nishida's
own expression, from "absolutely nothing," springs forth the "stream of
inner life" and it begins to act gradually but intensely as creative intuition.
As regards the body in authentic acting-intuition, Nishida writes:

> That we act with the "historical body" means that the self immerses it-
> self in the historical world; insofar as it is the expressive world's self-
> determination, we can say that we act or function. . . . As the creative el-
> ement in the historical world, our bodily self and the historical life
> actualize themselves through our bodies. The historical world forms it-
> self by means of our body. . . . To immerse [oneself] in the world does

not mean to lose the body, nor does it mean that it becomes universal. On the contrary, [the self] is deepened or, rather, it is thoroughly at the base of one's body.[18]

This passage from "Logic and Life" is extremely difficult, but we may attempt an interpretation based on what we have already said. First of all, there are frequent references to the "historical" as contrasted with the "natural scientific." A "historical body" is a body in the self qua *basho* which is beyond the body in its everyday dimension; that is, the historical body has overcome the disintegration into subjectivity and objectivity. When the self acts as a historical body, it enters into the *basho* vis-à-vis nothing, transcending the dimensions of the ego-consciousness or bright consciousness. Consequently, transcending the standpoint of self-consciousness, the self has "immersed" itself into the "historical world," that is, into beings' total interconnectedness in the world as the life-space. In this sense, the body's function is not the ordinary sense of "action," that is, it differs from the bright consciousness, from the everyday self in which one moves the body in accordance with the will's choices and decisions. But, as Nishida says, insofar as it is viewed as "the expressive world's self-determination," we "act or function" in some higher sense.

"The expressive world" means the world seen as the *basho* in which absolutely nothing (at the extremity of the *basho* vis-à-vis nothing) expresses itself. Here is Nishida's unique metaphysics: when this world is seen as the expressive world in which absolutely nothing expresses itself, the function of "our bodily selves," that is, the acting intuition in the self qua *basho,* becomes "the creative element in the historical world." For the "historical life," or the stream of creative intuition that springs from the ultimate, absolutely nothing, "actualizes itself through our bodies." In other words, "the historical world forms itself by means of our bodies."

This is no place to study Nishida's complex metaphysical system; we only wish to examine his mind-body theory. What, then, is left once we eliminate the metaphysics of absolutely nothing? Towards the end of the previously quoted passage, he said that to immerse onself in the world is not to lose the body, but rather the self is deepened and is thoroughly at the base of the body. In other words, in the self qua *basho,* the body's function in the acting intuition seems to disappear (for the self's self-awareness of the self), but, in reality it exerts even more completely the body's function. What does this mean?

In ordinary experience, the body's function is separate from the mind's; that is, one experiences the body as that which is inert in response to the mind's function. For example, those who have not acquired a skillfull knack for something or are not well trained in an athletic sport cannot move their hands and feet as the mind intends. This is because the self controls only the surface layer of the bright consciousness. As the self overcomes such a bright ego-consciousness and illumines the layer of the dark consciousness buried in the body, the body loses its heaviness and becomes unopposed to the mind's functioning. The body qua object is gradually made, as it were, subjective. At the same time, my mind comes to lose its character of being a subject opposed to objects. In this way, the body as object is subjectivized and mind as subject loses its opposition to objects; it gives up being an ego-consciousness. It enters into the state of selfless *samādhi* or what may be called "the self without being a self." By saying acting intuition "becomes a thing and exhausts it," Nishida claims that the ambiguity between subjectivity and objectivity disappears. To become a thing and exhaust it means, we might say, that "the mind [*kokoro*] becomes one with the thing and it strikes to the heart [*kokoro*] of the thing." Here we have an Eastern tradition's view of being human and of body-mind.

Problematics in Nishida's method

Although Nishida's approach is suggestive for our task, he is still inadequate in developing a theory of the relationship between mind and body. From a methodological standpoint, he leaves us with two problems.

First, Nishida's arguments do not clearly demarcate ordinary experience from the experience of *basho*. We have attempted to delineate the difference between the two and, in so doing, have tried to see the contrast with Husserl and Heidegger. Without such an effort on our part, Nishida's arguments disappear into recondite speculation. For example, TANABE Hajime, a critic of Nishida, rejected the acting intuition theory as being a quietistic, contemplative intuitionism. MIKI Kiyoshi, Nishida's beloved disciple, criticized him for taking a step backward into Eastern intuitionism without sufficiently seeing the practical character of action. Both of them interpreted Nishida as valuing intuition (quiet, passive contemplation) over action. Such views arose from Nishida's lack of clarity about intuition; so the heterogeneity of acting intuition's two dimensions (the everyday self and the self as *basho*) was left undeveloped.

Differently stated, Nishida did not consciously tell us how to transform the dimension of everyday experience into the dimension of experiencing *basho*. He did not see this as the problem that it is: this transformative process involves an important revision in our attitude about the mind-body relationship. At the same time, it seems that the mode of everyday thinking, based on the standpoint of ego-consciousness, must be overcome and negated. Thus, one important theoretical problem for Eastern philosophy may be the transformation and reversal of our ordinary grasp of beings.

The second point about Nishida is that he was strongly influenced by modern, especially Kantian, epistemology. In the preface added to a later edition of *The Study of Good,* he writes: "Today this book's standpoint may be considered to be that of consciousness and it might even be considered psychologistic. Such a criticism cannot be avoided." Here he rejects psychologism and takes logicism to be philosophy's correct standpoint. This is a direct influence of the Neo-Kantians, who maintain that psychological experience is relative and individualistic, thereby lacking logical necessity. Logical form must possess an absolute necessity transcending the relativity of psychological experience. Post-Kantian rationalistic philosophy strongly maintained this logicism and, broadly speaking, it is an idea found in Western idealistic metaphysics since Plato. What Western philosophers of old tended to think of as transcending the relativity and contingency of empirical knowledge was the necessity of mathematical proofs. They discovered in mathematics a model for philosophical reasoning. Moreover, an absolute necessity even transcending the necessity of mathematics came to be a philosophical ideal. The tradition of Eastern metaphysics, however, seriously questions the Western assumption about the superiority of intellectual speculation.

Now I shall make one final comment about Nishida. It has often been said that Nishida's philosophy made the Zen experience logical. Nishida himself did not claim this, however. Unlike D. T. Suzuki, he did not restrict himself solely to the study of Zen, nor of Eastern thought generally. Nishida simply tried to establish his own metaphysics and, in so doing, to go beyond Western philosophy. Yet, we cannot deny that his philosophy took root in the Eastern tradition; he himself admitted this. Taking Nishida's thought for our guide through the contemporary problems in philosophy and science, we want to see the Eastern tradition's implicit way of comprehending the relationship between the mind and body.

In this respect, we note that Zen's way of thinking begins by denying the superiority of intellectual speculation. This is the meaning of the famous Zen phrase "just sitting [in meditation]." From a broader perspective, the same essential idea runs throughout Buddhism and even all the Eastern traditions.

To try to make the content of the Zen experience logical by means of intellectual speculation would only trivialize Zen. Naturally, insofar as Zen inherits the Buddhist philosophical tradition, it does not necessarily reject *all* philosophical analyses. But to interpret its significance only in light of intellectual reasoning without taking into account its psychological and experiential content would be to stray into hazy speculation. Thus, we must seek anew a research method or attitude appropriate to understanding the traditional character of Eastern metaphysics.

Chapter Three

Method and Attitude in Studying Eastern Thought

The need for methodological reflection

In studying Eastern thought, it is common practice even in Japan to depend on the methods and theories of Western philosophy. For example, in Buddhist scholarship, KIMURA Yasumasa interpreted Early Buddhism in the light of Schopenhauer's philosophy, while WATSUJI Tetsurō based his innovative interpretation on phenomenology.[1] Although Buddhist studies have progressed such that this sort of straightforward approach is no longer prevalent, we still commonly find an analogous attitude in the study of individual thinkers. Comparative thought is quite fashionable in Japan today, and so there are numerous studies comparing, for example, Dōgen and Heidegger or Shinran and Kierkegaard. Such comparisons are indeed useful in both deepening our understanding of individual philosophers and in discovering new meaning in familiar ideas.

Still, in treating premodern Eastern thought, there is the danger of gross misinterpretation unless one carefully takes into account the fundamental philosophical differences between East and West. In contemporary Japan, knowledge of Western thought is widespread, and our thinking is deeply influenced by it. Consequently, we are liable to slip unconsciously into the tendency to investigate and evaluate Eastern thought in the light of Western modes. One example is Nishida's adoption of logicism in rejecting psychologism. Still, it is questionable whether such a Western-style approach is appropriate to understanding more traditional Eastern thought.

Among contemporary Western thinkers, those who have expressed the deepest interest in Eastern thought generally belong to such fields as psychiatry or clinical psychology, rather than philosophy. (For the present, I am excluding for consideration, of course, Western scholars in oriental studies per se.) For example, such names as C. G. Jung, Erich Fromm, and Medard Boss immediately come to mind. Jung expressed a deep interest in yogic meditation, Taoist meditation, and the special meditation method expounded in a basic text of Pure Land Buddhism, the *Amitāyurdhyāna Sūtra*. Moreover, his research also covered esoteric Tibetan Buddhism, Zen Buddhism, and the Chinese *I Ching*.[2] Even in his own psychological theory, the influence of Eastern thought is considerable, a point to which I will return later. Although Fromm's interest in the East is not as broad as Jung's, he did find an essential connection between Zen and psychoanalysis in their views of the nature of being human.[3] The Buddha's teachings, it is said, inspired Fromm's formulation of his own psychoanalytic theory. When Medard Boss visited India, he met with various Hindu sages. He too felt that he had found in their spiritual life the ultimate ideal for Western psychotherapy.[4]

Major Western philosophers, on the other hand, have generally not demonstrated an interest in the East equal to that of the psychologists and psychoanalysts mentioned above. Jaspers stands out as a possible exception: he dealt with Eastern as well as Western thinkers in his work, *The Great Philosophers*. Even in his case, however, the fundamentals of his own philosophical system have nothing to do with Eastern thought. In my opinion, Rudolf Otto expressed a comparatively deep, personal interest in the East, but still, as is evident from his *The Idea of the Holy*,[5] he was much more interested in psychological, experiential facts than in logical or philosophical speculation.

In short, Western philosophers do not have the substantial interest in Eastern thought often found among psychiatrists and psychologists. I have been bothered by this fact for a long time, but as I proceed in my research into Eastern thought and psychiatry, this situation seems less and less accidental. It is the result of a deep historical divide between the Eastern and Western traditions in their modes of thinking.

Depth psychology and Eastern metaphysics

Like Jung, the other psychologically oriented thinkers mentioned above are all offshoots of Freudianism. Upon its first appearance in the West, Freudianism was vehemently criticized as heretical. This adverse response was undoubtedly due in part to specific problems in Freud's theory, such as his pan-sexism and his tendency to reject Christianity. What is important theoretically and methodologically, it seems to me, is that Freud's method diverged from the accepted view of scholarship up to that time. That is, Freud wanted to regard psychoanalysis as a positive, empirical science, but in actuality went beyond the boundaries of empirical positivism so as to enter into philosophical and ideological issues concerning human nature, philosophy, and religion. Yet, if one were to ask whether the essence of Freudianism is philosophical, one must say it is not. In short, Freudianism is too speculative and philosophical for it to be a positive, empirical science and, conversely, it does not depart far enough from scientific, empirical positivism for it to be considered purely philosophical. Hence, modern scholarship, that is, scholarship that seeks theoretical and methodological rigor, criticized Freudianism as a quasi-science and quasi-philosophy.[6]

Nonetheless, Freudianism survived such criticisms. Interestingly enough, the contemporary world is infected by another quasi-science and quasi-philosophy, namely, Marxism. Marxism, too, while insisting that it is an empirical, positive science, enters into philosophical debates beyond those boundaries. This kind of thinking, which does not fit neatly under either the discipline of philosophy or science, seems to thrive in the contemporary West; I wonder if this is because there is a problem with the modern Western view of scholarship itself in that it distinguishes so sharply the roles of philosophy and science.

Kant's epistemology is representative of the modern view that tried to establish the two distinct domains and roles. For Kant, philosophy is a meta-science that reflects on the various presuppositions upon which the empirical sciences are based and of which the empirical sciences themselves are often unaware; hence, philosophy clarifies the methodological foundations of science, and there is a logical distinction between it and science. The theories and laws discovered by science, according to this account, have their foundation in empirical positivism and, to that extent, possess only *relative* validity. Philosophy seeks an epistemic necessity transcending the relativity of empirical knowledge. This, in short, is a rough approximation of modern philosophy's view as to what scholarship should be.

The reason that the Neo-Kantian school rejected psychologism was that psychologism relied on empirical positivism. Contemporary phenomenological ontology also inherits this modern epistemological standpoint; for it, science is an *ontical* operation lacking reflection on the principles concerning human being, that being which is the foundation of science itself. In contrast, according to these phenomenologists, philosophy is an *ontological* reflection upon this foundation of science. This, at least, is the basic position taken by Husserl and Heidegger.

Freudianism calls into question this modern Western view of scholarship. Jung says,

> I can hardly draw a veil over the fact that we psychotherapists ought
> really to be philosophers or philosophic doctors—or rather that we
> already are so, though we are unwilling to admit it because of the glar-
> ing contrast between our work and what passes for philosophy in the
> universities. We could also call it religion in *statu nascendi,* for in the vast
> confusion that reigns at the roots of life there is no line of division be-
> tween philosophy and religion.[7]

I shall refrain from elaborating on the Freudian view of scholarship, since
our present concern is whether Jung's rejection of the essential difference
between philosophy and empirical science (in his case, psychology) was
supported by his study of Eastern thought.

Jung's opinion concerning the difference between Western and Eastern thought can be summarized as follows. In the Western tradition,
metaphysics and psychology were originally separated, and became
decisively so with the advent of critical philosophy in the eighteenth century. In contrast, metaphysics and psychology in the East have always
been inseparable. In this regard, the East has never produced a "metaphysics" in the Western sense.[8]

It seems that Jung's opinion has many implications for our consideration of the fundamental differences between Western and Eastern
thought. The decisive separation between metaphysics and modern psychology in the critical philosophy of the eighteenth century refers us to
Kant's critique of the theory of the soul, a critique causing the philosophical concepts of "subject" and "consciousness" to become disconnected
from their experiential foundation in the deep regions of the psyche.
Jung points out, however, that this separation is not a problem that has
suddenly emerged in modern philosophy, but is derived from a long
tradition in Western intellectual history.

Although Jung is not very specific on this subject, we can elaborate a
bit on his statements.[9] One source of European metaphysics is Aristotle,
who established metaphysics as a science that is "after physics" (*meta-
physika*). Another important source is the Christian theology established
by the Church Fathers (of the Western Church especially). For our present
concerns, what interests us is the cosmology, the so-called "creation out
of nothing" (*creatio ex nihilo*). God, by virtue of this principle, tended to
become absolutely transcendent, cut off from the universe that is God's
creation. This is the first step toward logically distinguishing empirical
research into nature from the realm of metaphysical problems. This view
of an absolutely transcendent God came to influence not only cosmology
but also the Western view of humanity. God's personhood (*persona*) is the
"Highest Good," that is, God is Perfection, the absolutely Good itself,

and must be discontinuous from human nature, delimited as it is by the corporeal body through original sin.

At this point, psychological research aimed at the empirical investigation of human nature became, in principle, incompatible with metaphysics' concern for what is beyond natural experience. (Of course, even prior to modern psychology, there did exist in the realm of religion an empirical investigation of the human psyche, that is, there were attempts to reach the dimension of divinity through the empirical investigation of the deep psyche, as in ancient gnosticism and medieval mysticism, both offshoots of Platonism. The orthodox tradition of Christian metaphysics necessarily regarded these ideas as heretical, however, since transcendent divinity and the human nature endowed with a corporeal body were, in principle, separate.)

In contrast, Jung might say, metaphysics and psychology have always been inseparable in the Eastern tradition. What is meant by this statement will become clear in the next chapter. Here we may just note that what Jung means by "psychology" is a clinical psychology with a close relationship to personality formation and to various therapies for mental disease, such as psychiatry, depth psychology, and psychotherapy. To put it simply, if Western metaphysics is that which considers what lies behind the experience of "nature" (*physis*), Eastern metaphysics might be called "metapsychics," that is, that which aims beyond the experiences of the human "soul" (*psyche*); alternatively, the psyche may be called "inner nature" as opposed to "outer nature." A first issue in Eastern metaphysics is how the "soul" is the "inner nature" buried in the corporeal body. The point of departure is to investigate this in light of the *inseparability* of the mind and body.

Of course, this does not imply that Eastern thought does not cosmologically investigate "outer nature" as well. As Chu Hsi said, though, "Although the principle of things is certainly not outside our considerations, human relationships are the most immediate problem for us." The central issue in Eastern metaphysics lies in the practical problem of personality development rather than in cosmology. It is said that Shakyamuni remained silent toward those who asked him metaphysical and theoretical questions. This is because the investigation of theoretical problems does not have an immediate bearing on nirvana (*satori*); the foremost consideration in Buddhism must always be the practical issue of guiding the soul. Bearing this fundamental character of Eastern thought in mind, we can proceed in our investigations.

EDITOR'S SUMMARY

PART TWO

These four chapters investigate how the integrated, enhanced mind-body system is developed in Eastern meditative techniques, through personal religious cultivation (*shugyō*) and artistic training (*keiko*). As already pointed out, modern Western philosophy has shown little interest in studying the development of the personality, and even modern Japanese philosophers such as Nishida have analyzed the results of such personality development without giving us details on how the development itself actually takes place. To get this, Yuasa takes us within the Eastern meditative traditions themselves, explaining their own characterizations of the techniques, and adding his own observations on their relationship to acting intuition and the dark–bright consciousness theories developed in Part One.

Chapter Four examines the notion of *kairitsu* (precepts and canons) as it emerged in the development of personal religious cultivation in Indian, Chinese, and Japanese Buddhism. Yuasa explains the historical development of this tradition across cultures, emphasizing one particular theme that is especially important in Japanese Buddhism, namely, that the idea developed in such a way that mortality was seen as a religious cultivational practice in which one voluntarily imposed upon oneself a set of behavioral regulations that took one beyond what was required by the secular society. Yuasa points out that this pattern reiterates the idea that in personal development, the bright consciousness self-consciously imposes a pattern or form on the body-mind so that eventually the dark consciousness can act spontaneously in a creative and spiritually significant manner. In a sense, the bright consciousness trains the dark consciousness so that the dark consciousness can eventually take over. This is the most pertinent aspect of personal cultivation (*shugyō*) in the religious sphere.

Chapter Five shows how the Japanese sense of artistic training (*keiko*) derives from the idea of religious cultivation. Yuasa notes that the tradition of

artistic criticism is somewhat different in Japan from the West. Rather than having critics evaluate the completed works of art, Japanese criticism is traditionally done by the artists themselves as a way of transmitting the tradition of
how to train and express artistic creativity. Yuasa shows how *keiko* is exemplified in both the poetic criticisms of FUJIWARA Shunzei and FUJIWARA Teika
as well as the critique of Nō acting developed by Zeami.

   Chapters Six and Seven return to Japanese Buddhist personal cultivation as
developed in the philosophies of Dōgen and Kūkai. Yuasa is particularly interested in the role of the body in their analyses. Dōgen emphasizes the efficacy of *zazen* (seated meditation) for forgetting the self and "molting the
body-mind" (*shinjin datsuraku*). In his analysis, Yuasa shows that the normal
mode of experience in which the mind controls the body must be transcen-
ded. In *zazen* the body, with its intellectualized sensory experience, must take
the lead. When this is accomplished, the self-conscious self drops away and
the bright self-reflective consciousness yields to a deeper unity of body and
mind.

   Yuasa believes Kūkai gives the most comprehensive explanation of how
the dark consciousness comes to replace the bright consciousness in controlling many functions. First, Yuasa analyzes Kūkai's discussion of the ten stages of
mind, showing how this classification system differs from those developed in
China in that it primarily discusses doctrines as stages of religious insight available to the Buddhist practitioner, rather than as distinctions based on the
origin, age, or audience of the teachings. In short, Kūkai's ten stages map the
progressive stages in the enhancement of the self achieved through religious cultivation.

   The second teaching Yuasa considers in his discussion of Kūkai is that of
hosshin seppō (the *dharmakāya* expounds the *dharma*). That is, Kūkai maintains that the *dharmakāya* directly communicates with the Shingon practitioner. Here we have a metaphysical theory growing directly out of meditative
experience. But what exactly does this mean? Yuasa argues that for Kūkai this
religious experience has an implicit erotic dimension, that such practices as
meditation on the mandalas serve as a technique for sublimation (in a
specifically defined post-Freudian sense) resembling the theory of Kuṇḍalinī
Yoga. In this light Yuasa points out the profound significance of Kūkai's key
teaching of *sokushinjōbutsu*, attaining enlightenment in and through this
very body.

Part II

Cultivation and the Body

I say, for now, that there are two means to study the Way of the Buddhas: one is to study with the mind and the other with the body. To study with the mind is to study with all minds. . . . The body's studying the Way is to study with the body. The chunk of raw meat is what studies. The body comes from studying the Way. And in so doing, it is the body.

Dōgen

Chapter Four

What Is Cultivation?

B uddhist practice is usually called in Japanese "*shugyō*" (personal cultivation). The nature of personal cultivation is significant for our investigation of mind-body theories. The ordinary, common sense understanding is that cultivation is practical training aimed at the development and enhancement of one's spirit or personality. As already noted, however, Eastern thought traditionally tends to emphasize the inseparability of mind and body. Therefore, personal cultivation in the East takes on the meaning of a practical project aiming at the enhancement of the personality and the training of the spirit by means of the body. (Later we will develop these concepts of "enhancement of the personality" and the "training of the spirit"; for now, we will use them only in a general sense.) At any rate, "cultivation" is a distinctively Asian term with its own special nuances such that it does not correspond exactly, for example, to the Western idea of praxis. Thus, to understand this term, we must consider the history of the concept behind it, examining its relationship to Buddhist philosophies and taking into account the differences in the intellectual traditions of India, China, and Japan.

Kairitsu *in Indian Buddhism*

A fundamental doctrine of Buddhist philosophy is that of no-ego (*anattan*). *Anattan* in Pali is taken to have two senses: "that which is not mine" and "that which does not have an ego." The Sanskrit word, *anātman,* is also translated as "no-ego" but is usually understood to mean the denial of the existence of an *ātman* (authentic self) as described in Upanishadic philosophy. This is not really the Early Buddhist understanding of the term, but is more like the theories formulated later in Theravāda (Hīnayāna) Buddhism and in early Mahāyāna Buddhism.[1] The Buddha Shakyamuni himself, it is said, remained silent as to whether or not there is an *ātman*. He only opposed the interpretation of *ātman* as something that exists or functions objectively. How, then, should we understand the two meanings of *anattan* mentioned above?

The first meaning, namely, "that which is not mine," teaches us to detach ourselves from the egoism directed toward all things, including the self itself; this is because that which one sees as being one's own is, in reality, nowhere to be found. The second meaning, "that which does not have an ego," indicates the state of being free from the just-mentioned kind of egoism. Consequently, we may interpret the first meaning to indicate a practical process for reaching the second, ideal state. The second meaning, furthermore, does not refer only to the state of our being detached from egoism, but also means that in such a state, we will be able, for the first time, to see that which is true. That is, it indicates a true manner of cognition attained by means of a practical process of detachment from egoism. Therefore, the fundamental attitude of Buddhism as a philosophy lies in its contention that a theoretical cognition of the truth is possible only through this practice. Hence, there can be no theoretical philosophy apart from the practical one.

There is a book by Watsuji entitled *The Practical Philosophy of Early Buddhism*. He explains the significance of the title roughly as follows: It is written that the Buddha remained silent and did not answer metaphysical questions. This is because speculation on such theoretical questions is of no use in reaching nirvana (*satori*). What is most necessary for humanity is not theoretical speculation, but, rather, the practice that eliminates delusions from one's own soul and detaches one from egoism. The Buddha did not deny the significance of all theoretical speculations, however. If through practice one reaches the state of no-ego without any attachment to egoism, one will come to cognize, within this new horizon, the way the world truly is. According to Watsuji, this is the meaning of the Buddha's silence. In other words, the Buddha's silence teaches us that cognition through practice is alone truly deserving of the name "cognition."

True cognition is a "cognition that observes *dharmas* in no-ego." "*Dharmas*" here means "truth" as well as "beings." In the terminology of contemporary philosophy, when one cognizes the mode of the Being of beings in the state of non-ego, one will be able to know the configuration and the meaning of the real. This cognition—that is, the "observation of *dharmas* in no-ego"—unfolds only through "practice to reach the state of no-ego." Consequently, there is no separation here between cognition and practice. "Herein we find a cognition that does not distinguish the theoretical from the practical, that is, a cognition of actuality itself. It is this which characterizes philosophical cognition in Buddhism."[2] If it is legitimate to understand the theoretical content of Buddhist philosophy in this manner, we must first investigate the concrete content of personal cultivation before we examine Buddhist theory.

The actualities of Buddhist cultivation come down to the so-called "precepts and canons" (*kai-ritsu*). This compound term itself is a Chinese neologism not found in Indian Buddhism, but we will use it as a general term in discussing its specific cultural meanings. In my interpretation, *kairitsu* has four meanings. First, it is *ritsu* in the sense of *vinaya*, the regulations internal to the Buddhist monastic order or *saṃgha*. Leaving the secular world and entering the *saṃgha*, one renounces all secular responsibilities and submits to the constraint of the canons. The articles in the canons are called *prātimokṣa* and one will be punished for violating them, that is, one must atone for wrongdoing. The contents of the *vinaya* include the regulation of property, as well as ethical issues, and even details about daily schedule, garments, eating, and living quarters. The maximum punishment for violating the regulations is excommunication from the order. Consequently, the *vinaya* is a self-governing system of laws for maintaining the order's organization.

In this respect, the *vinaya* is similar to canon law in Christianity, but we must also note a deep, fundamental difference between Christianity and Buddhism vis-à-vis their social systems. The *saṃgha* in Buddhism is an organization only for those who have left the secular world; a lay person cannot become a member of the order. In this respect, the *saṃgha* resembles monastic Christianity, but again, the monastery is just a special organization within the Church; the nucleus of Christianity lies in the church structure as it tends to the needs of the laity. There is no organization in Buddhism exactly corresponding to the idea of "the Church."

Max Weber distinguished two types of faith: master religiosity (*Virtuosen-religiosität*) and mass religiosity (*Massen-religiosität*).[3] According to this classification, Indian Buddhism belongs to the former type because of the structure of traditional Indian society. That is, the Indian religious order generally forms a sacred region with extraterritorial rights beyond the intervention of any secular power. Consequently, those who have left the secular world are free of all the constraints of secular laws. In this sense, there exist in India two legal systems which do not interfere with each other: the secular and the religious. Freedom from secular law is a right claimed by the *saṃgha* itself, and the secular powers of Indian society have traditionally recognized this right. Therefore, the religious world and the political world are completely separate social systems.[4] This indicates a dualism in the Indian view of the world between religion and politics, and consequently, between the sacred and the secular. In this regard, to regulate one's everyday life in accordance with various determinations of the *vinaya* may rightly be called "practice outside the secular world." "Cultivation" in Buddhism begins here.

The second meaning of *kairitsu* is precepts (*kai*) or *śīla*. These are essentially the norms for daily life that a lay person, either wishing to enter the *saṃgha* order or to become a devout Buddhist lay person, adopts autonomously through his or her own resolution. The content of the precepts is different depending on whether one enters the order of the *saṃgha* or remains a lay person. The precepts (*śīla*) and the canons (*vinaya*) are, in principle, the same for anyone who leaves the secular world, for in such a case, one submits oneself to the constraints of the *vinaya*. But, although the contents of the *vinaya* are also referred to as "precepts" (*śīla*), the constraint of the *vinayas* is not autonomous like the *śīla* for lay persons, but heteronomous in that it involves externally imposed sanctions.

The precepts for the lay person are the famous Five Precepts: not to kill, steal, lie, commit adultery, or drink intoxicants. The Five Precepts, insofar as they are precepts, are accepted out of the believer's own resolve. Consequently, at least theoretically, they are not prohibitive imperatives of the "Thou shalt not . . . " sort, but, rather, they express the positive resolution of the will, "I will not. . . . " In this respect, the precepts essentially differ from the Judeo-Christian moral commandments. To accept the precepts is to impose upon oneself constraints beyond the norms of ordinary life. In spite of the fact that the content of the Five precepts seems to resemble closely the moral laws of our ordinary understanding, they theoretically involve something else—one's own choice of a way of life above and beyond the social norms under which ordinary people in society are constrained.

This brings us to the following question. If the Five Precepts designate something above and beyond the ordinary social norms, how were killing, stealing, lying, drinking, and committing adultery generally regarded in the secular morals of India? Although it is difficult to give an unqualified, specific answer to this question, the reason that the precepts developed as they did is due to the unique circumstances of Indian society. Ordinarily, in any society, conventional norms are at first naturally generated and, if they are religiously purified, come to be exalted as moral laws. India, however, is a society where numerous races dwell together in the same region; languages and conventions differ among the respective races. Consequently, the life norms take on varied forms even in the same society; that is, in Indian society, the correct significance of *dharmas* (as moral teachings) depends upon the status and profession of the individual involved. (Herein lies a basis for the caste system.) Max Weber, noting this point, says that there is no universally valid, personal, or social ethic in India.[5] The precepts of Buddhism arose under these circumstances. Consequently, this presupposes that they do not have to deny the existing systems of norms in the secular society. In this respect, the precepts differ decisively from Western Christian moral laws. When Christianity has entered a society, it has tended to deny the existing, conventional, moral norms and to Christianize the social norms' fundamental character.

Another fact to note is that Buddhists did not have to accept all Five Precepts. Apparently, one could follow the precepts of one's own choice and determine the period or time for accepting them. According to the *vinaya* among the Sarvāstivādin, for example, it is considered a "small good" when a woman accepts the nonadultery precept only for the daytime while still committing adultery at night, or when a hunter accepts the precept of nonkilling only for the nighttime.[6] At first glance, this may seem ridiculous, but this is probably derived from the limitations placed on them because of their professions. The spirit of the precept is to accept the resolution in order to enhance onself even one small step further as a human being; thus, women in the lower statum of society whose profession is prostitution, or hunters whose work is to kill animals, refrain from performing these acts for at least certain periods of time, regretting their sins among the agonies of having to live such a life.

Kairitsu *in China and Japan*

These two terms, *vinaya* and *śila,* constitute the rudiments of *kairitsu,* but since they are rooted in traditional Indian society, their content changed radically as Buddhism spread to East Asia. First, with respect to *vinaya* the Indian duality between religion and politics did not have a correlate in China. Weber frequently compares the authority of the Chinese emperor with that of the Roman emperor.[7] A Roman emperor held the office of the Supreme Pontiff (Pontifex Maximus) in the traditional Roman religion and, at the same time, he was the supreme secular ruler as well. Similarly, religion and politics were integrated in China, and there was no tradition of recognizing extraterritorial privileges for religion. It was from the Northern and Southern Dynasties through the Sui and T'ang Dynasties that Chinese Buddhism achieved its unique development. By the end of the T'ang Dynasty, almost all Buddhist orders in China were subsumed under the sovereignty of secular law. Although there was a trend in the Buddhist orders of the Northern and Southern Dynasties to recognize, at least to a certain extent, the autonomy of the *saṃgha* (especially in the South), it became customary by the end of the T'ang Dynasty to appoint lay bureaucrats to the Office of Monks governing the Buddhist world.[8] Under such conditions, it is natural that the *vinaya* in its Indian form did not find a place in Chinese society.

We can cite the monastic rules (*ch'ing kuei*) of the Ch'an (Zen) Buddhist school, a development unique to China, as an example of the Sinification of the internal regulations of the Buddhist orders. Although much of its concrete content is similar to that of the *vinaya,* these monastic rules differ as a social system in that they are not considered to be outside of secular law. An example is the *Monastic Rules of Pai-chang,* a representative set of Ch'an Buddhist monastic rules first instituted in the T'ang Dynasty by Pai-chang Huai-hai (A.D. 720–814) and revised in the Yüan Dynasty. The revisions were made under imperial order, and it starts by prescribing the ceremonies for the "Holy Day," rites, that is, for the emperor's birthday. Such a capitulation to politics would be inconceivable in the original Indian context of Buddhism.

This comparison is of more than historical interest to us. In Indian Buddhism, a life of observing the *vinayas* meant a complete separation from the secular order and, consequently, religious cultivation can be termed an *extrasecular* practice. But China is different. There cultivation came to mean an *intrasecular* practice, having the characteristic ambiguity of going beyond the secular standards of life while still in the midst of the secular order. In this sense, the theoretical Indian distinction between the *vinaya* and the *śīla* is lost.

The Japanese Buddhist orders fundamentally followed the pattern of Chinese Buddhism. The supervision of the orders in ancient Japan was by means of the secular laws—the monastic edicts in the state constitution and laws (*Ritsuryō*). The *kairitsu* were introduced full-scale in Heian Buddhism [ninth through twelfth centuries], but the system of internal regulations for the order (corresponding to the *vinaya*) was not established at that time. In later Kamakura Buddhism, Dōgen* instituted the *Eihei Monastic Rules,* introducing regulations into daily monastic life similar to those of the Chinese Ch'an (Zen) monasteries. Still, his school is a minority within the total Japanese Buddhist world.

In this respect, the Japanese Buddhist orders were generally far more secular in operation than were those of Chinese Buddhism. In contrast with China, however, the political supervision of Japanese Buddhism was not intense. Since the earliest Japanese Buddhist orders were derived from the Southern Dynasties by way of Korea (Kudara) and since the

---

*Dōgen (1200–1253) is the founder of the Japanese school of Sōtō Zen Buddhism. He is discussed in Chapter 6.

power of the Chinese emperors in the Southern Dynasties was weak (there being a strong aristocratic tendency toward an antisecular, Taoist-influenced "pure discussion"), the India-like principle of "those who have left the world do not respect the king" was advocated. That is, the political supervision of the Buddhist world in this period was indirect.

The Office of Monks was established in ancient Japan as the executive office for the monastic edits and its system was apparently based on the structures of Southern Dynasties Chinese Buddhism; supervisory officers were, without fail, monks rather than laymen.[9] In this respect, we may say that in Japan, unlike China, there was a moderate dualism between religion and politics. Once Saichō's Tendai order was freed from the supervision of the Office of Monks in the Heian Period, political supervision of the Buddhist world became nominal; Buddhist orders actually came to possess (during the next four hundred years of the Heian period) extraterritorial rights opposed to the secular power. Here we find the basis for the Japanese world view in regard to the sacred and the secular, one quite different from that of China. This, however, is not our present concern; what we must recognize for now is the fact that Japan did not develop the unique internal regulations of the Buddhist orders we find in the Indian *vinaya*.

Now let us examine the transformation of *śīla*. As has been observed earlier, the Buddhist *śīla* did not originally reject the existing customs and moral norms. There were only the Five Precepts for lay devotees, a very lenient number when compared with Jainism, for example. This helped in Buddhism's transmission to East Asian regions where customs and conventions were completely different. Still, there were many cases in which the practical teachings of Buddhism did not completely coincide with the existing social norms. In China, for example, the relationship with Confucian ethics became problematic. Concentrating on those who have left the secular world, Buddhism did not seriously consider issues such as family ethics and behavior toward the emperor. In China, however, these ethical ideas were critically important. In this instance, the Chinese Buddhists transformed Buddhist teachings so as to make them agree with traditional Chinese ethics, rather than worrying about remaining true to the letter of the Indian tradition. For this task, the Mahāyāna forms of Buddhism introduced into China were convenient in that they respected at least the relative values of the secular world. Through this process, Buddhists in the Sui and T'ang Dynasties came to think of the Five Precepts as being comparable to the Confucian Five Constant Virtues (humanity, righteousness, propriety, wisdom, and sincerity). Moreover, although filial ethics between parents and children does not have any importance in Indian Buddhism, it came to be regarded as extremely important in Chinese Buddhism, relating it to the idea of "favor" (*ên*).[10]

In this process, when translating Buddhist *sūtras,* the Chinese often intentionally used wrong translations or made alterations so as to be more in accord with Chinese morality.

Śīla in Indian Buddhism, as already mentioned, theoretically meant to choose for oneself norms more strict than the norms by which the ordinary person conducts oneself. If the prohibitive imperative, "Thou shalt not . . . " is the standard for norms concerning the conduct of the average person, *śīla* means, in addition to this, to impose upon oneself a positive vow of the form "I will not. . . . " It is in this latter respect that *śīla* means "personal cultivation." In Chinese Buddhism, where *śīla* was placed on the same level as secular morality, this special sense was obscured. This does not mean, however, that the original spirit of *śīla,* that is, to live autonomously beyond how an average person does (*Leben mehr als*) disappears. In other words, while remaining within the order of secular morality, an attitude arose in China such that one accepted these moral norms actively and autonomously out of a desire for character formation rather than out of heteronomous constraint. Moral practice arises, not out of the constraint "Thou shalt not . . . ", but is, instead, a positive, willed attitude of "I will not," that is, a resolve "to become such a person who does not. . . . " Such a spiritual attitude behind the reform movements of Confucianism in the Sung, Yüan, and Ming dynasties arose from the interaction with Taoism and Buddhism.

The Wang Yang-ming school, influenced by Ch'an (Zen) Buddhism, is one example of this interaction. As SHIMADA Kenji points out, this school emphasized the contrast between "inward" and "outward."[11] "Outward" refers to human relations, society, and politics. Generally speaking, this amounts to the Confucian norms of etiquette, music, punishment, and government: the Five Relations and Five Constant Virtues. In contrast, "inward" refers to the "I" as a subject of "innate wisdom." Wang Yang-ming established the inward/outward distinction, maintaining the primordial superiority of the former. The spirit of the Wang Yang-ming school is to change first what is inside the self while still recognizing that social and moral norms exist outside the self. At the same time, it strongly demands the external society to change from within.

The important issue for us is the possible spiritual influence from Buddhism such that moral practice was regarded as a path to character formation, that is, it is comparable to the cultivation through which one can live a life better than that of the average person. This derives from the self-imposition of norms that are not considered heteronomous constraints. This Chinese attitude was carried out as far as possible within intrasecular practice. This development parallels the Chinese transformation of the *vinayas* we observed earlier.

How, then, was *śīla* treated in Japan? There was no system of moral laws to speak of in pre-Buddhist Japan, and there were only the conventional norms of Shintoism in its ancient, primitive form. Certainly, Buddhism had a considerable influence on the moral concepts of the Japanese, but no system of Buddhist moral law developed. As stated earlier, Buddhism does not try to change the original, existing social norms and it does not embody a developed and organized system of moral laws capable of such change. Consequently, in Japan there were conventional norms of life only where Buddhistic ideas overlapped with Shintoistic conventions, as in Shintō-Buddhist syncretism (*shimbu-tsushūgō*), for example. Although the Chinese idea of moral practice was introduced to the Japanese *bushi* (warrior) class in the premodern period, this Confucianist influence (especially by the Wang Yang-ming and Chu Hsi schools) did not permeate much into the general Japanese populace.

As far as can be determined, in Japan from the ancient through to the modern period, there has been no moral legal system in the sense of objective norms. Needless to say, there is an ethical ethos forming the core of moral ideas, but no attempt has been made to systematize this so as to make it lawlike with respect to the various aspects of the social order. For example, Watsuji's *History of Japanese Ethical Thought* is probably the only complete work written thus far on this topic, but surprisingly, he does not treat Buddhism in the book. Although Buddhism has had considerable impact on Japanese moral ideas, it is possible, nonetheless, to do a rough history of Japanese morality without dealing with it. "The morality of a clear, bright mind" in ancient Japan and "the morality of self-sacrifice" in the medieval *bushi* were Watsuji's primary concerns and these do not constitute a moral system of laws at all, but rather an ethos or ethical sentiment inseparable from conventional norms. In short, the idea of *śīla* in the Buddhist concept of *kairitsu* did not really take hold on Japanese soil. Herein lies a great difference from China.

Kairitsu *and cultivation in Japanese Buddhism*

I stated at the beginning of this chapter that there are four meanings of *kairitsu*. The preceding discussion was concerned with precepts and canons. Although the other two meanings are derivative of the authentic Indian sense of "precepts and canons," they are more important than the previous two (which did not really take hold in Japan) in understanding the distinctively Japanese notion of personal cultivation.

Kairitsu in its third meaning is related to "meditation" (*samādhi*). There is a single term even in the *Vinaya-piṭaka* and *Agama Sūtras* of early

Buddhism, "the Three (Practical) Studies" (triṇi-śikṣāani): precepts (śīla), meditation (sampatti), and wisdom (prajñā). These indicate the fundamental procedure or path for practicing Buddhism. Since these Three Practical Studies constitute the path originally designed for those who have left the secular world, "precepts" here means, more specifically, vinaya. The spiritual point in calling them "precepts" is because the vinaya should be observed in daily life by one's own autonomous resolution. Those who have left the secular world should learn "meditation" only after they pass the stage of understanding the "precepts." Meditation in Buddhism is derived from yogic meditation, a dimension of all Indian religions from ancient to contemporary times.

The ultimate purpose in practicing Buddhism is to attain the third of the Three Practical Studies, namely, wisdom. To reach it, however, one must pass through the stages of practicing precepts and meditation. To be more concrete, "wisdom" here refers to the theories in Buddhist philosophy propounded by in the sūtras (scriptures) and abhidharmas (commentaries). For Buddhism the theoretical cognition of the world can only be reached through these two practices. Specifically, Buddhist practice or "cultivation" has the dual sense of practicing the precepts and meditation and, consequently, embraces all aspects of the Three Practical Studies.

Meditation was originally cultivated only by those who had left the secular world; lay persons were not required to perform this practice. As Mahāyāna Buddhism developed, however, the concept of the lay practitioner arose. The Vimalakīrti-nirdeśa Sūtra is well-known for its exultation of such a lay disciple, for instance. Such a Buddhist tradition, in which both monks and lay persons alike may participate, was highly developed in China. This phenomenon also applies to Zen Buddhism in Japan: Nishida was such a lay follower, for example. In this regard, we should also note that Japanese Buddhism typically considers meditation to be a central part of kairitsu.

This trend began with Saichō* and Kūkai,† the two key figures in Heian Buddhism. Breaking away from the Nara Buddhism of the eighth century, Saichō instituted a new system of accepting the precepts, the so-called "Mahāyāna bodhisattva precepts." In their institutional form, these represented a ritual for entering the Tendai order unsupervised by the previously dominant Office of Monks in Nara. The philosophical implications are even more important, however. In establishing this new ritual, Saichō emphasized "self-vow precepts" (jiseikai), a form neglected

---

*Saichō (767–822) is the founder of the Japanese Tendai school of Buddhism.—Ed.
†Kūkai (774–835) founded the Japanese Shingon school of Buddhism. He is the focus of Yuasa's discussion in Chapter 7.—Ed.

in previous systems. These self-vow precepts originated in the tradition of lay devotees' taking the vows on their own without the guidance of a monk. This custom apparently originated in Indian Mahāyāna Buddhism, perhaps as an expedient for Buddhist devotees in remote districts where clerical guidance was not available.[12] Therefore, these precepts for lay persons marked their becoming believers, that is, they were one kind of *upāsaka* (lay person) precepts. They were lower in value than the formal, monastic, *upasaṃpadā* precepts for monks.[13] Saichō, on the other hand, placed them in the center of the rite for entering the order; they were the core of the precepts to be observed by those who leave the secular world. Here we have a uniquely Japanese interpretation of *kairitsu*.

Saichō got the idea of the self-vow precepts mainly from the *Brahma-jāla Sūtra*. According to it, after taking the vows in front of the Buddha, one should continue contemplation (*meisō*) and repentance for seven days, training oneself so as to see the Buddha's "meritorious appearance" (*kōsō*), the Buddha's spiritual form as it appears in meditation.[14] Psychologically speaking, it is an hallucinatory vision from the depths of one's psyche. If one can see this appearance, it is a sign that the Buddha accepts one's undertaking the precepts. If one cannot attain this vision within seven days, it is prescribed that one continue contemplation and repentance for a year or even two. Obviously, the very idea of the "self-vow precepts" assumes that one can reach the Buddha's world by means of contemplative cultivation. That is, here we find the precepts joined with meditation. This unique understanding of *kairitsu* began with Saichō and gradually became a characteristic of Japanese Buddhism as a whole.

According to the system of receiving precepts (that is, entering into the order) that Saichō established in his *Sanga-gakushō-shiki,* one first goes up to the ordination platform and invokes the presence of Shakyamuni, Manjuśri, Maitreya, and others so that one will be initiated ("bestowed with the precepts") by these invisible Buddhas.[15] Needless to say, monks on the platform actually performed the ceremony, but Saichō's view is that, spiritually speaking, Buddhas, not humans, perform the initiation. Although Kūkai took his *samaya* precepts from the *Essentials of Meditation by Śubhākarasiṃha (Shan-wu-wei-san-ts'ang-ch'an-yao)*, he fundamentally followed the same interpretation as Saichō. Although this understanding of the true meaning of receiving the precepts is not authentically Indian, its basis may be found in India, nonetheless. Still, it is significant that this interpretation took root so strongly in Japan. This is probably because of the convergence with ancient Shintō conventions.

This convergence between Heian Buddhism and Shintō mountain worship probably emerged from the common tradition of pursuing religious cultivation in the mountains. According to Japanese mountain religions' world view, the mountains were where the gods (*kami*) were in attendance; a beautiful mountain was called a *kan'nabi* (god's mountain). Usually, a sacred stone area was constructed on it and called an *iwasaka* (divine throne), and the appropriate gods attended the rites there. Consequently, the ceremonial rites invoked the gods' presence. Both Saichō and Kūkai had the experience of cultivating themselves in the mountains, and they always paid due respect to the ancient Japanese gods. The idea of receiving the precepts by invoking the Buddhas at the initiation platform, making one's vows in front of them, converges with this Shintō tradition. At any rate, understanding *kairitsu* in this manner, placing the cultivation method of *samādhi* or meditation at its center, it a uniquely Japanese Buddhist idea shaping later tradition in Japan.

The fourth and final meaning of *kairitsu* is that of "ceremonial rites." In Indian Buddhism, these rites were required either for entering the *saṃgha* or for initiating a lay believer. When wishing to leave the secular world to enter the *saṃgha,* one vows, under the guidance of a monk, to observe the Ten Precepts. (Added to the standard five are precepts about not wearing ornaments, not participating in song and dance, and not eating after noontime.) This is called the *tārayati* and one who has undergone this rite is called *śrāmaṇera*. After a certain period of cultivation, one formally becomes a monk (*bhikṣu*) by accepting the precepts (*upasaṃpadā*) as witnessed by ten monks. This ceremonial rite is usually called the "Three Masters and Seven Witnesses" and was introduced into Japan by the T'ang Dynasty monk, Ganjin (Chien-chên). The rite for a lay person is relatively simple. Called the "Three Vows and Five Precepts," one promises to revere the Three Treasures: the Buddha, *dharma,* and *saṃgha,* that is, the Buddha, his teaching, and those who preach that teaching. After that, the person accepts the Five Precepts.

Such rites gradually come to possess a meaning similar to the sacraments in Christianity. A kind of charisma (the so-called "embodiment of the precepts") is generated by the performance of the rites, and the one receiving the precepts is regarded as obtaining virtues or benefits. This tendency became increasingly prominent, especially in Mahāyāna Buddhism. Absorbing from the outset many folk religions, it has a variety of rites. Weber regarded Mahāyāna Buddhism and Hinduism as being typical of the Asian "Magic Garden" (*Zaubergarten*) model. The ancient notion of magical rites converged with bestowing and accepting the precepts within the Buddhist order. For example, the "bodhisattva precepts" originated in Mahāyāna, the term "bodhisattva" referring to all practitioners of Mahāyāna Buddhism, whether monastics or lay persons. Unlike the *upasaṃpadā* rite for entering the order, the bodhisattva precepts can be received by either a monastic or lay person and can be received again and again. Unlike the rites for entering the order or for becoming a lay believer, the bestowal of the bodhisattva precepts is performed for the purpose of endowing charisma. Saichō's Mahāyāna bodhisattva precepts incorporated the spirit of the previously mentioned self-vow precepts into the bodhisattva precepts, giving them the significance of being the rite for entering the order.

The ceremonial aspect of Japanese Buddhism developed markedly when it merged with Esoteric Buddhist rites initiated by Kūkai in Japan. Esoteric Buddhism did not really prosper in China, having disappeared after the T'ang Dynasty, perhaps because it could not compete with the already existing Chinese Taoist rites. In contrast, having merged with the Shintō rites, Japanese Esoteric Buddhism developed considerably after the medieval period and became a pervasive influence on Japanese Buddhism as a whole. We should note that the ritualistic endowment of charisma was thought to depend on the magical power of the executor of the rites. Consequently, rites came to have a close relationship with the cultivation of contemplation discovered in the third meaning of *kairitsu* discussed above. This magical activity is, as it were, a supernatural ability or, in contemporary terms, a parapsychological or paranormal ability. In India this is understood to be the result of contemplative cultivation through yoga; in Buddhism it is called the "divine power" (*ṛddhi*).

Although it is said that early Buddhism admonished against magic, in reality, it must have been tacitly approved since it was practiced among the populace. At any rate, esoteric Mahāyāna Buddhists certainly very much valued the attainment of magical powers. For them, performing Esoteric Buddhist rites is called a "cultivation method" and these rites have efficacy only when performed by a person with magical ability attained through meditation. In other words, a cultivation method is meaningful only insofar as it presupposes accomplishment through cultivation, so much so that there arises a tendency to regard a cultivation method itself as a form of cultivation. For example, the repetitive recitation of *sūtras,* worship, *nembutsu* [expressing faith in Amida Buddha], and *daimoku* [paying homage to the *Lotus Sūtra*] came to be considered kinds of cultivation, rather than merely rites performed by one who has already cultivated oneself through other means. As Japanese Buddhism extended to the masses in the later ancient and medieval ages, this form of cultivation was widely practiced. In terms of depth psychology, the repetitive recitation of *sūtras, nembutsu,* and *daimoku* has an autohypnotic effect and, in this respect, overlaps contemplative cultivation.

The meaning of cultivation

In conclusion, cultivation amounts to the following: First, theoretically speaking, cultivation is to impose on one's own body-mind stricter constraints than are the norms of secular, ordinary experience, so as to reach a life beyond that which is led by the average person (*Leben mehr als*). The "enhancement of the personality" or "character building" means, in concrete terms, this sort of practical training.

In actual form, Buddhist cultivation somewhat resembles the Christian monastic life of prayer and labor. Christian monastic prayer corresponds to what medieval philosophy termed "contemplation" (*contemplatio*) but the distinctiveness of Buddhism lies in the fact that prayer and the techniques of contemplation have developed in various ways through yogic meditation. What we usually call religious cultivation in Buddhism is the "precepts" and meditation, the former meaning the control of one's desires by the imposition in everyday life of constraints upon one's body-mind. This corresponds to labor in Christian monastic life. We may call this the "*outwardly* directed practice," oriented toward the external world. As noted, the conceptual meaning of the practice does differ somewhat across cultural and social systems (as we saw in the comparisons with India and China, for example), but the narrow sense of precepts is still the practice established between the everyday self and the external world.

In contrast, we shall refer to the stages of contemplative cultivation represented by *samādhi* (meditation) as "*inwardly* directed practices," that is, practice oriented towards one's mind. This parallels more the praying or contemplative aspects in Christian monastic living. Contemplation is an attempt to attend to the interior of one's mind, to make one's way into its depths. Although, in view of its original meaning, we should not call meditation a kind of "action," it may, nonetheless, be considered a type of *practice* in that it aims at spiritual enhancement and the building of character.

Cultivation's ultimate goal is wisdom (*prajñā*), seeing the true profile of Being in no-ego. Buddhism contends that this goal can be attained only through cultivation. When a self becomes connected to the invisible, ultimate point of primordiality or no-ego, when one becomes, as it were, an authentic self, the person comes to command a new perspective on openness (*Offenheit*) and will cognize correctly the true meaning of the Being of beings. Such is the teaching of the Buddha.

Chapter Five

Theories of Artistry

The Buddhist notion of cultivation has influenced Japanese intellectual history in a variety of ways. We shall here deal with a few historical examples, examining their grasp of the relationship between the mind and body. In this chapter, we shall be concerned with "artistry"* and then, in the next two chapters, we will cover Buddhist philosophy.

Cultivation and training in the waka *theory of poetry*

The Japanese theory of artistry is not simply a theoretical investigation of the arts. It differs from our modern day literary and artistic critiques in that it represents a performer's or artist's attempts to describe his or her own experience of production or composition so as to pass this knowledge down to future generations of artists. Obviously, such an approach is still a theoretical investigation of the arts, but it is a theory formulated only in light of the *practice* of artistic creation. Here it parallels Buddhist philosophy in that theory derives from the practice of personal cultivation. This parallel is not just due to similarity in goals. Rather, the very modes of thinking about artistry arose through the influence of Buddhist cultivation theory.

The theory of artistry began historically with the critique of *waka* (thirty-one-syllable poems) by the father-and-son team of the FU-

---

*"Artistry" translates *geidō,* literally, the "way of the arts." Whereas Western aesthetic theories usually focus on the form and style of the completed artwork, the Japanese tradition has most often emphasized the form and style of the creative act itself.—Ed.

JIWARA † family (namely, Shunzei and Teika) towards the end of the Heian Period. Later, in the Muromachi period, this came to be called the theory of *renga* ‡ poetry. The theory of *waka* and *renga* is called the "way of poetry" (*kadō*). Zeami applied such a theory of artistry to Nō drama in the Muromachi period, and Rikyū to the tea ceremony (*chadō*) in the Azuchimomoyama period. (In the modern period, the notion of "way" [*dō*] was extended from poetry and the tea ceremony to cover martial arts such as *kendō*, "the way of swordsmanship," and *judō* as well.)

What is usually cited as the very first critique of *waka* poetry is FU-JIWARA Shunzei's *Summary of Ancient Styles* (*Korai fūtei shō*). The beginning of this book refers to the "great cessation and discernment" (*makashikan*), a meditative cultivation method employed in the Tendai school. "Cessation" (*shi*) here means to arrest disordered or delusional functions; "discernment" (*kan*) means to observe the configuration of all *dharmas* (things) from a quiescent mental state. We see here that the act of composing *waka* was compared to religious cultivation. Obviously, since *waka* composition does not require physical training, we will be hard pressed to find passages in literary criticism referring to the body. The one example I did find is from FUJIWARA Teika's, *Monthly Summaries* (*Maigetsushō*).

> In composing *waka*, one should prepare onself to assume the correct posture. If one becomes accustomed to composing in an unrestrained posture such as standing or lying down, one cannot compose at all on formal occasions, thinking that the rules [for composition] are not right. . . . [My father, Shunzei] admonished me not to compose *waka* even for a short while without the correct sitting posture.[1]

This passage precedes the explanation that "the first step in learning [to compose] *waka* is, above all, to have a very clear mind." That is, FU-JIWARA Teika says that when one's mind becomes clear, good poetry is produced, by assuming the correct posture. This contention may seem strange or even laughable when considered from the perspective of modern aesthetics, but it is rather natural if we take into consideration the fact that the theory of artistry derives from cultivation theory, the idea that one's bodily form directly expresses the mind. Striving for expression and entrance into a deeper aesthetic feeling, the poet resembles the cultivating monk, attempting to concentrate the mind and deepen the meditation and *satori*. As with cultivation, what yields a good poem is not some momentary, skillful display of know-how.

FUJIWARA Teika states his own experience as follows.

† FUJIWARA Shunzei's dates are 1114-1204, while FUJIWARA Teika's are 1162-1241.—Ed.

‡ A *renga* is a classical form of linked verses.—Ed.

At times of fervor when I am perturbed to the bottom of my mind, I cannot create the "substantial profundity" [*yūshintai*], no matter how much I may try to compose the *waka*. If I struggle to compose it in spite of myself, I weaken more and more my natural ability and end up not being myself.[2]

The "substantial profundity" here is the ideal in *waka* poetry, what was later called "profound mystery" (*yūgen*). Such an ideal state cannot be attained in a momentary conscious effort. At times, the mind is in such disorder that one is helpless, but still, if one undergoes a long period of training (*keiko*), forgetting the "I" and immersing oneself in writing poetry, the way to artistry opens of itself.

An excellent poem is composed not when the author has a definite, thematic plan and clear vision [of his composition], feeling he can expedite it immediately, but, rather, when a thematic plan and vision for *waka* poetry comes to him out of the blue without his initiating it. . . . Don't strive for an excellent poem. With much training, it will be composed naturally.[3]

This instruction is based on FUJIWARA Teika's experience as a poet. This resembles a practicing monk's meditation. There are times when delusions and random thoughts distract the mind, no matter how much effort one makes. But when one continues to cultivate onself for a long time, the personal experience of "insight into one's nature" (*kenshō*), or a certain level of *satori*, arises spontaneously (from beyond, as it were). Here there is a correspondence between artistic training (*keiko*) and Buddhist cultivation (*shugyō*). Whether training or cultivating, if one forgets the self with its efforts and failures, then a new world will unexpectedly open up and a new self be born.

The waka-dhāraṇī

The medieval view of *waka-dhāraṇī* developed the theoretical relationship between *waka* artistry and cultivation. Following its opening line, "There is a deep principle in the way of *waka*," the Kamakura period work, *The Sand and Pebbles Collection (Shasekishū)*, states the following:

Giving an account of the way of *waka*, I would say that it has the quality of stopping a turbulently unfocused mind and bringing a quiescent calmness. Though its words are few, it nonetheless envelopes the mind. There ought to be a sense of "total preservation" [*sōji*]. This total preser-

vation is itself *dhāraṇī*. . . . In total preservation, there are originally no
words, yet one expresses total preservation; one expresses words. In
what words of what language is there the quality of expressing this total
preservation? The Master of Mt. Kōya [that is, Kūkai] also said, "The
five elements all have sounds; the six sense objects are all words."[4]

A *dhāraṇī* is an incantation with mystical significance used in Esoteric
Buddhist cultivation. Etymologically, it is derived from the term *dhāraṇa*,
a yogic method for maintaining mental concentration on a definite place
or object. It concentrates the consciousness on some point such as the abdomen just below the navel, the tip of the nose, or the place between the
eyebrows. It is this term which is translated into Japanese as *sōji* (total
preservation) or *nōji* (ability preservation). Theoretically speaking, the
dhāraṇī is used to invoke the Buddha's protection and in Esoteric
Buddhism is considered a method of cultivation. The recitation of the
nembutsu in Pure Land Buddhism, or of the *daimoku* in the Nichiren sect,
arose from such cultivation methods in ancient Japanese Buddhism. In
actual practice, the cultivator attains the *dhāraṇī* state of one-pointed concentration by reciting repeatedly the incantation phrase. Thus, this
Kamakura period work thinks that to submerge oneself in training (*keiko*)
for *waka* has the same significance as such recitation in that it stops "the
turbulently unfocused mind."

The *dhāraṇī* connects the Buddha's protective power with the mind
of self-cultivation. The person approaches the Buddha qua *satori* through
the *dhāraṇī*; the *dhāraṇī* are words, a *symbolic language*, pointing to the
Buddha's invisible realm. Kūkai's words cited above are taken from his
"Significance of Sound-Word-Reality" (*Shōjijissōgi*), meaning essentially
the following: If with a deluded mind we observe the universe—the five
elements (earth, water, fire, wind, and sky) and the surrounding world of
the six sense objects (form, sound, scent, tastes, textures, and thought-
objects)—we do not understand reality, the genuine mode of Being. Once
we realize (*satoru*) that this actual world is intrinsically filled with the
Buddha's power, however, we know that both the sounds that preach the
dharma (truth) in the Buddha's voice, as well as the invisible words that
also preach the *dharma*, are expressed in the vibrations of Nature and in
the configuration of things in our surrounding world. This is Kūkai's contention. Consequently, the claim that the essence of *waka* lies in the
dhāraṇī means that one intuits the working of an invisible life transcending
the world of sense impressions.

In the Muromachi period, Shinkei* perfected the medieval theory of
waka vis-à-vis this *dhāraṇī* view. In *Murmurings* (*Sasamegoto*), he states:

---

*Shinkei (1406–1475) was a famous *renga* poet.—Ed.

Whatever the way [of practice], shouldn't one's mind change greatly through training [*keiko*] and diligence? If so, no matter how much one is exposed to sacred teachings and books, attainment is not his unless he knows for himself what is cold to be cold, what is hot to be hot. Saint Saigyō* says "the way of waka is nothing but a way of *meditation* and *cultivation. . . .* " The way of *waka* poetry is, in essence, our country's own *dhāraṇi*. When intellectually engaged with elegant words, even to read *sūtras* and their commentaries or to cultivate oneself in meditation is delusion.[5]

Here, "training" and "diligence" in composing *waka* poetry is regarded as essentially the same as the Buddhist "meditative cultivation." The phrase, "to know for himself what is cold to be cold, what is hot to be hot," is a common Zen expression meaning that cultivation can be understood only by personally experiencing with the whole body-mind; it cannot be grasped by the intellectual understanding of books. Shinkei takes this to be leaving behind intellectual elegance.

Just as the practicing monk leaves behind his own egoism and deepens his *satori* by experiencing cultivation with his body-mind, so too, the poet enhances his or her state of mind as a poet by training in composition. Therefore, training in artistry is a kind of personal cultivation: one not only studies a certain technique but also, in so doing, enhances one's own personality. Certainly, the word "way" (*dō*) of "the way of poetry" (*kadō*) supports such an interpretation.

Shinkei characterizes the ultimate state of *waka* poetry:

It is the first eight levels of consciousness that stir the stormy waves of delusion about right and wrong. Once one reaches the tenth consciousness, one is unmoved by the distinction between good and evil. Awakening to the wisdom about dreamlike transformation [that is, impermanence] and eliminating all delusions, both the environment and wisdom [that is, both the object and subject] are no longer dreamlike. Simply awakening to nonrelational [nondiscriminatory] compassion, one must relationally condition the state of nondistinction [that is, one must express the ultimate state of emptiness transcending the opposition between being and nonbeing].[6]

This terminology about the eighth and tenth consciousness comes from Kūkai's *Ten Stages of Mind* (*Jūjūshinron*), which distinguishes ten levels of religious experience, from delusion to *satori.*

---

*Saigyō (1118–1190) was a famous monk and *waka* poet of the late Heian period.— Ed.

We will discuss these later, but here we should note that this theoretical system of the ten-tiered consciousness assumes a process for enhancing the spirit or personality. The ultimate *satori,* the tenth consciousness, is the nondiscriminatory, compassionate mind that first thoroughly experiences and deals successfully with this transient world and then, from such a transcendent mental state, proceeds to feel compassion toward all sentient life. Similarly, the ultimate state for *waka* artistry is to attain such heights that one sees through this world's human afflictions and delusions, and yet, for that very reason, one is the mind of Great Compassion in the face of this world's delusory forms. This is a free mind that can empathize and share in the pain found in the various profiles of human life. In this manner, Shinkei contends, true artistic expression becomes possible.

Performance and mind in Zeami

In his theory of Nō drama, Zeami* also adopted the idea of artistic training as personal cultivation. Since Nō drama, unlike poetry, is a theatrical art, let us bear in mind that the concept of the body is naturally more prominent. In his *Transmission of Stylish Form and the Flower* (*Fūshikaden* or *Kadensho*), there is a section entitled "perennial training" (*nenraikeiko*). Perennial training is a mental readiness for training in accordance with one's age, from childhood to one's late years. The aim is to obtain the so-called flower (*hana*). The word "flower" means specifically an artistic dramatic skill or the beauty of performance. Abstractly, this is the essence or ideal of all performance; it is the symbol of artistry.

In this chapter, Zeami explains first the "timely flower," that is, the charming beauty in the boy's body. He then discusses the "temporary flower," the resolute beauty mastered by the well-trained youth. Finally, he moves on to the "true flower" which does not wither away in spite of the decline of the body; one achieves the state of the "flower remaining on the old bones." The point here is that true art cannot be mastered merely through the conceptual understanding, but must be acquired, as it were, through one's body. In other words, it is a bodily acquisition by

---

*Zeami (1363–1443) is regarded as a central figure in the theoretical development of Nō (sometimes romanized "Noh"), an ancient form of Japanese drama characterized by controlled, graceful movements accompanied by chanting and stringed, wind, and percussion instruments.—Ed.

means of a long, cumulative, difficult training (*keiko*). What then is the relationship between the mind and the body according to this account?

In the chapter "Questions and Answers," Zeami compares training to Zen cultivation. In Zen cultivation, whether one is engaged in seated meditation or in everyday chores, one is instructed to assume a certain "form" (*katachi*) or posture for meditation, eating, worship, or working in compliance with the monastic regulations. At any rate, Zen corrects the mode of one's mind by putting one's body into the correct postures. Zeami seems to understand artistic training in a similar manner. Training, it seems, is a discipline for shaping one's body into a form. Art is embodied through cumulative training; one comes to learn an art through one's body. We all have had such an experience in sports, for example. Training or disciplining means to make the mind's movements accord with the body's. In this respect, theatrical performance, athletic activity, and vocational skills are all similar.

Initially, the body's movements do not follow the dictates of the mind. The body is heavy, resistant to the mind's movement; in this sense, the body is an object opposing the living subject's (*shutai*) mode of being. That is, the mind (or consciousness) and the body exhibit an ambiguous subjective–objective dichotomy within the self's mode of being. To harmonize the mind and body through training is to eliminate this ambiguity in practice; it amounts to subjectivizing the body, making it the lived subject. This is a practical, not a conceptual, understanding. Although we tend to forget that which is cerebrally understood, we do not forget what we learned through our body. What we acquire through our body can be unconsciously, naturally expressed in body movements fitting "form." The "mind" here is not the surface consciousness, but is the "mind" that penetrates into the body and deeply subjectivizes it.

Through training one will gradually master the "true flower," the essence of art. In Zen meditation, through the training of the body-mind, one attains *satori*. Zeami summarizes the process of mastering "flowers" through training and quotes the *gatha* (hymn) of the sixth Ch'an (Zen) patriarch, Hui-nêng, to conclude the passage:

> The timely flower, the flower of voice and the flower of *yūgen* [the boy's beauty]—all these are apparent to the eye, but since they blossom from out of the performer's technique [*waza*], since they are just like the blooming flowers, here is soon the time for them to wither. . . . But for the true flower, both the fact of blossoming and that of withering should be in accord with the mind. . . . What should you do to understand this principle? . . . You should keep in mind the various types of performance through "perennial training" from the age of seven. After you carry your diligence to the extreme and exhaust all your faculties,

know that this flower cannot be lost. The mind that penetrates this is the seed of the flower. Since this is the case, if you want to know the flower, first know its seed. The flower is the mind and its seed the technique [*waza*]. The ancient master [Hu-nêng] says:

> The ground of the mind contains many seeds. All of them sprout completely in the universal rain. If one suddenly realizes the mind of the flower, the fruit of *bodhi* (enlightenment) matures of itself.[7]

It is the lifelong accumulation of training and diligence that makes the true flower blossom. In the above passage, the term *waza* (technique) occurs twice. Literally, it means "performance" but, more generally, it indicates the mode of being a body. The *waza* is the seed and the artistic mind is the flower blossoming out of it. The *waza*, such as a beautiful voice or a boy's natural beauty, temporarily enables the flower to bloom, but since it is connected with the youthful body, it will soon wither. Zeami contends, however, that the *waza* enabling the true flower to bloom can make the unwithering flower blossom at any time, since it is mastered through cumulative training.

When we examine and compare Zeami's explanation with Hui-nêng's *gatha* at the end, we can detect a subtle difference. In Hui-nêng's verse, the seed of Buddha-nature is at the ground of the mind. This seed sprouts if one cultivates oneself in compliance with Buddhist teachings, the *dharma*-rain. When the flower of *satori* blooms in due course, it is naturally the nucleus of the Buddha's *satori* (*bodai*). Thus, the great ground that contains seeds is compared to the mind, the rain to cultivation, and the flower or fruits to *satori*. Missing here is any specific reference to the body. Zeami quoted Hui-nêng not only for the metaphors of seed and flower, but also, obviously, to draw a parallel between artistic training and Zen cultivation.

But the parallel is not perfect. For Zeami, the seed is the *waza*, that is, the bodily modality that acquires a performative technique through training (*keiko*). *Waza* is an ideal "form" (*katachi*) for the bodily modality; the bodily form acquired through training is the seed and the artistic mind is the flower. In other words, the beauty displaying the artistic ideal is said to be a flower which blossoms from such a seed. Consequently, the claim is that one should first acquire the correct bodily mode, for only then can the correct mental mode be opened up.

No-mind and body-mind oneness

Zeami presents a serious point for a theory of body-mind. Art cannot be achieved through conceptual, intellectual understanding but must be acquired with one's body through training (*keiko*). Conceptual understanding is a conscious judgment and inference having the form, "if such and such, then I should do so and so." In this case, the mind, the function of consciousness, leads the action, that is, the body's function. When ordering an action in ordinary experience, the conscious mode dominates the bodily mode.

Zeami seems to realize that we should not interpret the essence of what we call the human mind from such a standpoint. In order to grasp the mind's authentic mode of being, we must first reverse the ordinary view that puts the mind before the body, and place priority on the form of the body. Only then can one seek the authentic or essential mode of that which we call "the mind." For the true mind, that is, the mind of the flower, is attained anew only via the comprehension of technique (*waza*), the body's correct form (*katachi*), through its training (*keiko*).

What then is the mind of the flower that blossoms through cumulative training? In the *Flower Mirror* (*Hanakagami*) and in his later works, Zeami roughly distinguishes two levels of the performer's art: the "easy rank" (or mind at ease) and the "matured rank" (or no-mind). The easy rank is the state wherein expressive technique and the fullness of the inner mind accompany each other to a certain degree. And this easy rank is further divided into "the skilled one" and "the masterful one." The skilled one can handle music, dance, acting, excelling in theatrical technique. In contrast, the masterful one has attained the artistic mind. "To act in a Nō-play, mindfully and deeply aware of its attractive experience, is not found in the skilled one, but it is what deserves the name the masterful one."

At any rate, these two "easy ranks" are so named because one can express through them the technique of performing as the mind wishes. What distinguishes the merely skilled from the masterly, however, is whether one attends to the body's technical aspect or to the mind's fullness. Zeami characterizes "the full operation of the mind with seventy per cent of the body" as the quotient of the skilled performer on the stage. While operating one's mind to the fullest, one performs the dance in such a way that "the mind causes [the body] to be activated less than itself, stopping at the more interior." We may say that such an actor performs with a self-possessed mind, without exaggerating the outward, performative expression. Still, we might add that the mind in this instance implies "consciousness" in the sense that the actor's mind attempts to activate the body.

The ultimate state of art, the "mature rank" or "no-mind," is where one penetrates through the state of the "easy rank" or the "easy mind." Achieving this state, even if one performs a technique usually considered wrong, it may appear right. If we may say of the art of the easy rank, "form is emptiness" (*rupa* is *śūnyatā*), of the matured rank it may be said, "emptiness is form."

> Even when there is mellow-sounding music of an uncertain variety, while certainly sounding exotic, it almost makes no difference whether it is good or bad, or right or wrong. It is "emptiness is form." When the music is fascinating with its right–wrong ambiguity, there should be no [consideration of] right or wrong.[8]

The term "form" (*rupa*) probably refers here to the performing technique. In contrast, "emptiness" (*śūnyatā*) means the "mind." Although the easy rank is a free state, indicating that one can express a performing technique as the mind wishes, there is still a small gap between the mind and the body's performance. In contrast, the matured rank is the mind's being emptied such that one's awareness of performance disappears.

Such a no-mind, Zeami contends, produces such states as: "observing with a detached seeing" and "observing with the same mind as one observing from the audience." "Observing with a detached seeing" is the state in which the self's consciousness of itself (the observing self) disappears and the actor sees even his own dancing figure from the outside. And "observing with the same mind as one observing from the audience" means the state in which an actor observes his own performance as from a seat in the audience. These two forms of self observation are the same in that one sees one's own figure not only from the inner, but also from the outer, perspective. Here there is no consciousness distinguishing self and others, or performer and audience. The world is fused into one.

As a theory of body-mind, Zeami's no-mind parallels Nishida's "acting intuition" in the "*basho* vis-à-vis nothing." In the state of no-mind, the subjective-objective ambiguity between one's mind and body disappears, and the body as an object is made completely subjective. The body already loses that object-like weightiness which resists the mind's function as subject; the body acts by passively receiving the power of creative intuition brimming forth from the dimension that transcends the dimensions of everyday self-consciousness. When the body is made completely subjective in this manner, the mind is no longer a subject dominating the body as a resistant object. Thus, the mind is made completely objective.

The bodily form dancing on a stage signifies, at the same time, the *mind just as it is.* In the active state of body-mind identity, the ambiguous dichotomy of the body disappears.

Zeami says that "there is an end to life, but Nō is endless"; there is an infinite depth to artistry. It is a path without end that renders the self into nothing.

> If we speak in terms of the bifurcation between being and nothingness, being is observation [expression] and nothingness is a container [the mind]. What expresses being is nothingness.[9]

When the mind becomes nothing, it freely expresses all beings, all that has a form. Alive in this notion is the Buddha's teaching of no-ego.

Chapter Six

Dōgen

Zen's practical character

Dōgen* is the founder of Japanese Sōtō Zen. More than that, he is a distinguished, representative Japanese monk as well as an unexcelled philosophical thinker. In dealing with his philosophy, we encounter a rigorous attitude rejecting idle speculation.

A famous anecdote, which appears in all his biographies, recounts that upon first entering China at Ming-chou in 1223, Dōgen spoke with a *tenzo* from Mt. A-yü-wang (a Ch'an or Zen monastery); a *tenzo* is the monk in charge of cooking meals at the monastery. Because of his personality and erudition, this sixty-year-old unknown monk made a favorable impression on Dōgen. Stopping him, Dōgen asked for Zen teaching that night but the *tenzo* declined, informing Dōgen that he had not obtained

---

*DŌGEN Kigen (1200–1253), a highly creative thinker and writer, is generally considered to be one of Japan's greatest philosophers. In recent years, much scholarly attention has been focused on Dōgen by Western scholars. Of the available translations of parts of his *magnum opus, Shōbōgenzō* [The treasury of the correct *dharma*-eye], the most scholarly renderings are those by Norman Waddell and Masao ABE found in various issues of *The Eastern Buddhist* beginning with Volume 4 (1971). For a more popular work, one may consult Reihō MASUNAGA's translation of *Shōbōgenzō Zuimonki, A Primer of Sōtō Zen* (Honolulu: University Press of Hawaii, 1971). Among secondary sources, the best book-length treatment is Hee-jin Kim's *Dōgen Kigen—Mystical Realist* (Tucson: University of Arizona Press, 1975). A shorter, more philosophical discussion can be found in chaps 6 and 7 of T. P. Kasulis, *Zen Action/Zen Person* (Honolulu: University Press of Hawaii, 1981). For a critical review of Dōgen materials available in English, see T. P. Kasulis, "The Zen Philosopher: A Review Article on Dōgen Scholarship in English," *Philosophy East and West* 28:3 (July 1978), pp. 353–373. Two important recent contributions to Dōgen scholarship are William R. LaFleur (ed.), *Dōgen Studies* (Honolulu: University of Hawaii Press, 1985) and the translations by Thomas Cleary in *Shōbōgenzō* (Honolulu: University of Hawaii Press, 1986).—Ed.

permission from the temple to stay away for the night. Dōgen asked:

> "Why do you labor diligently on the troublesome work of a cook, instead of applying yourself to the Way of the Buddhas, studying *kōans*, reading the sayings of the ancient masters, sitting in quiet meditation, undertaking the Path? Is there any virtue to this work you do?"

The *tenzo* laughed:

> "Young man from a foreign land, you don't know what words *are* nor what undertaking the Path means."

The monk's laughter was as much a shock to Dōgen as if he had been slapped in the face.

"What, then, are words? What is the undertaking of the Path?" The *tenzo* replied:

> If one does not make a false step in handling a question, can one not be a person [of insight]?

This meant that if such an inquirer does not stumble over his own feet in questioning, he can be called a true person practicing the Path. Dōgen was twenty-four years old at the time; we can imagine the shock the ambitious young monk received from his Chinese senior.

One can probably take this conversation in various ways. But our immediate concern is the question: in Zen Buddhism, what is the relationship between practice and theory? When one asks about "words" or the "undertaking of the Path," that is, when one asks what Buddhism is, there must be at its foundation (one's own feet) a premise about practice as the mustering of one's body-mind. Any theoretical speculation that misses this premise will result in misunderstanding Zen's aims. For now, we will leave our interpretation of the *tenzo* story at this.

Among the Buddhist schools, Zen explicitly demands a rigorous practice. The distinctive teaching of the Zen school is its classification of Buddhist schools according to "two gates:" doctrines and meditation (*zen*). Zen sees the standpoint of the other Buddhist schools as the doctrinal gate; each school is established in light of a theoretical system set out in particular *sūtras* and *abhidharma* commentaries. In contrast, the Zen school emphasizes the meditation gate, believing that personal cultivation via seated meditation is fundamental.

Four mottos expressing the fundamental Zen spirit are found in such works as *The Gateless Barrier* and the *Blue Cliff Records:* (1) no dependence on words; (2) special transmission outside of doctrines; (3) pointing directly to one's own mind; (4) becoming a Buddha upon seeing one's own nature. Concretely, "No dependence on words" means not to use any particular *sūtra* or commentary as the standard. The teachings propounded in *sūtras* have their own unqiue theories as systematically organized thought, and, obviously, since each is derived from the Buddha's teaching, each probably expresses some aspect of Buddhism. Still, there is the danger of missing the fundamental spirit of Buddhism were one to attach oneself to any verbalized theory.

There is something else important to be transmitted besides teachings: the "special transmission outside of doctrines." What is this special transmission? Clearly, the Buddha's experience of *satori*. Seated meditation tries to re-experience, in one's own body-mind, the Buddha's *satori*.

The point is not to understand intellectually a systematic set of teachings but to inquire directly, through seated meditation, into the essence of human nature within the interiority of one's own self. This is the meaning of the third motto, "Pointing directly to one's own mind." Thus, the Zen inquiry is not intellectual, but, rather, the introspective experience of one's mind.

The goal is to be connected with the Buddha's mind. Therefore, the fourth motto, "Becoming a Buddha upon seeing one's own nature," means to actualize the Buddha-nature within the self.

In the rigor of Chinese Zen, one senses a spiritual aura in its broadest sense, what might also be termed a strong ethical ethos. Indian Buddhism appears more theoretical and speculative. The ethical character of Chinese Zen Buddhism is influenced by the traditional Chinese spiritual climate represented by Confucianism. The Sung Dynasty, when Zen blossomed, was a period of Confucianist revival and high spirituality among government officials. The schools of Chu Hsi and Wang Yang-ming resulted, in part, from a spiritual exchange between Confucianism and Buddhism. Still, the fundamental attitude of Zen, with its emphasis on subjective practice over theoretical thinking, and its rejection of the superiority of intellectual speculation, is of Buddhist heritage. As already observed, Buddhism teaches the three studies—the precepts, meditation, and wisdom. As we discussed earlier, the term "cultivation" subsumes the first two: the precepts (an outward-oriented practice) and meditation (an inward-looking practice). The former means that the human subject acts towards the world in a field of interconnected meanings involving ordinary experience. The practice (*prāxis*) discussed in contemporary philosophy is such action. In contrast, meditation is an inward-looking practice because it faces the self's inner world, the interior of one's mind. The ultimate goal of Buddhism—*prajñā,* the wisdom accompanying *satori*—can be attained only through this meditation. The ideas and theories presented in *sūtras* or commentaries are simply its resultant wisdom. Consequently, one cannot correctly understand Buddhist philosophy without first passing through these two stages (obeying the precepts and meditation) in the order mentioned.

Since the three studies indicate the Buddhist spirit as a whole, it was naturally recognized in ancient Japanese Buddhism. The Tendai sect divides Buddhism into the doctrinal and the meditative gates, while the Shingon (Esoteric) school distinguishes the doctrinal and concrete aspects. In the Tendai sect, the meditative gate is the actual practice of meditation and cultivation as set out in *The Great Cessation and Discernment.* The concrete aspects of Esoteric Buddhism are often interpreted to be cultivation methods, since, as we have already noted, the method of performing ceremonial rites and cultivation are inseparable. It was a premise, even in ancient Japanese Buddhism, that the practical, concrete aspect must accompany the doctrinal aspect, that is, theoretical study. For various historical and social reasons, though, ancient Japanese Buddhism was monopolized in the late Heian period by aristocrats. So the cultural and intellectual side of Buddhism was greatly stressed at that time. In *Gakudōyōjinshū* [What to bear in mind while studying the way], which Dōgen wrote when he opened the Kōshō Temple at Uji after returning from China, we find the following critique of this development.

> How regrettable! Mistaken teachings easily take root in this hinterland [Japan] and the Correct Dharma has difficulty. The Correct Dharma has already been heard even in Korea, but never in our country. This is because all the previous monks, who went [to China] during the T'ang Dynasty [in Japan's Heian period] were trapped in the entanglement of written doctrines. They brought back Buddhist *sūtras* but have forgotten the Buddha *Dharma*.[1]

The "entanglement of written doctrines" means undue reliance on the theoretical aspects, a pedantic approach to Buddhist *sūtras* while forgetting the essentials, the Buddha Dharma. This is Dōgen's criticism of one aspect of the Buddhist world at the end of the ancient period. In this sense, Zen sought to renew the practical character originally found in Buddhism; it tried to restore to Japanese Buddhism the searching attitude of original Buddhism.

Cultivation's reversal of the ordinary understanding of being

In *Gakudōyōjinshū,* Dōgen discusses the preparation of mind for studying the Way of the Buddhas:

When one enters the gate [of Zen] to study the Way of the Buddhas, one listens to the teaching of a learned master and cultivates oneself accordingly. One must know at such a time the [two] teachings: (1) one moves the *dharma* and (2) the *dharma* moves the self. When one moves the *dharma* well, the self if strong and the *dharma* weak. When the *dharma* moves the self, the *dharma* is strong and the self weak. In the Way of the Buddhas, there have always been [these] two situations. Only authentic *dharma* successors know this. In fact, it is rare to hear this mentioned by anyone other than me. One who does not know this ancient fact has not yet undertaken the study of the Way. How can one tell the authentic [cultivator] from the inauthentic one? Since those [of you here] who study the Way through seated meditation will be transmitted this ancient fact without fail, you shall not be led astray. There is nothing like this in other sects. Those who diligently seek the Way of the Buddhas can know the true Way exhaustively only through seated meditation.[2]

This quote is not too difficult. Those who study the Buddha Way for the first time must do so under a master and cultivate themselves according to his or her teaching. They must note that there are two different attitudes, one in which the *dharma* moves (literally, "turns") the self, and the other in which one moves the *dharma*. For now, I interpret *dharma* here as meaning "Buddha Dharma," the truth of Buddhism. Knowledge of these two attitudes is the difference between the authentic and inauthentic understanding of Buddhism. Obviously, Dōgen regards the former, the *dharma*'s moving the self, as the proper alternative. Dōgen's claim that he alone reveals this truth is not a boast, but an expression of his resoluteness in understanding Buddhism through the strict distinction between these two attitudes. Dōgen, then, concludes that the authentic Way, that is, the *dharma*'s moving the self, is seated meditation.

The quoted passage rejects the attempt to understand Buddhism by means of "higher" intellectual speculations. In other words, we can reach the correct understanding of Buddhist philosophy only through the practice of seated meditation. The problem to consider here is the relationship between the self and the *dharma*. Although the term *dharma* can mean the Buddha Dharma, the true teachings of Buddhism, it also means "that which exists," so we find phrases like "all *dharmas*" or "the myriad *dharmas*" in the sense of all things, that is, the Being of beings. Since the Buddha Dharma is what clarifies the true mode of the Being of all beings, we may collapse these two senses by saying the Buddha Dharma is the true aspect of the Being of beings. The distinction between "the self moves the *dharma*" and "the *dharma* moves the self" can then be seen as two attitudes of understanding the Being of beings.

In trying to understand Buddhism from the standpoint of theoretical speculation, one attitude understands the Being of beings by postulating a self. Thus, the self becomes strong and the *dharma* weak; the true aspect of the Being of beings will be covered over. Conversely, if one takes the attitude achieved through the strict path of personal cultivation, the true aspect of the Being of beings will be revealed and the self is moved. Then the *dharma* is strong and the self weak. By our interpretation, therefore, the quote expresses two attitudes for understanding the Being of beings, and seated meditation is the practice that directs one to understanding Being in an authentic way.

In the "*Genjōkōan*" [Presence of things as they are] fascicle of *Shōbōgenzō* [Treasury of the correct *dharma*-eye], there is a famous passage that corresponds to the one already quoted from *Gakudōyōjinshū*:

> To cultivate-authenticate all things by conveying the self [to them] is delusion; for all things to come forward and cultivate-authenticate the self is *satori*. . . . To model yourself after the way of the Buddhas is to model yourself after yourself. To model yourself after yourself is to forget yourself. To forget yourself is to be authenticated by all things. To be authenticated by all things is to effect the molting of body-mind, both yours and others.'.[3]

In this passage, the relationship between the self and all things (or all *dharmas*) is again examined. (Incidentally, the fascicle, "*Genjōkōan*," was written in August 1223, whereas *Gakudōyōjinshū* is thought to have been written in March of the following year. Thus, the relation between the self and *dharmas* was most important to Dōgen as a new Zen master, just beginning his teaching.)

What does Dōgen mean by "to cultivate-authenticate all things by conveying the self to them"? TAMAKI Kōshiro translates this passage as, "the self, becoming a subject (*shutai*), verifies the surrounding world."[4] "All things" (all *dharmas*) means everything that exists, the totality of which is the surrounding world. Dōgen says that it is delusion to grasp the world through the self as a subject. In the expression of the *Gakudōyōjinshū*, this is the attitude in which "the self moves the *dharma*," the inauthentic way to understand Buddhism. If this is correct, how should we interpret Dōgen's point in modern terms?

To use a more contemporary expression, the "self" here probably refers to being a self-conscious subject. Therefore, to grasp the world by verifying it through the self qua subject means to cognize the modes of being by understanding that things in the world are objects opposed to the subject, or to consciousness. This attitude is natural in ordinary human experience. In the language of Part I, it is thinking with a pre-determined, delimited human subject who, as a being-in-the-world, has its place in the everyday life-space. Dōgen contends that the path to *satori* is opened only by the daring rejection of natural, everyday cognition as a "delusion." Why? According to Dōgen, the self is not forgotten in such an ordinary attitude. That is, the self attempts to understand intellectually the Being of beings (the meaning of what is) in light of self-conscious experience.

What, then, is *satori?* Dōgen says, it is to model oneself after oneself (through seated meditation) and to forget the self. As one forgets the self, the standpoint of self-consciousness disappears and the self becomes, as it were, a "self without being a self." There is a transition from the self's moving the *dharma* to the *dharma*'s moving the self. All things (*dharmas*), all beings in the world, reveal the true profile of Being and, on their own, they illuminate the true meaning of the self's authentic being. So says Dōgen. In other words, when one experiences, as it were, the dimension of the *non-everyday* such that self-consciousness is "forgotten" and the self is no longer a self, the self changes into Being. This Being exists by virtue of its being illuminated by all the objects experienced in ordinary experience. The whole world is made, as it were, into an absolute, transcendental subject, and the self, here and now, becomes the Being illuminated by this single, absolute subject. The self merges into the whole universe and there is no distinction between self and other. This is the true profile of the self. For now, we may understand Dōgen's point in such a way, but this is only a verbal expression and cannot really grasp the full significance of *satori.*

Dōgen says it is delusion to posit the self. In other words, the human subject's everyday attitude of understanding the world is inauthentic and must be reversed. But how? In the words of *Gakudōyojinshū,* one must "study the Way through seated meditation"; in *"Genjōkōan,"* it says one must "molt the body-mind." Thus, it seems that in seated meditation, the body and mind are to fall away, but no clear answer is given as to where and how this takes place. This is because we are seeking the answer on the theoretical level. Speculation is a self-conscious thinking, and is the very positing of the self which Dōgen rejects. We have, therefore, come to an impasse.

The impasse stems from our attempt to understand intellectually and verbally the meaning of the molting of body-mind. This molting in seated meditation is not an event which can be understood by ordinary intellectual cognition. It is an event that each person has to experience for oneself through practice, outside ordinary experience. Dōgen states in *Hōkyōki,* a memoir of his sojourn in China, the following to be the teaching of his master Ju-ching (Nyojō):

> Seated meditation is the molting of body-mind. It is not burning incense, worshiping [the Buddha's image], calling on a Buddha [*nem-*

butsu], repentance rituals, or reading sutras. It is only sitting [*shikantaza*]. What then is the molting of body-mind? It is seated meditation itself.[5]

Dōgen liked the expression, "seated meditation is the molting of body-mind," using it repeatedly in such *Shōbōgenzō* fascicles as "*Gyōji*" and "*Sammai Ō Zammai.*"

When we wish to place ourselves in the position of seeking the Way of the Buddhas as a Zen cultivator, we must abandon our pen. However, we are not in such a situation. Our standpoint is to take what Dōgen's teaching means as a contemporary issue in philosophical thinking, or more directly, to gain from it a new suggestion for a mind-body theory. In order to do this, we must think this out on our own, guided by Dōgen but going beyond him.

Body-mind relation in seated meditation

Experience in the everyday world is common to us all; everyone has it naturally. In contrast, the lived experience of "body-mind molting and falling off" through seated meditation, of which Dōgen speaks, is not immediately given in the field of natural, ordinary experience. It is possible to experience it only through a specific, practical means of personal cultivation. In this sense, it may be regarded as a *non-everyday* or *supra-everyday* experience, and consequently as an *extraordinary* experience: that is, cultivation is an inevitable passage as well as a detour for reaching the field of supra-everyday experience by way of everyday experience. Let us now take note of the relationship between the mind and body in cultivation before we investigate the character of such a supra-everyday experience.

TAMAKI Kōshirō gives the following interpretation of the *Shōbōgenzō* fascicle, "*Shinjingakudō*" [Studying the Way with the body-mind]:

> Ordinarily, we tend to think that the spirit is more fundamental and important than the body, but it is the opposite with Dōgen. The title reads "Studying the Way with the Body-Mind," placing the body before the mind. Moreover, this fascicle discusses the mind first and then the body, indicating that the body is rather more important than the mind.[6]

According to Tamaki, the fundamental attitude in cultivating the Way of the Buddhas is to reserve the ordinary thinking that places the mind (spirit) above the body. This emphasis on the body captures the meaning of cultivation for Dōgen as well as for Buddhism in general.

What is personal cultivation? Earlier we said it covers both the stages of the precepts and of meditation in Early Buddhism's threefold study: the precepts, meditation, and wisdom. In our terminology, the precepts are the outwardly oriented practices in ordinary experience, and meditation (*samādhi*) is the inward-looking practices of extraordinary experience. In either case, what is first required is the placing of the body into a definite *form*.

In the Zen school, one must comply with monastic regulations and engage in the daily routine of washing, working, and cleaning. Dōgen regarded these everyday tasks so highly that there are fascicles in *Shōbōgenzō* such as "Washing the Face and Hands" ("*Senmen*"), and "Cleansing" ("*Senjō*"). In the conversation with the elderly monastic cook quoted at the beginning of this chapter (from the book *Tenzokyōkun*), Dōgen discovered the fundamental spirit of Zen, of Buddhism generally, to be living as did that *tenzo* monk. To place oneself into such a form is to train one's body in compliance with established regulations, and thereby, to correct one's mental mode. In other words, the departure point of cultivation assumes not the mind's dominating the body, but rather, the body's dominating the mind. To sit in meditation is to carry out this attitude more thoroughly than one can in the stage of outwardly oriented practice.

Earlier, Tamaki said it is our common view to think of the spirit as being more fundamental and important than the body. Although this value judgment relates to the history of thought and its emphasis on the superiority of the spirit, for the present we shall leave the historical issues moot. Instead, we shall consider it in a more phenomenological and immediate maneuver.

When we reflect upon our body-mind in ordinary experience, the spirit usually dominates the body. For example, I am thinking now (in the mind) that I would like to write on this paper. I am controlling my hand (a part of my body) in accordance with this mental mode. In principle, it is the same with other actions, so we find in the field of our ordinary experience the actual fact that the mind dominates the body. Based upon this fact, the value judgment arises that the mind *should* dominate the body. As long as we live in the everyday life-world, this is the natural human mode and, consequently, insofar as we remain human it is a matter of fact that we dominate the body through the spirit. This approach has its foundation in the ordinary experience of the self as a conscious subject relating itself to the world; it is natural to inquire into the meaning of human being based upon such experience.

The philosophy of self-consciousness in the modern West has clearly established such an attitude. For example, in his *Critique of Practical Reason,* Kant says that to observe moral laws is to control the sense functions in compliance with practical reason (the rational will); the essence of being human has to be sought therein. The sense functions are the emotions, passions, or impulses that are connected with the body's desires. To explain it in terms of the mind and body, the "mind" here means rational judgment, whereas the functions of emotion, pathos, or eros are considered to belong to the "body." In this sense, the mind is superior to the body.

Dōgen's demand that we "study the Way with the body-mind" is the reversal of the ordinary experiential view just discussed. Dōgen maintains that the body must dominate the mind. Here we must think more rigorously about the difference in the two stages of cultivation distinguished earlier.

Precepts, the stage of outwardly oriented practice, overlaps with secular moral laws, although the precepts are stricter. For example, the proper way of eating is required, to a certain extent, of the lay person as well as the monastic. In this case, putting the self into a form is not sufficiently freed from the idea that the spirit dominates the body. Consequently, the authentic meaning of cultivation must be sought in the second stage, the inward-looking practice of meditation or *samadhi.* How is the relationship between the mind and body grasped in this case?

When one sits in meditation, one has to suspend all actions pertaining to the external world. One has purposely to cut off behavioral relations with and caring for all beings in the world. Dōgen explains the method of seated meditation in the *Shōbōgenzō* fascicle, *"Zazengi,"* [Principles of zazen]:

Meditation under a Master is seated meditation. A quiet place is best and one should use a thick cushion [to sit on]. Do not let any wind or smoke blow in, and do not let rain or dew enter. Take care of the place for your body. There are citations of [Buddhas] having sat on the Diamond [seat] and on big rocks; but they all sat on thick grass. Keep the sitting place lit, not letting it be dark either during the day or night. Keep it warm in winter and cool in summer. Give up all relationships and let all things be. Neither good nor evil are thought of. They are not conscious in the mind. . . . [After this follows some detailed remarks about the method of sitting: correct posture, closing the eyes half-way, breathing quietly through the nose.] After preparing one's body-mind in this way, there should be a deep exhalation. Sitting immovably, thinking is not thinking. (Even as it is thinking something, consciousness achieves the state of not thinking while thinking.) How do you think in not-thinking? This is without thinking. (It is the nothingness of conscious thinking.) This is the true method for seated meditation.[7]

This is a kind instruction. To sit in meditation, one places a mat in a quiet place away from wind, smoke, rain, and dew, keeping the place warm in winter and cool in summer. This prevents the sense organs of the body from receiving stimuli from the external world and, consequently, prevents the mind from wandering toward the external world. At this time, all ties between the self and the world must be such that one "gives up all relationships and lets all things be."

The next statements, that "neither good nor evil are thought of" and "they are not conscious in the mind," are more difficult, but not thinking of good and evil probably means to suspend all judgments about the world of everday experience (in phenomenological terms, an attitude of *epoché*). To enter into the extraordinary experience of meditation, one must abandon all value judgments concerning the secular dimension. In this way, the self qua conscious subject must deny its being conscious. Meditation is an inward-looking practice facing the self's inner world, an attempt to transcend toward a world that is not the conscious mind. Theoretically, meditation performs an *epoché* (the suspension of judgments) with respect to the conscious subject's natural attitude in ordinary experience. But it is not simply an *epoché* like a theoretical operation in phenomenology. It is a practical operation through which the self becomes that which does not judge. Being such a practical operation, meditation also performs the *epoché* in a *theoretical* mode.

The judgment that the spirit dominates the body is thus suspended. Through practice one willfully rejects the human subject as a "being-in-the-world," grounded in the everyday life-world. When this change occurs, the spirit can no longer dominate the body. Rather, the self is confined to the reversal of the everyday mode of being, and the body dominates the spirit. In this situation, what are the horizons of the self?

As noted earlier, the value judgment that the mind ought to dominate the body is based upon the fact that the mind does dominate the body. In Kant's moral principles, the rational mind rejects the pathos of the passions and the eros of the impulses conjoined to the body, placing them under the control of self-consciousness. This is simply an *ought,* however, and it does not mean that consciousness completely dominates the body.

Indeed, the passions and impulses sometimes rebel against rational consciousness. The body qua pathos is heavy and vehement, resisting the consciousness qua *logos;* this is the substrate's restriction on the rational human subject. Nonetheless, when we relate ourselves caringly and actively to the everyday life-world, we often forget about the substrate's restriction, and the layer of the bright *cogito* flows so as to become a conscious subject in the field of ordinary experience.

The bright consciousness thinkingly judges vis-à-vis the passive function of seeing the external world as perceived contents. Based upon this judgment, the subject (*shutai*) attempts to direct its body to the active mode of acting towards the world. According to Nishida's theory of acting intuition discussed in Chapter Two, the subject (*shutai*) is linked to the life-space by establishing a passive-active circuit of relationship. The layer of the bright *cogito* is what indicates this superficial structural relationship, represented by the stream of perception and thinking.

But beneath this surface layer is concealed the dark *cogito*, tightly bound by corporeality. This body qua pathos is the substrate's restriction. A meditative sitting opens our eyes to this substrate concealed from the dimension of ordinary experience. It confronts the dark consciousness and its meaning for the human subject.

Generally speaking, meditative thinking first puts the body prior to the mind by letting the former comply with a set form. By setting up such an artificial situation, one realizes that the everyday understanding of the self is inauthentic. We are led to experience that the body, as the determination of the human subject, is an object that does not originally belong to the sovereignty of rational consciousness. Consequently, we recognize that it is the body that dominates the spirit, even in the everyday mode of the self. Ordinarily, we simply forget this fact. When you suffer physical pain and delusions during meditation, in the delusions arising from the depths of your own body-mind, you are asked: "Have you, as a person, not been dominated in your life by bodily desires?" Through this question, the self is directed to the primordial passivity of life found in the substratum's basal restriction on the human subject. In other words, the self realizes the destiny of human nature thrown into the world: one originally comes to live in this world as a carnal, objective being. When sitting in meditation, one penetrates the meaning of such human destiny.

Molting the ordinary dimension

Let us summarize Nishida's theory of acting intuition alongside what we have been investigating through examining Dōgen. In Nishida, the process that takes one from the dimension of ordinary experience to the dimension of *basho* was not clearly recognized. As a being-in-the-world in

ordinary experience, when considered in light of the relationship between the mind and the body, the human being has an ambiguous
subject-object character. The relationship between the self and the world
is therefore maintained by the active-passive structure, based on the two
moments of action and (bodily) intuition. In the everyday dimension, the
self is aware of its being a conscious subject. Nishida considers this mode
to be inauthentic. When the self becomes grounded in the *basho* vis-à-vis
nothing, which is hidden from the dimension of ordinary experience, the
structure of the acting intuition is authentically revealed: to act toward the
world as a "self without being a self," by receiving the (creative) intuition
activated through the *basho* vis-à-vis nothing. Nishida did not, however,
ask *how* the self can change from the ordinary to the *basho* dimension; this
was a life-and-death issue for Dōgen.

Dōgen rejected as delusion the ordinary attitude that attempts to understand the world while positing the self as a conscious subject.
Although sharing his departure point with Nishida, Dōgen thinks we
must note the mode of the body-mind so as to reject the ordinary attitude. We must adopt the attitude that the body dominates the mind, and
reject the conscious, everday belief that the mind dominates the body.
Meditation regulates and dominates the mind while complying with the
body. At this point, the dual passivity and activity structure holding the
self and the world together in ordinary experience is artificially suspended, and the self rejects on its own (via practice) its being a conscious subject at the center of such a structure. As Dōgen says, this is to "disregard
all relationships and stop the working of all things." From a theoretical
point of view, this means the practical suspension of all judgments on the
part of the conscious subject in ordinary experience.

Concealed at the base of conscious experience in the everyday
dimension, the substrate's restriction on the human subject is manifest.
In Nishida's expression, this is the entrance to the *basho* vis-à-vis nothing,
the layer of the dark consciousness or of the body qua pathos. Dōgen
demands we leave the everyday dimension of being-in-the-world dominated by the bright consciousness, and effect the molting of the body-
mind at its base. This is where we have come so far. For our next step, we
investigate Kūkai's works.

Chapter Seven

Kūkai

Kūkai,* or Kōbō Daishi, is a cultural hero in Japan, his life enshrouded by legend. He lived in the ninth century, a time when most Japanese were still at the mythic stage. Kūkai himself was an archaic man with the primitive sensitivities of an inhabitant of such an age of myth. Yet, he was also an intellectual of the highest caliber, not only in terms of his fellow Japanese but even on a worldwide scale. For example, his versatile talents amazed even the Chinese intellectuals in Chang-an, the capital of the great T'ang Empire. Kūkai's rare combination of the primitive and the intellectual succeeded in establishing Buddhism firmly in Japanese soil. The Japanese Buddhism of the earlier Asuka and Nara periods was only a cultural import limited to the capital and its vicinity. Buddhism did not become Japanese, did not take root among the populace, until Kūkai initiated his Esoteric Buddhism (*mikkyō*).

In his youth, Kūkai undertook ascetic practices in the mountains and by the sea, areas sacred in the archaic world view. Kūkai revered and respected the deities (*kami*) who dwelt there. When he opened his monastic center at Mt. Kōya and built Tōji, a temple in the Heian capital of Kyoto, he began by establishing a pantheon of deities to guard those places, and only then started construction.[1] It is no accident that the syncretism of Buddhism and Shintō later sprang from the Esoteric Buddhism that

---

*Kūkai (774–835) is probably the first great systematic philosopher in Japanese history. Some illuminating scholarly work on Kūkai has recently appeared in English. Yoshito S. HAKEDA's *Kūkai: Major Works* (N.Y.: Columbia University Press, 1972) includes a translation of most of the central writings, a biographical sketch, and an overview of Kūkai's basic doctrines, whereas Minoru KIYOTA's *Shingon Buddhism* (San Francisco: Buddhist Books International, 1978) presents a more thorough study of the conceptual intricacies of Kūkai's elaborate system.

Kūkai initiated; Shugendō, the mountain religion unifying Buddhism and Shintō, was also deeply tied to Esoteric Buddhism. These faiths constituted the ground of Japanese mass religion through to the modern period. It was Kūkai who first connected this religious ground to the heights of Buddhist philosophy. We will not here go into the problems of spiritual history, and for now, we shall simply investigate briefly Kūkai's view of personal cultivation from the standpoint of body-mind theory.

Chinese Buddhism and the Indian character of tantric Buddhism

A basic and systematic exposition of Kūkai's philosophy is found in his major work, *Jūjūshinron* [Discourse on the ten stages of mind] and its abbreviated version *Hizōhōyaku* [Jeweled key to the secret treasury]. *Jūjūshinron* organizes the process of religious consciousness or experience into ten stages, starting with delusion and culminating in *satori*. From the fourth stage on, the doctrines of the various Buddhist schools are dealt with, the final, tenth stage being reserved for Esoteric Buddhism. Although this presentation adopts its form from the "doctrinal interpretation" (*p'an-chiao*) tradition of Chinese Buddhism, the principles behind the theory, it seems, are substantially Indian.

The doctrinal interpretation tradition is a method in Buddhist dogmatics which achieved a unique development in China. It is a categorizing and arranging of teachings derived from various *sūtras* and commentaries. It developed in light of either doctrinal content or the form, method, and procedure of Buddhist preaching. In Buddhism, there is no unified, orthodox teaching such as one finds in Christianity. Moreover, since the various *sūtras* and commentaries were imported almost all at once into China, independently of their historical development in India, the need arose to classify the scriptures from some definite standpoint. Thus, making their own *sūtra* or commentary the focal point, each school of Chinese Buddhism criticized the ideas of the other *sūtras* and commentaries. From this critical attitude arose the division into the "Thirteen Schools of Sui and T'ang [China]," and there arose many dogmatics, for instance, the "Scriptural Treasuries and the Three Wheels" of the Mādhyamika (*Sanron*) school, the "Five Periods and Eight Teachings" of the Tendai school, and the "Five Teachings and Ten Schools" of the Kegon school. (The "Two Gates of Doctrine and Meditation" in Zen is also an offshoot of this tradition, although it is unique in emphasizing "no dependence on words.")

As an example of how this Chinese system works, we shall briefly examine "the Five Periods and Eight Teachings" instituted by Chih-i, the founder of the T'ien-t'ai (Tendai) school and a figure well-known in Japan as Tendai Dāishi. First, the Five Periods theory categorizes the teachings of the various *sūtras* according to when the Buddha was supposed to have preached them. The first, the Wreath Period, is the Buddha's teaching upon attaining *satori* at Buddhagaya and is represented by the *Kegon (Gaṇḍavyūha) Sūtra*. The second, the Deer Park Period, started with the Buddha's preaching at Benares, and covers the teachings of Hīnayāna *sūtras* like the *Agamas*. The third, the Development Period, includes the teachings of Māhayāna *sūtras* such as the *Vimalakīrti-nirdeśa, Śrīmālā,* and *Suvarṇaprabhāsottama*. The fourth, the Wisdom Period, covers the teachings of the *prajñā sūtras* emphasizing emptiness (*śūnyatā*). Finally, the fifth, the Lotus-Nirvana Period, represents the teachings of Shakyamuni's last years, as depicted in the *Lotus (Saddharmapuṇḍarīka)* and *Nirvāṇa (Mahāparinirvāṇa) Sūtras.*

The Eight Teachings outlined by Chih-i refer to the four methods of teaching (sudden, gradual, secret, indefinite) and to the four categories of doctrinal content aimed at different audiences (the [Hīnayāna] Tripiṭaka, the Common [Māhayāna] Teachings of the Three Vehicles, the Distinctive [Māhayāna] Teachings, and the Complete Teachings). More detailed explanations can be found in specialized works.[2]

Although the doctrinal interpretation categorizes and arranges the teachings of various Buddhist schools from a quasi-theoretical or scholastic viewpoint, it is not, of course, done with modern philological methods. In categorizing the Five Periods and Eight Teachings, for example, the *Lotus Sūtra* is considered "unexcelled." This is a value judgment arising out of the Tendai dogmatics dependent on the *Lotus Sūtra* itself. Insofar as the doctrinal interpretation is a form of dogmatics, parallel to Christian dogmatics, it is natural that a sectarian attitude is assumed.

This form of doctrinal interpretation presents a way of thinking uniquely Chinese, combining what we will call "classicism" and "sageliness." The doctrinal classification systems assume the truth to be contained in the teachings of *sūtras* recorded in words and to be attained verbally. Furthermore, the criterion for the truth of a teaching lies in the *sūtras'* having been taught by Shakyamuni, the Buddha, as a sage. For example, a main reason that the *Lotus Sūtra* is judged to be the most doctrinally excellent is that it was preached in Shakyamuni's final years from his mature, perfected perspective. (This historical claim is rejected by modern scholarship, of course.) Although every religion reveres its scriptures and founder, there is an especially strong tendency in China on the one hand to make the classics into the standard and, on the other, to seek truth using the ancient sages as a criterion, as in Confucianism. Thus, the classificatory doctrinal interpretations may be said to represent a quasi-philological method, displaying a distinctly Chinese cultural tendency.

We do not find this attitude at all in Indian Buddhism. First, in the religious traditions of India, there is no sanctification of historical figures qua historical beings. When historical persons are regarded as sacred, it is usually as *avatāra,* or embodiments of various transcendent gods. These embodiments are the gods' appearance on earth in a disguised form for redemptive purposes. Although present in Indian Buddhism, this phenomenon is most frequently observed among Vishnu cults in Hinduism, in which many historical and legendary figures, such as Krishna and Rama and even Shakyamuni, are regarded as divine embodiments. We do not find in India the Chinese version of the sage, the sacralizing of Confucius or Mencius, for example, while still recognizing them to be historical individuals. That Mahāyāna Buddhism regarded Shakyamuni to be important as a historical figure was a temporary phenomenon in its development. Emphasis on a historical figure, even Shakyamuni himself, was completely absent from the early teaching. The last preaching of the *Nirvāṇa Sūtra* is typical: "Do not rely on the man but on the Dharma." In Theravāda (Hināyāna) Buddhism, the *dharma* (teaching) was also the center of concern, but since Mahāyāna Buddhism took the form of a redemptive religion (*Heilsreligion*) born from the needs of the populace, it came to worship Shakyamuni, a historical figure, as a savior, taking him to be sacred, like Jesus in Christianity. But as Mahāyāna Buddhism developed, Amida and various other Buddhas, legendary and transcendent, appeared on the stage alongside the historical Buddha. The focus of belief gradually turned toward them and the status of the Shakyamuni as a historical figure gradually diminished; finally, he was relegated to a corner of the Mahāyāna pantheon.

Esoteric Buddhism is the last phase in the historical development of Indian Mahāyāna Buddhism. One of its prominent characteristics is that its teaching is not dependent upon Shakyamuni. Naturally, since Mahāyāna *sūtras* were created in approximately the first century A.D., long after Shakyamuni's death, they contain many points that deviate from the teaching of Shakyamuni himself. Yet Mahāyāna *sūtras* prior to Esoteric Buddhism were all believed to be, in principle, the record of Shakyamuni's teachings; for example, they all begin with the statement by some disciple of the Buddha, "Thus have I heard," and they depict a setting with Shakyamuni sitting on his throne and preaching the Dharma. On the other hand, Shakyamuni does not appear at all in the *sūtras* of Esoteric Buddhism, and Mahāvairocana, the cosmic Buddha, directly preaches the Dharma. Thus, the existence of Shakyamuni as a historical figure is completely ignored. Mahāyāna Buddhism reached this state because there was no idea of the sage in India as in China, that is, there was no tradition of historical figures, as such, being sacred.

There also was no Chinese-style reverence for classicism in India. Since Chinese words (characters) are ideographs, they frequently appeal to visual perceptions. Although China is a multiracial society with a variety of languages and dialects, the Confucian classics could be the common property of intellectuals since they were interpreted through visual, rather than auditory, perception. There naturally arose an aura of respect and sanctity around the written classics, specifically, the Confucian texts. On the other hand, the Buddha's teaching in India was received from the outset through auditory perception: It was heard, not read. Today, when we compare the Chinese classics and the Buddhist *sūtras* in their printed forms, the initial impression is that the Buddhist *sūtras* contain numerous repetitions and redundant explanations in contrast to Chinese classics like the *Analects,* in which the explanation is simple, yet full of implications. Although Mahāyāna *sūtras* endlessly cite the names of bodhisattvas lined up around the throne where Shakyamuni preaches the Dharma, this is irrelevant to understanding its content. It becomes significant only when we realize that repetitious descriptions appeal to auditory perception. Since sounds disappear quickly, unlike the words we read, repetition and redundancy are necessary to make an imprint on the memory. We might say that a characteristic of the Indian tradition is to think as if in a dream, with an emotive mood created by the rhythm of sounds.

We should also note that the Buddhist *sūtras* range from those of Early Buddhism, such as the *Vinaya* and *Agamas,* to contemporary ones, in theory. In contrast, the Chinese classics are restricted to those available up to the early Han dynasty (206 B.C.–25 A.D.). In the case of the Indian Mahāyāna *sūtras* of a later date, however, they are no less valuable as *sūtras*. In India, unlike China, there is no value in the historical age of an idea; the passage of time does not have much significance. The *Mahāvairocana* and *Vajraśekhara Sūtras* of Esoteric Buddhism were produced in India sometime in the seventh century A.D. Since they were translated into Chinese in the T'ang period (the eighth century), their appearance in China was contemporaneous with Kūkai. According to the Indian criteria, however, Buddhist teachings of a thousand years ago and contemporary *sūtras* have exactly the same value, for the Buddha existed thousands of years ago and still exists eternally now without change. The Buddha is a being who is preaching the Dharma to us right now. With such a spiritual tradition, there is no way for India to generate a set of classics like China's. If an Indian Buddhist were to encounter the doctrinal classification system of Chinese Buddhism, he would say that the Chinese people do not know what the Buddha's teaching is.

Cultivation and the ten stages of mind

Now we can return to Kūkai. Although he learned Buddhism in China, Kūkai's temper of mind, his mode of thought is more Indian. The theoretical organization of his *Jūjūshinron* is adapted from the chapter, "The Stages of Mind," in the *Mahāvairocana Sūtra.* In his Preface, Kūkai writes, "Now, by relying on this *sūtra,* I shall reveal the process through the stages of the mind for a cultivator of the Shingon approach." A "Shingon cultivator" is one who practices Esoteric Buddhism, and "the stages of mind" are the stages of religious experience. Thus, the theoretical organization of *Jūjūshinron* is based on the actual experience of enhancing and developing one's spirit and personality by means of religious cultivation. Understanding the fundamentals of Buddhism lies not in the systematized theories of written materials, but in the experiential fact of cultivation.

In the "Stages of Mind" chapter of the *Mahāvairocana Sūtra,* the process of cultivation is divided into ten stages according to a very simple explanation. It compares the initial development of mind to the growth of a plant: (1) the seed in the mind of a cultivator; (2) the sprout; (3) the bud; (4) the leaves; (5) the blossom; (6) the fruit. As a result, (7) the self-cultivator is born into a heaven transcending the human world—enjoyment of the seed; (8) there one cultivates oneself under the guidance of heavenly deities—creating an infantlike mind with no fear; (9) one seeks liberation—the unexcelled mind; and finally (10) one attains *satori*—the resolved mind.

Kūkai established his own unique system by freely interpreting this chapter. In Kūkai's version, the first stage of mind is called "the goatish mind of lowly people, filled with desire"; this is the delusory mind of the ordinary person who, in repeated transmigrations, merely follows, like a ram, his sexual desires and appetites. The second stage (the childlike, ignorant mind with a sense of morality) is the stage of moral consciousness as represented by Confucianism. The third stage of mind is the infantlike mind with no fear, the stage at which a religious consciousness is awakened. In this stage, Kūkai deals with religions other than Buddhism, the so-called "heretical paths." The fourth and fifth stages represent Hīnāyana Buddhism. From the sixth to the ninth stages, Kūkai deals with the teachings of the other schools of Mahāyāna Buddhism (Yogācāra [Hossō], Mādhyamika [Sanron], Tendai, and Kegon, respectively.) The tenth and last stage is, obviously, that of Shingon Esoteric Buddhism (the "secret, glorious mind").

After the fourth stage, the form of Kūkai's ten stages resembles the Chinese doctrinal interpretations, since the theories of the various

Buddhist schools are critiqued. Since the Chinese classifications categorize only Shakyamuni's preaching of the Dharma, however, they do not include stages prior to Buddhism, such as the awakening of moral consciousness from delusion or the entrance into the religious world view. Kūkai's structure is unique because the principle behind it is the process of enhancing one's personality and deepening religious consciousness. Consequently, even though the theories of various Buddhist schools are treated after the fourth stage, Kūkai's purpose is not to compare and determine the superiority of various teachings by means of some theoretical speculation. On the contrary, the principle in Kūkai's structure is that the meaning of those theories becomes intelligible as the religious experience of the cultivator deepens. Consequently, like Dōgen, Kūkai rejects the necessity of a prior intellectual understanding of Buddhism.

In Indian Mahāyāna Buddhism, however, there is the tendency to sort out the stages of cultivation for enhancing the personality or deepening one's religious consciousness. As two representative examples, we shall mention the theory of the bodhisattva's fifty-two ranks and the structure found in the *Daśabhumika Sutra* as absorbed into the *Gaṇḍavyūha Sūtra*.

The fifty-two ranks are the stages of cultivation for the bodhisattva up to the perfected rank of Buddha or Tathāgata. These are the ten ranks of belief, the ten ranks of the quiescent mind, the ten ranks of discipline, the ten ranks of practicing virtue, the ten grounds of benevolence, the rank equal to Buddha, and the ultimate, unexcelled rank of *satori*. The first forty stages, from the ten ranks of belief through to the ten ranks of practicing virtues, are the state of the ordinary person. The first ten stages, the ten ranks of belief refer to the "ordinary outsider," and are on the lowest plane. The next thirty stages collectively refer to the "ordinary insider" and are know as "the three sagacious stages." The promotion to the rank of sainthood, or the ten grounds of benevolence, come only after one has ascended the first forty stages. Strictly speaking, it starts with the forty-first stage of "the beginning ground." (The "ground" here refers to the state of having benevolence for all sentient beings, just as the earth itself nurtures all things.) In this way, a cultivator who has completed these ten stages attains the last, fifty-second, rank equal to that of the Buddha; but one is not a buddha (*tathāgata*) yet. The highest rank, that of the ultimate, unexcelled *satori*, extinguishes all delusions, and then possesses the most perfect wisdom. Only when the cultivator goes beyond this ultimate, unexcelled rank of *satori*, does one finally become a buddha, a *tathāgata*. (The theory of the fifty-two ranks arose from the Tendai school's addition of the ten ranks of belief to the forty-two ranks originally propounded in the *Muktāhāra Sūtra*.) This scholastic explanation indicates that the process of

cultivation is an infinite path ascending to heights beyond one's imagination. It is, for the Indian, an imaginative product to transcend the illusion
(*māyā*) in everyday life, to think of ascending gradually from the creeping
life on the earth to the zenith filled with the splendor of illumination.

The *Daśabhumika Sūtra* divides the process of personal religious
cultivation into ten stages. According to ARAMAKI Noritoshi's interpretation, the ten stages are: (1) the blissful rank; (2) the rank free from
impurity; (3) the rank of the bright splendor of illumination; (4) the rank
of the dazzling splendor of illumination; (5) the rank truly difficult to con-
quer [the stage difficult to penetrate]; (6) the rank in which the true wisdom presents itself; (7) the rank of going afar; (8) the totally immovable
rank; (9) the rank of true wisdom everywhere; (10) the rank of the endless
dharma-cloud. Aramaki calls this the "phenomenology of the Boddhi-
sattva path," using Hegel's *Phenomenology of Spirit*. It advances to "the community of the ones who have attained *satori*," while observing the mode of
"the community of deluded, ordinary people." Returning to the community of the deluded from the community of the enlightened, it
gradually ascends in a spiral, as it were, and finally reaches the ultimate
height, the highest *satori* in which the enlightened community is immediately identical with the deluded community.[3]

This, indeed, reminds us of Hegel's *Phenomenology of Spirit*, which
starts with the natural consciousness and culminates in absolute knowledge. Unlike Hegel's systematic stages for the world of ordinary consciousness, science, and history, however, the bodhisattva path is a
"phenomenology of inward practice" rising through the mind's inner
world. If we call Hegel's dialectic a *horizonal* phenomenology, reducing all
the phenomena of the external world to concepts and logic, the phenomenology of the bodhisattva path may be called a "phenomenology of illusion" (*māyā*), or a dialectic ascending the self's inner world *vertically*
from ground to zenith. But actually, it is not theoretically correct to call
this "illusion," because in Indian thought, it is the actual world that is il-
lusory (*māyā*). The profile of the world disclosed in the mind, on the other
hand, is the true reality. It is a higher reality transcending the everyday, as
in Schleiermacher's "higher realism." Behind this Indian way of thinking
is, obviously, the experience of cultivation through yogic meditation.

Kūkai articulates a thorough cultivation theory with his own unique
method. He propounds the theory of "the *dharma* body expounding the
dharma" taken from the Mahāyāna Buddhist triple-body theory of the
Buddha, which can be compared to Christology in Christianity. The
theory is that the Buddha has three bodies (*trikāya*). The first is the incarnate body (*nirmaṇa-kāya*), the Buddha as appearing in the flesh in order to
teach all sentient beings. The second is the reward body (*saṃbogha-kāya*),

the Buddha as enjoying the results (rewards) of his past cultivation. Amida Buddha, for example, is of this form. From the religious cultivator's perspective, this is the spiritual Buddha perceived in meditative cultivation. The third buddha body is the *dharma* body (*dharma-kāya*), the ultimate, absolute Buddha. It is the true body itself without matter or form; it might even be called a cosmic body. Even though Chinese Buddhism adopted this theory, it regarded the Dharmakāya as a transcendent secret, believing that "it is possible to expound the cause but impossible to expound its effect," that is, it is possible to expound the method and stages of *satori* but impossible to expound the ultimate *satori* itself. Going beyond this Chinese view, Kūkai says that Mahāvairocana, the absolute Dharmakāya Buddha, takes off the secret veil and expounds the *dharma* himself to the souls of each cultivator. TAMAKI Kōshirō says that the theory of "Dharmakāya's expounding the *dharma*" was not only a revolution in Japanese Buddhism but it "possesses an epoch-making significance in the history of all ideas developed in India, China, and Japan."[4] The theory of "Dharmakāya's expounding the *dharma*" is not found in the *Mahāvairocana* and *Vajraśekhara Sūtras,* the basic *sūtras* of Esoteric Buddhism, but was first formulated by Kūkai.[5]

How, then, does the ultimate, absolute Dharmakāya speak to a person cultivating his or her religious development? In Kūkai's poem, "Wandering in the Mountains Longing for a Mountain Sage," he writes:

A family [of boddhisattvas] are like the [Dharma] rain.
Mahāvairocana sits in the center.
Who is called Mahāvairocana?
From the start, it is the king of my mind.[6]

In the mandala map of Esoteric Buddhism, Mahāvairocana is depicted in the center, accompanied by numerous buddhas and bodhisattvas. Kūkai says that the absolute Dharmakāya (Mahāvairocana) in the center of the mandala is no other than one's mind. The term, "the king of my mind" (*citta rāja*) is often used in the *Abhidharmakośa* and the Jñanāmatiptra school, indicating the mind's essence or substance, in contrast to its various functions. Kūkai claims that if the cultivator directs oneself to the mind's interior, investigating its profound world, he or she can hear the voice of the ultimate, absolute Buddha. Cultivation aims to hear the voices from the ultimate heights.

The body and sexuality

As is apparent from what has been said so far, Kūkai's philosophy tries to systematize the cultivation experience. How then is the issue of the body handled in his system? We must discuss the problem of *eros* in Esoteric Buddhism.

In his historical novel, *Kūkai no fūkei* [Kūkai's landscape], SHIBA Ryōtarō says the following:

> Does anyone other than Kūkai raise human sexuality to such majestic magnificence in the metaphysical world? But more, he brought its edifice down to earth from an intellectual system to the formative arts, and he continues to bring a trembling intoxication to people today.[7]

Shiba notes that Kūkai regarded the *Ardhaśatika Sūtra* to be highly important. This *sūtra* begins with a famous description of sexuality: "Purified *surata* is the very locus of the bodhisattva." *Surata* means a state of sexual intercourse. As a novelist, Shiba does not go into whether Kūkai approved or disapproved of sexual desires. But it is obvious that this issue occupies an important place in Kūkai's philosophy.

The first stage in Kūkai's *Jūjūshinron* is that of the goatish mind. The goat here is actually the ram, symbolizing the mind that races around, driven by sexual desires and appetites. Although this word is taken from the *Mahāvairocana Sūtra,* it is Kūkai's creative idea to place it at the beginning of his theoretical organization. We cannot understand the essence of human life unless sexuality is investigated, since all life, nonhuman and human, issues forth from sexual intercourse.

We must turn, at this point, to the relationship between Kūkai and the *Mahāvairocana Sūtra.* There is a legend that Kūkai, in his youth, discovered a copy of this *sūtra* by the pagoda of the Kume Temple in Nara. Moreover, it is said that he resolved to go to China because there was no master in Japan who could explain this *sūtra* to him. Thus, the *Mahāvairocana Sūtra* was highly important to Kūkai's life. Although Esoteric Buddhism generally considers both the *Mahāvairocana* and *Vajraśekhara Sūtras* to be central, Kūkai thought the latter not as important. For example, in the arrangement of the buildings in the Kongōbu Temple at Mt. Koya, the main pagoda is placed in the center, symbolizing the *garbha* Matrix, or noumenal world, as described in the *Mahāvairocana* tradition. And the West pagoda symbolizing the *vajra* Diamond, or phenomenal world, is placed in a subordinate position.[8] The names and layout of the pagodas, more than anything else, indicate Kūkai's emphasis on the *Mahāvairocana* over the *Vajraśekhara*.

Furthermore, according to Esoteric Buddhism, the *garbha* and *vajra* realms indicate a relationship between the female and male principles, respectively. The former is the substance or essence and the latter is the function or phenomenon. Etymologically, "*garbha*" means the uterus, womb, or embryo. In short, the female principle occupies a more fundamental position in Kūkai's philosophy than does the male. His master, Hui-kuo and Hui-kuo's master, Pu-k'ung, handed on to him the esoteric Buddhism of the *Vajraśekhara Sūtra,* while the esoteric Buddhism belonging to the literature of the *Mahāvairocana Sūtra* was transmitted by Śubhākarasimha and I-hsing. Since Hui-kuo also studied under I-hsing, however, this latter tradition was also transmitted to Kūkai. Thus, it is Kukai's own creative contribution to regard the principle of *eros,* concealed in the *Mahāvairocana Sūtra,* as so important. (From the standpoint of Japanese spiritual history, Kūkai noted the importance of *eros* because he was still a person with an archaic, primitive mind. Among all races, primitive religion begins with glorifying the abundant *eros* of Mother Earth, as in the worship of sexual organs, for example.)

What is human sexuality? It is the source of life, the source of the body's existence in this world. By virtue of having a body through sex, the self is a being-in-the-world. This is obvious as long as one lives in the world of ordinary life. Where, then, can one seek this self's ground of being? As long as we attempt to find the answer in the everyday dimension, no solution can be found. As long as we seek the answer, to use Nishida's terms, in the *basho* vis-à-vis being, we shall only receive the tautological response that the ground of the self's living existence is sexual intercourse. What is Kūkai's view?

As noted already, Kūkai's first stage of mind in *Jūjūshinron* is "the goatish mind of ordinary people, filled with desires." Kūkai creatively joins together the "ordinary people" (*ishō*) and the "ram or mountain goat" (*teiyo*). The *Mahāvairocana Sūtra* simply states that "ignorant people are just like the ram," but Kūkai neologized the combined term (*ishō-teiyo*) because the correct interpretation of *bonpu* (the ignorant people) was explained to be *ishō* (ordinary people) in Śubhākarasimha's *Commentary on the Mahāvairocana Sūtra.*[9] The original Sanskrit word is *puthujana, puthu* meaning "many, various, or different" and *jana* meaning "person or persons." The full term means to be reborn in various forms, repeating the cycle of birth and death, that is, continual transmigration.

Kūkai seems to have had a deep concern for transmigration since his youth as a mountain ascetic. For example, in his maiden work, *Sangōshīki* [Indications of the goals of the three teachings], there is a scene where a poor self-cultivator named Kamei-kotsuji (Mr. Pseudonym Mendicant), modeled after Kūkai himself, is asked by Kyobu-inshi (Mr. Taoist Nothingness): "Who are you; where are you from?" Kamei-katsuji responds, "From no house in the triple-word. . . . I may be either your wife or your parents."[10] That, in a former life, "I was either your wife or parents," means that it is foolish to ask "who" and "where" about the "I" found in the body. In *Goshōraimokuroku* [Memorial listing newly imported *sūtras* and other items], there is the following story. On the night Hui-kuo

(Kūkai's master) died, Kūkai was praying in total concentration within the
meditation hall of Ch'ing-lung Temple in Chang-an; Hui-kuo's appari-
tion, as if alive, appeared and told Kūkai: "There is a long accord in
thought and intention between you and me, and we vow to promulgate
the secret teaching. I shall be born again in the Eastern Country [Japan]
and will surely be your disciple."[11] For Kūkai, transmigration was an un-
questionable fact.

What then is transmigration? The hymn in the beginning of
Hizōhōyaku [Jeweled key to the secret treasury] reads:

> The deranged in the triple-world do not know they are mad.
> Blind people in the four kinds of life do not recognize their blindness.
> Born time and time again, they are in the dark from the beginning of
> their lives.
> Dying time and time again, they are enveloped in the darkness at the
> end of their deaths.

One who believes only in tangible realities is like a mad person who does
not know that he or she is mad. Where does the life of a self come from
and where does it go? Without understanding the beginning and the end
of life, one fully believes the true self to be the self that exists merely in the
body and is bound to die. This is the life of a ram or mountain goat. The
life of the ram is the bodily self of sexual intercourse. In other words, it is
the everday self as a being-in-the-world. The theory of transmigration
demonstrates in concrete terms that such a self cannot be the true self.

Kūkai's inquiry resembles Socrates' discussion of transmigration in
Plato's *Republic*. When people are born on this earth, they leave the former
life in "the place of oblivion" (Lethe). For this reason, the self in its new
body cannot see the world of truth (*alētheia*). In this sense, life on earth is
like life in Plato's cave, where Truth (*alētheia*) is forgotten (in Lethe.)[12]

In order to know the true self, one has to search the invisible darkness at the base of the body born through sexual intercourse. Whence
does my life come and whither does it go? Cultivation's departure point is
to question the meaning of one's own living existence in the direction of
the darkness at the mind's core, to search for the secret illumination.

Sublimation of eros in the mandala

I have said that Kūkai's intellectual temperament is basically Indian. This
is especially true with regard to *eros*. We are amazed by the opulent, sen-
sual beauty of Indian art. Indian religions grew in the garden of *eros*. In

contrast, Chinese philosophy never talks about sex, as if sex did not exist for Chinese intellectuals. The Chinese people are, from the outset, ethical, not religious. It is really surprising that in China Kūkai could grasp the essence of Indian religion. This is probably because the primitive mind still alive in Kūkai corresponded to the vital, primitive base of Indian religion, coming together in the internationalism of Chang-an, the Chinese capital.

Esoteric Buddhism is often called tantric Buddhism. *Tantra, giki* in Japanese, refers to the rules of iconography or to the methods of ritual offerings and incantations. *Sūtras* valuing the intellectual significance of the *tantra* were also called tantric. This is a common phenomenon in later Indian Esoteric Buddhism and Hindu Tantrism. To modern rationality, tantrism may seem a strange and obscure magic garden, but the secret behind sexuality cannot be cut through with the sword of intellectual logic. In Kūkai's writings, there is no theoretical analysis of sexuality. From the fundamnetal standpoint of Buddhism, a theoretical analysis or resolution would be irrelevant anyway. What is needed is a practical approach. Therefore, we must deal with the tantras as a systematic, pragmatic approach. Since the tantras are not like a doctrine that has been fixed in written words, it is inevitable that our investigation will be somewhat hypothetical. At any rate, we must note that we have already set foot in the Freudian realm, the world of depth psychology.

A Buddha image unique to Esoteric Buddhism is the so-called "*vidyā-rāja*." Acala-nātha (Fudōmyo-o) is especially popular in Japan. Whether depicted in sculpture or picture form, Acala-nātha has an angry expression, carries a sword, and is backed by a burning fire. All the *vidyā-rāja* images have such features, and present a marked contrast to the quiet and peaceful bodhisattva or *tathāgata* [buddha] images. The fierce mien is to subjugate the heavenly beings threatening the Buddha Dharma. Seen from the standpoint of psychology, though, it expresses the struggle with the dark passions at the base of the human mind. According to SAWA Ryūken, the term, "*vidyā-rāja*" (literally, "bright king"), means the brightness of intuitive wisdom (*prajñā*) accompanying the king who uses the Shingon incantations to break through the darkness of carnal desires (*kleśa*) and karmic hindrances.[13] *Kleśa* means delusions, that is, it is a general name for the spiritual functions assaulting and torturing the body-mind. Usually, the three poisons—desire (*kāma-rāga*), hatred (*dveṣa*), and ignorance (*moha*)—are regarded as its representatives. (There are other categorizations, but they will be omitted here.) In contemporary terms, they roughly correspond to passion, impulse, and desire. The *vidyā-rāja's* anger and fiery intensity parallel the intensity of deep psychological passion.

The image of the *vidyā-rāja* was originally constituted as part of self-cultivation practice. One meditation method in Indian Esoteric Buddhism cited by Sawa is the *sādhanamala,* a meditation employing active imagination:

> Cultivator, imagine in your meditation that you are Śrī Candamahārosaṇam. His color is like that of the *atasī* flower. His posture is in the immovable (*acala*) form. He has a face, two arms, and squinting eyes. His facial expression is fearsome with his fangs exposed. His head ornaments are jewels and his teeth are biting his [lower] lip. Several garlands decorate his neck. His eyes are reddish and he carries a sword in his right hand. A rope is entwined on his pointing finger that is extended to his chest, the sacred rope being a white snake. His is garbed in a tiger hide and decorated with several kinds of jades. His left foot touches the ground while his right leg is slightly raised. His body radiates like the sun and the top of his head is always crowned with an imperturbable *tathāgata*. Thus contemplate to the end![14]

This Śrī Candamahārosaṇam image is another name for "Acala (-nātha)." Thinking to oneself that one is Acala-nātha, the cultivator imagines in meditation the concrete details as to face, ornaments, the sword, and the snake. Psychologically, this kind of meditation has some resemblance to the method of "active imagination" used in Jungian therapy. Although this meditation method is not limited to Esoteric Buddhism as such, Esoteric Buddhism placed a unique emphasis on such grotesque figures, symbolizing anger, fear, and vehement passion. (Incidentally, the cultic aspects of Acala-nātha hardly developed in India or China, but enjoyed a considerable development in Japan.[15])

Obviously, among the various *kleśas,* the enemies of the *vidyā-rajā, eros* is the most important. In this respect, the organization of the mandala, something unique to Esoteric Buddhism, is significant. A mandala is an iconographic form utilized in personal religious cultivation. C. G. Jung was especially interested in its psychological meaning.[16] He heard an explanation of the mandala (*khilkor* in Tibetan) from the head monk at a lamasery near Darjeeling in 1938. According to the head monk, a mandala is *dmigs-pa,* an image produced by the spirit, and only an advanced lama can form it via the imagination. No two mandalas are identical, and the mandalas hung in temples do not have a great significance, since they are simply the outward expression of an inner image. A true mandala is gradually formed in the mind when the cultivator works through his or her own thoughts. In short, the mandala is a sketch of the inner world through which the cultivator makes his or her way in meditation.

The *garbha*-realm mandala and the *vajra*-realm mandala are the best known in Esoteric Buddhism. The *garbha* realm is divided into the thirteen Halls shown in Figure 2. Following the explanations by MIYASAKA

Fig. 2: The Garba Mandala

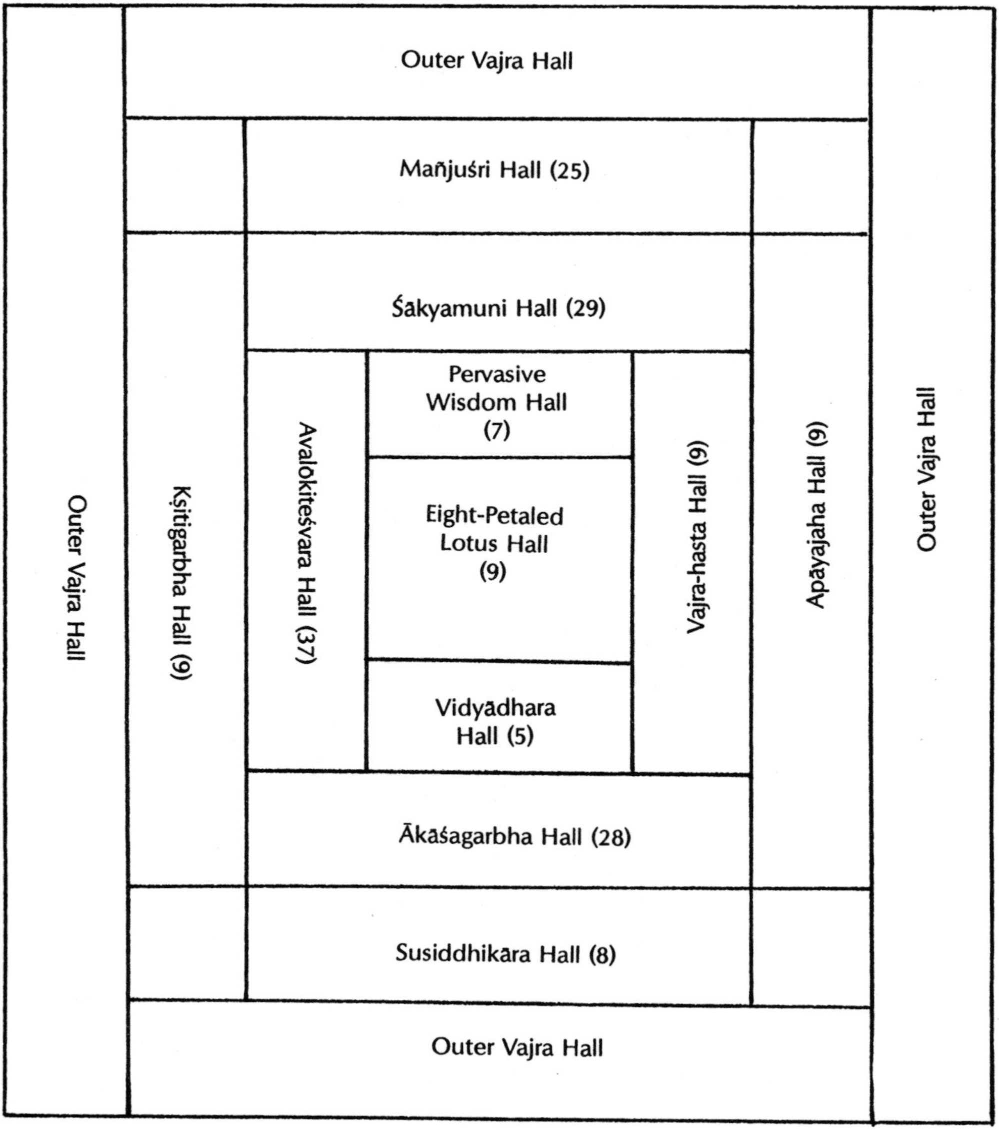

Note: (n) = Number of Buddhas or Bodhisattvas located in the Halls.

Yūshō and by KANAOKA Shūyū, the central eight-petaled lotus and the image of Mahāvairocana seated on it express the principle of "becoming a buddha in this very body" (*sokushinjōbutsu*) such that the person's body is essentially the same as the Buddha's body.[17] The eight lotus petals, which form the Buddha's throne, are an Indian symbol for the heart, and so they express the carnal body. This eight-petaled lotus flower is given only potentiality, however.

We must note here the relationship between the Pervasive Wisdom Hall and the Vidyadhara (Bright) Halls located just above and below the Central Eight-Petaled Lotus Hall. The Pervasive Wisdom Hall has other names as well: The Mother Buddha Hall and Mother-Buddha-with-Buddha's-Eyes Hall. In the center of this Hall are depicted a female Buddha, "Mother Buddha-Tathāgata with the Buddha's eyes," and a triangle, pointing upwards, that is enclosed, as in Figure 3, by flames. The Mother Buddha-Tathāgata with the Buddha's eyes is the mother giving birth to all buddhas, and is, in Jung's terminology, "the Great Mother." Also, according to the rules of Indian iconography, a triangle pointing upwards symbolizes the male principle. Thus, in the configuration of the Pervasive Wisdom Hall, the male principle is enclosed by a female principle.[18]

In contrast, the Vidyādhara Hall, below the central Lotus Hall, is surrounded by Acala-nātha and three other male *vidyā-rājas* with the female *prajñā*-bodhisattva as their center. The female *prajñā*-bodhisattva sym-

Fig. 3: Pervasive Wisdom Hall

bolizes the religious self-cultivator who seeks the *prajñā* wisdom. The male *vidyā-rājas* surrounding this bodhisattva symbolize the power of wisdom to destroy the darkness of ignorance (*avidyā*), that is, the various *kleśas,* or in contemporary terms, the instinctive impulses and dark passions lurking beneath consciousness. A meditator endeavors to overcome the *kleśas* by imaginatively forming the flames behind the *vidyā-rājas'* backs and the fierce anger subjugating the *devas* or gods. Here again, the *vidyā-rāja* image, which exhibits a masculine power, is surrounded by the *prajñā*-bodhisattva, the female principle. Various images in the fringe of this *garbha*-realm mandala indicate the depth-psychological conditions of ordinary people. A cultivator gradually enters the region of the deep psyche through meditation, reaching Mahāvairocana at the center. The greatest barrier to enlightenment is the struggle with *eros,* as represented in this mandalic structure.

It is said that the *garbha*-realm mandala with its female principle indicates the source of all beings. In contrast, the *vajra*-realm mandala is based on the male principle, with the life-functions emerging from this source. The *vajra*-realm mandala, in Figure 4, is divided into nine sections. If we take the state of the ordinary person as our initial point, we start with the Trailokyavijaya-samaya Assembly (1) in the lower right and go through the remaining assemblies in sequence, (2, 3, 4, and so on), in a counterclockwise spiral (the ascending process) until we reach the five buddhas in the center of the 9th frame, named the Karma Assembly or the Attaining–Buddha-Body Assembly.

What interests us here, from a depth-psychology standpoint, is that the image of the counterclockwise movement indicates the mind's turning to the unconscious.[19] A figure with a counterclockwise design is regarded as having religious significance, both in the East and West (ancient examples in the West are found at the downstream region of the Danube). For example, the Buddhist swastika (卍) has a counterclockwise design and is the symbol of Truth (Dharma). The reverse clockwise swastika (the Nazi symbol) stands for black magic.[20] This is probably because the clockwise movement is associated with demonic images, arising from the mind's dark region. The cultivator must step into this dark passage, starting with the Trailokyaviyaya-samaya Assembly of the *garbha*-realm mandala. For this, one must soulfully pray to receive benevolent guidance from the Buddha. Consequently, we must note the clockwise descending process starting from the Karma Assembly at the middle around through (8) to (1).

The Esoteric Buddhist experience of meditation is expressed as "the self's entering the Buddha and the Buddha's entering the self." Egotistical prayer and meditation takes one to magic haunted by demons. The as-

Figure 4: Vajra Mandala

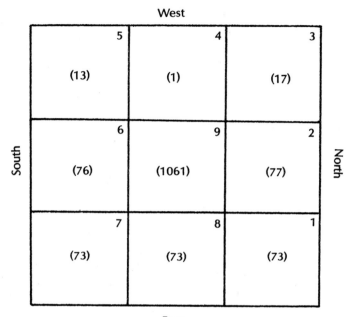

West

5 (13)	4 (1)	3 (17)
6 (76)	9 (1061)	2 (77)
7 (73)	8 (73)	1 (73)

South — North

East

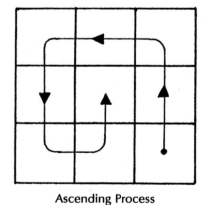

Ascending Process   Descending Process

(n) number of Buddhas or Bodhisattvas

1. Trailokya-vijaya Samaya Assembly
2. Trailokya-vijiya Karma Assembly
3. Nayaḥ Assembly
4. Ekamudra Assembly
5. Caturmudra Assembly

6. Pūja Assembly
7. Sūkṣma Assembly
8. Samaya Assembly
9. Karma Assembly

cending path to the Buddha, which takes one up to true *satori,* must depend on the descending path through which the Buddha guides the person. So, first comes the Trailokya-vijaya Samaya Assembly (1): the prayer of the cultivator entrusts the mind to the *vajra-hūṁkara vidyā rāja's* compassion, which saves all sentient beings. When the cultivator reaches Trailokya-vijaya Karma Assembly (2), one fights in one's mind with the devil, imagining oneself to be a fearful *vidyā-rāja.* The next stage (3) is the famous Nayaḥ Assembly: In its center is Vajrasattva, at once an embodiment of Mahāvairocana and the self-cultivator as well. Surrounding him are young and beautiful female bodhisattvas: desire, touch, love, and pride. Desire (*iṣṭa*) is the erotic craving for the opposite sex. Touch (*kelikila*) refers to the touching of one another's bodies. Love (*raga*) indicates an ever increasing sexual love resulting from touch. Pride (*māna*) symbolizes the state of sexual ecstasy. Vajrasattva, at the center of this panoramic *eros,* indicates a cultivator's outlook which, in spite of this panoramic *eros,* is not defiled by desire (*kleśa*). This idea of the Nayaḥ Assembly is taken from the *Aradhaśatika Sūtra* mentioned above. It is interesting from depth-psychology's standpoint that *eros* is placed next to the angry mind of *vidyā-rāja.* As long as the self-cultivator does not pass through the stage of this burning fire and the struggle with *kleśa,* one cannot see nor hear the transcendent Buddha, that is, the sacred numinous dimension, beyond this earthly world.

Comparison with meditation in Kuṇḍalinī Yoga

What did Kūkai think about sexuality? Among his writings, there is a book entitled *Gobu darani mondō gesan shūhiron* [The secret poems of the dialogue on the Five Dhāraṇīs]. This book deals with an explanation of virtue and the meaning of *dhāraṇī*. It follows a poetic (*gāthā*) form in a dialogue between a lay self-cultivator, Shushin-koji (Mr. Truthseeker) and a monk named Himitsu-shōnin (Saint Secret). In it, there is the following conversation.

> SECRET: That there are five princesses (*vidyā-rājñī*) in the palace means that a king is most noble. They please the king's mind with the five [sensuous] desires and living long, they inherit the throne.
>
> TRUTHSEEKER: Shingon also preaches on these princesses, but I do not understand it fully. What does it mean?
>
> SECRET: When I preach on the princesses of Shingon, they do not have the significance of long life. I am just comparing the truth to secular talk; expressing the Dharma is like this. Sthamaprapta puts to rest the five psychophysical constituents, dispersing far and wide everyone's reflective minds. Moreover, in the mud of the five desires, all sentient

beings [attempt to] protect their bodies so as not to destroy them.
The princesses match the seeds and bear the principle of virtue.
Firmly keeping the *bodhi*-mind, they lead [sentient beings] to the
Buddha Land.[21]

Since this book has not been well studied and lacks any commentary,
we shall give a tentative interpretation. The king is the bearer of secular
power, who occupies the most noble position. He is in a position to satisfy
all secular desires, the greatest of which is sexual satisfaction. Consequently, the five princesses (*vidyā-rājñī*) surround him in the palace. The phrase
in the second line, "living long, they inherit the throne," can be interpreted as meaning the king is captivated by the erotic, beautiful princesses, but this does not simply refer to a king in the actual world, but also
expresses symbolically the everyday mode of being-in-the-world.

By this interpretation, the first two lines of Secret's response to
Truthseeker's question mean the following. The Shingon cultivator is of a
nobility comparable to the secular rank of a king. But in expounding on
the princesses, Shingon does not intend such a secular perspective: it uses
the secular to express the transcendent truth metaphorically. The next
two lines also go together. Sthamaprapta, who "puts to rest the five psychological constituents," is a bodhisattva occupying a position in Avalo-
kiteśvara's quarter of the womb-realm mandala. As a benevolent guide,
he evokes the self-cultivator's mind to seek the truth (*bodhi*). The five psychophysical constituents (*skandhas*) are: matter, form, sensation, cognition, volition, and consciousness. Although the cultivator seeks the Way
of the Buddhas, entrusting himself to the compassions of bodhisattvas
like Sthamaprapta, he still inclines to protect his body derived from the
mud of the five desires. He does not want the self to be extinguished. It is
the princesses of the last two lines who guide the cultivator to overcome
this difficulty.

More problematic is the interpretation of the final two lines, "The
princesses match the seeds and bear the principle of virtue. Firmly keeping the *bodhi*-mind, they lead [sentient beings] to the Buddha Land."
Although "seed" has various meanings, in reference to cultivation it often
means the potential to reach *satori*. In addition, though, it seems to suggest in this case a sexual meaning. If so, "the princesses match the seeds"
probably means the princesses respond to the wish or desire of the
cultivator. When the mind, seeking the Way, struggles with the *kleśa*, the
eros responds to the individual's wish. Yet the beautiful princesses, who
symbolize *eros,* also guide the cultivator to the Buddha world. Here we
find a paradox.

There seems to be no further clue in Kūkai's writings. In examining the relationship between Esoteric Buddhism and the tantric Yoga of Hinduism, however, some suggestions for a resolution present themselves.

One of the five great *vidyā-rājas* in Esoteric Buddhism is called Kuṇḍalī. In the main hall of Tō-ji, a famous Shiṅgon temple in Kyoto, this image is placed to the left front of Acala-nātha. The *tantra* for this *vidyā-rāja* was apparently brought back from China by Kūkai, and in his *Goshōrai mokuroku,* he lists two specifically related books: *Yogic Meditation Method for Sweet Kuṇḍalī [Kanro Gundari yuge nenju hō]* and *Sanskrit Mantras for Thousand-Armed Sweet Kuṇḍalī [Bonji senpi kanro Gundari shingon].* This name, Kuṇḍalī, is often found in tantric Yoga. There is a book entitled *Ṣaṭ-Chakra-Nirūpaṇa* [The investigation of the six cakras (wheels)], which was translated by a British Indologist, Sir John Woodroff (under a pseudonym, Arthur Avalon). This *sūtra* belongs to the Śakti Sect of the Shiva cult, and there is an original copy dated from the sixteenth century.[22] It is relatively well known among Yoga scholars. I first read this book almost twenty years ago, when I first took an interest in Eastern religions, and found it totally perplexing. It is a handbook for yoga meditation, and its method is known as "*kuṇḍalī yoga.*" The fundamental idea is that one can reach enlightenment through the transference and sublimation of sexual energy. Since it seems relevant to the paradoxical expressions concerning the *vidyā-rāja* and the princesses of Kūkai's *Shūhiron,* I discuss it briefly.

Kuṇḍalī means "that which is coiled," and in the text mentioned above, its image is a snake coiling around a penis. Kuṇḍalī expresses the power of a sleeping female deity, the Kuṇḍalī Śakti. *Śakti* is usually translated into Japanese as "sexual power" (*seiryoku*), but Avalon (Woodruff) explains it as "the divine cosmic energy in the body," translating it symbolically as "serpent power." In depth-psychology, the snake symbolizes the unconscious.

Yogic meditation is the means of awakening the power of this sleeping, coiled snake. The six *cakras* mentioned in the text's title are invisible "hubs" or "wheels" in the body, the places upon which one concentrates in meditation. It is said that a well-trained cultivator can see the light of the six *cakras.* In this respect, the *cakras* have the same significance as the mandala already noted. They exist in the six places in the *nadis* (routes) that run from the coccyx to the top of the skull. When the power of *kuṇḍalī* is awakened through meditation, it is said that the snake gradually ascends through the *nadis* and when it has passed through the six *cakras,* reaching "the gate of Brahman" at the top of the skull, one reaches complete liberation.

These six *cakras* coincide, to a considerable extent, with the concentration points in Buddhist and Taoist meditation. For example, the position between the eyebrows is called, in Buddhist iconography, "*byakugō*" (a thin white hair). We see in Genshin's* *Ojōyōshū* [Essentials of salvation], for example, a description of *byakugō* meditation. In the Yogic text already mentioned, the *cakra* between the eyebrows is also mentioned as the *ājñā-cakra*. Moreover, in Taoist meditation, the three *tanden* are considered important: the space between the eyebrows, the chest, and the lower abdomen. These also correspond to the *cakras* and are respectively called *ājñā-cakra, anahāta,* and *svādhiṣṭhāna.*

The *cakras* closely associated with sexuality are the *svādhiṣṭhāna* and *manipūra* wheels. The six *cakras* are depicted with lotus flowers, inside of which are the *vidyā-rāja,* princesses, an animal, or a Sanskrit syllable.

Svādhiṣṭhāna is depicted as a white lotus flower within a red lotus flower where *vidyā-rāja* Hali and *vidyā-rājini* Lakini dwell along with monstrous fish, *makuala,* in a half-moon shape, symbolizing the region of water. According to the explanation in the text, by meditating upon this region, a self-cultivator detaches from the ego, is freed of hate, and becomes like the sun illuminating the darkness of ignorance.

Above this *cakra* the next one, near the navel, is called "*manipūra*" and is the region of fire. Within a ten-petaled lotus flower colored like a rain cloud and cloaked in gloom shines an upside-down triangle, colored the red of the rising sun. Within the fire is a ram. The *vidyā-rāja* is the storm god king Rudhola and the princess is Lakhini. The cultivator drinks the nectar of the divine world and gains the power of creation and destruction through meditation on this *cakra* (see Figure 5).

This sort of description goes on and on, so that the reader unfamiliar with tantric symbolism cannot make heads or tails of it. Overall, though, the principle of *kuṇḍalini yoga* is to transform the lower sexual energy, *ojas,* into the cosmic creative power, *śakti.* This is accomplished by meditation on the *cakra's* creative power. In a physiological context, *ojas* means "sperm," but the modern split between the psychological and the physiological is not appropriate in interpreting this kind of symbolism. The *manipūra cakra,* the region of fire, destroys the *kleśa* and produces a new creative power. This *cakra* is symbolized by the radiantly red triangle, the ram, the storm god Rudola, and the princess Lakhini. These symbols, it would seem, are analogous to those of Esoteric Buddhism, such as the fiery triangle (Figure 3), the ram, and the angry *vidyā-rāja.*

When seen from the viewpoint of depth psychology, this tantric Yogic and Esoteric Buddhist way of thinking has special significance. Robert Assagioli, an Italian clinical psychologist influenced by Freud and

---

*Genshin (942–1017) was a Tendai monk from Mt. Hiei near Kyoto in the later Heian period. His *Ojōyōshū* was a highly influential work, setting the foundation for the development of the major Pure Land Buddhist schools in the Kamakura period.—Ed.

Fig. 5: The Maṇipūra Cakra

Jung, advocates "psychosynthesis" in opposition to Freud's psychoanalysis. He has devised practical methods for initiating creative activity by tapping the possibilities of the deep psyche. In discussing the relationship between sexuality and culture, he touches on the ideas of Freud, Jung, and Evelin Underhill, the investigator of mysticism. He claims that superior cultural activities are often generated by the transmutation and sublimation of sexual desire. Wagner, for example, composed *Tristan und Isolde* out of his passionate love for Mathiede Wesendonck. Upon completing this piece, his love disappeared.

Schopenhauer, too, recognizes this phenomenon:

> In the days and in the hours in which the tendency to voluptuousness is stronger . . . just then also the higher spiritual energies . . . are apt to be aroused more strongly. They are inactive when man's consciousness has yielded to lust, but through effective effort their direction can be changed and then man's consciousness is occupied, not by those lower and tormenting desires, but by the highest activities of the mind.[23]

Assagioli argues from such examples that sublimated sexual energy is utilized in creative activities and can be directed towards the enhancement of the spirit and personality. Psychosynthesis is a theory that develops a technical method for achieving this sublimation. The notion of sublimation is not new to Freudians, of course, but psychotherapy generally aims only to bring the patient back to normality. Going beyond that goal, Assagioli attempts to exalt sublimation in order to develop creative activities beyond those of the average person. In this respect, his thought parallels the Eastern notion of cultivation, which aims at a better life than the ordinary (*Leben mehr als*).

In short, Kūkai's view of sexuality gives every appearance of being consonant with both tantric Yoga and the post-Freudian theories of sublimation. In the Christian moral tradition of the West, on the other hand, *eros* was supposed to have been suppressed ever since Adam and Eve were expelled from Paradise. Since the Renaissance, though, the Western tradition has moved towards the liberation of sexuality. In the West there is an ambivalence between affirmation and negation, but the Eastern world has discovered the wisdom to utilize *eros* for the creation of a spiritual culture.

The body-mind relation as sokushinjōbutsu

The central idea in Kūkai's philosophy is "becoming a buddha in this very body" (*sokushinjōbutsu*). This phrase is derived from Pu-k'ung and Hui-kuo, and was originally used to emphasize the quickness of becoming a buddha through Esoteric Buddhism. Apparently, Pu-k'ung preached "becoming a buddha at this very time," and Hui-kuo changed it to "becoming a buddha in this very body."[24] Inheriting their theories, upon returning from China Kūkai wrote:

> If you direct your *mind* to the Exoteric teaching, it will take three *kalpas* [eons], [but] if you keep your *body* in the Esoteric treasury [of teachings], the lives of the sixteen is [attainable] instantaneous[ly].[25]

"The lives of the sixteen" refers to the sixteen boddhisattvas in the mandala, who surround the Buddha in the center; they signify the cultivators who have attained enlightenment.

The "three *kalpas*" signify an immeasurable span of time. This term is derived from the *Jataka* stories of the Buddha's prior lives. The term originated in the belief that Shakyamuni accumulated merit and cultivated himself from rebirth to rebirth for three *kalpas* until attaining *satori* as a buddha. This exaggeration of time emphasizes the greatness of Shakyamuni and the difficulty of cultivation. But Mahāyāna Buddhism, in turn, started boasting of the quickness of becoming a buddha so as to show the superiority of its teaching to that of Hīnayāna Buddhism. Esoteric Buddhism went so far as to claim one could become a buddha immediately in this body.

Kūkai, however, not only maintained the quickness of becoming a buddha; he also added a new significance to the phrase, "in this very body." In the preceding quote, the *mind* of the exoteric teaching is juxtaposed to the *body* of the esoteric treasury. We are, therefore, given a glimpse of Kūkai's emphasis on the body. In A.D. 815, he wrote:

> If you cultivate yourself according to the preaching [of the Dharmakāya] and the [right] principles, without passing through the three *kalpas,* you will immediately enter the Buddha-mind. In the body your parents gave you, you will transcend the ten grounds of benevolence.[26]

The term, "the body your parents gave you" is taken from the *Bodhicitta Śastra*. In *Sokushinjōbutsugi* [The significance of becoming a Buddha in this very body] Kūkai quotes from the *Vajraśekhara,* and *Mahāvairocana Sūtras* and the *Bodhicitta Śastra* such statements as: "authentically attaining bliss in this life," "achieving the unexcelled awakening in this life," and "immediately authenticating the great awakening in the body your parents gave you." So we may say that Kūkai's phrase "in this very body" emphasizes the meaning of "in the flesh," and "in this world" more than just "quickness." We see here that the issue of the body is very important to Kūkai's philosophy.

Kūkai's treatise, *Sokushinjōbutsugi,* is the theoretical systematization of this idea. Its summary is expressed in the following well-known verse:

> The six great elements do not obstruct each other and are forever joined. (essence)
> The four kinds of mandala are inseparable. (aspect)
> When there is the grace of the three mysteries [of Mahāvairocana], [enlightenment] immediately appears. (function)
> "This very body" is the manifold of [Indra's] net. (nonobstruction)[27]

The first line of the verse (the essence) discusses the nature of the universe as constituted by the six great elements: earth, water, fire, wind, sky, and consciousness. Among these, the first five were found in the ancient Buddhist *sūtras,* going back to the Indian mythological view of the universe. Kūkai added a new element: consciousness. Kūkai says that "in exoteric Buddhism, some consider the four elements to be nonsentient, but when Esoteric Buddhist expounds on them, they are the *samaya* body of the Tathāgata." In the earlier interpretation, earth, water, fire, and wind are simply the material forces constituting the universe. According to his interpretation, however, they express the body of Mahāvairocana as the

Buddha-body, that is, as the essence of the universe. Conesquently, Mahāvairocana is the *essentia* of the universe itself, not in the material sense, but in a metaphysical dimension. This is why Kūkai added consciousness, an immaterial principle. Although the six elements are said to indicate the *samaya* body of the Tathāgata, the term "*samaya*" indicates a state in which metaphysical, true being has appeared in the phenomenal regions. In short, seen from the domain of a truly lived religious experience, the universe is the phenomenal form of the metaphysical Buddha-body. The first line says that the six great elements are inseparable and always in the state of being fused or joined (*yoga*). *Yoga* here refers to yogic meditation, a state in which all discriminations disappear, as in the *samādhi* state.

The second line says that the aspects expressing the essence of the universe are the four kinds of mandala: the Mahā Mandala, in which the Buddhas and boddhisattvas are depicted; the Dharma Mandala, in which the Sanskrit letters, that is, the teaching of the Buddha, are inscribed; the Samaya Mandala, in which the tools for meditation, that is, the activities of the Buddhas are depicted; and the Karma Mandala which is not iconographic, but is a set of activities. According to Kūkai, the Mahā Mandala expresses all sentient beings whether of this deluded world or another; the Dharma Mandala, all the teachings either of this deluded world or any other; the Samaya Mandala, all of the world of conditions; and the Karma Mandala, all karmic events, that is, all activities.[28] In short, all living beings, all language, all conditions, and all activities of the world, when seen from the standpoint of religious experience, are expressive forms of the metaphysical Buddha body. Since these are essentially one, they are said to be "inseparable."

In considering the relationship between the body and cultivation, the phrase in the third line, "the grace of the three mysteries," is crucial. The three mysteries are the functions of the body, mouth, and intention, that is, body, language, and mind. In Buddhism up to Kūkai's time, the phrase, "body, mouth, and intention," traditionally designated the "three *karmas*," and meant the good and evil deeds performed by a sentient being in its life. That is, the mode of human action in ordinary experience is indicated by the three *karmas* or by the functions of body, language, and mind. In esoteric Buddhism, these are called the "three mysteries," mysteries in the sense that they cannot be understood in ordinary experience. The actions in the everyday dimension are truly, essentially, these three mysteries, but this cannot be understood as long as one remains within the everyday dimension. Cultivation presents a possible vehicle to understanding what transcends ordinary experience.

"Grace" (*kaji: adhiṣṭhāna*), as in "When there is the grace of the three mysteries," originally meant a controlling or mysterious power. It expresses the Buddha's protection of all living beings through that power. In order to receive the Buddha's grace, one must reach by cultivation the state through which one can realize the Buddha's power. So the term "grace" (*kaji*) came to possess the sense of cultivation. Kūkai says:

> If a Shingon cultivator observes this principle—forming *mudras* with the hands, reciting *mantras* with his mouth, and letting the mind dwell in the state of *samādhi*, one will quickly attain the great ground [the perfection of *satori*]; because the three mysteries respond to one another in grace.[29]

If a cultivator realizes that the three everyday karmic actions are, in their origin, the three mysteries, that is, if one forms the *mudras* with the hands, recites *mantras* with the mouth, and places the mind into a *samādhi* state, the three functions of body, mouth and intention reach a state commensurate with the Buddha's. To form a *mudra* is a corporeal function; to recite a *mantra* is a verbal function; meditation is a mental function. These three mysteries are synthesized in cultivation. That is, the grace of the three mysteries indicates cultivation's disclosure of the place hidden beneath the everyday world: It is the everyday function of the three karmic acts transformed into the three mysteries having the Buddha power and originating in the metaphysical dimension. The true aspect of the metaphysical universe, as exhibited in the six great elements and the four mandalas, is clarified through this experience.

For Kūkai, cultivation is an inwardly oriented practice probing the deep psyche inside the soul, breaking through the darkness of *kleśa* symbolized by *eros*. At the same time, however, it is a process in which a light radiates from beyond this darkness, and the cosmic energy issuing from the metaphysical dimension flows into the self and fills it. To use the expression of later Buddhism, we might say that cultivation by means of self-power (*jiriki*) and salvation by means of other-power (*tariki*) stand in an inseparable relationship. Dividing the term *kaji* (grace) into *ka* (adding) and *ji* (holding), Kūkai offers the following explanation:

> *Kaji* [grace] means the great compassion of the Tathāgata and also the faith of all living beings. *Ka* is the image of the Buddha sun that appears in the reflecting minds of all living beings; *ji* indicates that the cultivator's all-reflecting mind mirrors the Buddha sun.[30]

We find a similar explanation in Kūkai's *Dainichikyō kaidai* [Commentary on the *Mahāvairocana Sūtra*]:

Kaji used to mean that which the buddhas protect and preserve, and was also called *kahi* [receiving a divine power], but these interpretations do not yet get at its full implications. *Ka* receives its name because [the Buddha's three secret functions] are added from upward to downward to that of man. *Ji* has its significance by virtue of man's holding on to the Buddha's downward guiding [of sentient beings] without separation. That is, [*kaji*] means "I enter into [the Buddha] and [the Buddha] enters into me."[31]

In other words, if one interprets "*kaji*" simply as the incorporation of Buddha's protective power, its significance is not sufficiently clear. "*Ka*" means that the Buddha's power, radiating like the sun, flows into (interpenetrates) the cultivator's mind. "*Ji*" means that the cultivator realizes the Buddha's sunlike power and embodies it within the self, becoming one with it. Thus, the person's cultivation ascends to the metaphysical dimension "from the bottom to the top," as it were, and this ascent intersects with the top-to-bottom direction of the Buddha's power springing forth from the metaphysical dimension. The phrase, "I enter [the Buddha] and [the Buddha] enters me" indicates the activity of the Buddha's three mysteries entering into the self and the activity of the self's three karmic actions entering into the Buddha. Since the self and the Buddha became one, the activities of the three karmic actions are transformed into the activities of the three mysteries.

Kūkai's explanation obviously presupposes the religious experience of cultivation. Cultivation is a practical means for breaking through the invisible place hidden at the ground of ordinary experience, and for overcoming and transforming the manner of understanding the self in an everyday manner. Characteristic of Kūkai's thought is his emphasis on the Buddha's power *disclosed from above.* As already noted, the systematic organization of his *Jūjūshinron* was based on an ascent from delusion to *satori.* The forerunner of this idea can be found in Indian Mahāyāna Buddhism, such as in the "stages of mind" in the *Mahāvairocana Sūtra, Daśabhumika Sūtra,* and others. What is distinctive to Kūkai's view, however, is that the ascending process in cultivation is simultaneously taken to be the descending process of the Buddha's compassion and salvation. In *Hizōhōyaku* [Jeweled key to the secret treasury], for example, Kūkai explicitly takes the advance to a higher religious experience as being the Buddha's power disclosed to the cultivator, and guiding him or her to that state. For instance, Kūkai says, "If you happen to encounter the Tathāgata's wonderment, your mind turns to the generosity of the bodhisattva [that is, from the fourth to the fifth stage]," and "your mind, being endowed with wonderment, turns to the palace of nondiscrimination [the Mahāyāna standpoint, that is, the sixth stage]," or "[since] the

Dharma realm is not the ultimate, [you] advance immediately [from the ninth to the tenth stage] in being endowed with wonderment,"[32] and so on. This is sometimes referred to as "disclosure fo realization in wonderment," and it probably corresponds, in the terminology of the study of religion, to "revelation" (*Offenbarung*) or Eliade's "hierophany." Thus, according to Kūkai, the Buddha is not only the being who transcends ordinary sense experience, but who is also grasped in its overbrimming function, its descent from the metaphysical to the physical. Returning to Tamaki's interpretation noted earlier, Kūkai's theory of "the Dharma body's expounding the Dharma" represents a revolution in the development of Buddhist intellectual history in India, China, and Japan. The descent of absolute, transcendent being to the physical dimension, the absolute's speaking to the soul—these probably come from the wondrous revelation of the mysteries. Moreover as already observed, Kūkai regarded as most important the womb realm, that female principle depicted in the *Mahāvairocana Sūtra*. In the womb realm, *Mahāvairocana* is the ultimate source and nurturer of all the universe. Our existence is possible only by virtue of the power brimming over from that source. At the foundation of such ideas is the experience of the archaic man amazed at the mysterious power of "Mother Earth." This is probably connected to the concept of "spirit producing" (*musubi*) in ancient Shintoism.

Overcoming the body's ambiguity through cultivation

Kūkai's philosophy not only laid the foundation for the Japanese view of personal cultivation, it also established an intellectual tradition for Japanese Buddhism. We can now summarize the investigation of Parts I and II by giving it a contemporary expression.

Cultivation reverses the way we understand the world in ordinary experience. It is a practice revealing this point: To understand beings merely from the common standpoint of the self as a being-in-the-world is simply to understand them inauthentically. Thus, Kūkai took the body to be more important than the mind. In the *Seireishū* [Essays and letters of Kūkai] he writes:

> My *body* is wherever the six great elements permeate; wherever the ten worlds exist, they are, accordingly, my mind.[33]

The six great elements, as already noted, are the essence of the universe, and "the ten worlds" means the various aspects of the life-world, ranging from delusion (hell) to *satori* (the *tathāgata*). In this quotation, the six great elements as *essentia* are designated by the body, and the world as phenomena (the ten worlds) is designated by the mind. In this case, the body has the status of "active creation" or "generation," whereas the mind stands in the position of the "created" or "generated."[34] The body has to take precedence over the mind because cultivation corrects the mind's mode of being by first placing the body into a "Form," enabling the mind to be directed towards the base of the body. It is an attempt to disclose the body's invisible ground.

Dōgen inherited from Kūkai the tradition of giving precedence to the body over the mind. Dōgen understood seated meditation to be "the study of the Way with one's body-mind," and put the body ahead of the mind. In the field of ordinary experience we think the essence of human being lies in the fact that the conscious mode regulates and controls the bodily mode; the mind is put ahead of the body. Dōgen's "just sitting" (*shikantaza*) reverses such an everyday understanding. One must discard ordinary thinking which objectifies the world from the standpoint of self-consciousness. To effect this, one must "throw away all the relationships with the world, putting everything at rest" (as we saw in Dōgen's *Shōbōgenzō* fascicle "Zazengi"). All relationships connecting the self to the world are discarded and all judgments based on self-consciousness are suspended in practice. Meditation is an inward-looking technique designed to discover and to enter, by means of the practical suspension of judgments (*epoché*), the dark base-layer concealed at the bottom of the stream of consciousness. Dōgen characterizes this state as follows in the *Shōbōgenzō* fascicle "Bendōwa":

> The Buddhas and Tathāgatas have the wondrous art of nondoing: they directly transmit to each other the wondrous Dharma, and authenticate perfect enlightenment. Being passed on directly from Buddha to Buddha, this [transmission] is without distortion, that is, *jijuyū* [self-fulfilling] *samādhi* is the touchstone.[35]

The true mode of the Buddha's *satori* is truly transmitted not from Buddha to the ordinary person, but from Buddha to Buddha. This mode of disclosure is *jijuyū* (self-fulfilling) *samādhi*. The term *jijuyū* is originally derived from Esoteric Buddhism, where it is contrasted with *tajuyū* (fulfilling others). *Tajuyū* is "for the sake of others" or "for the sake of ordinary people."[36] We might say that it is the mode of being relational or of being for others (*für anderes*). In contrast, *jijuyū* is "for one's own sake" or "for the sake of the Buddha himself." It is the mode of being absolutely for itself (*an und für sich selbst*). This is not the experience of truth where the transcendent dimension has been pulled down to the ordinary level, but rather it is the state of experiencing truth as it is in the transcendence of the everyday. Dōgen maintains that such a state is attainable through "the participation in seated meditation." Truth presents itself in the inward experience of meditative cultivation.

We can restate our contemporary understanding of this in light of our investigation of Nishida's philosophy. The practical suspension of judgment by means of cultivation is to deny the validity of understanding the Being of beings from within the field of ordinary experience. Accordingly, one must reject the mode of the everyday self-consciousness, which seeks the ground that supports the Being of beings (the "what is") in the *basho* vis-á-vis being. The self must transform itself into the authentic self in the invisible *basho* vis-á-vis nothing. That is, it becomes a self that has discarded its conscious mode in order to become "a self without being a self." It is "to forget oneself" (see *Shōbōgenzō* fascicle "Genjōkōan"). At this point, the beings in the world do not exist in the *basho* vis-á-vis being but in the *basho* vis-á-vis nothing. They appear under a new, numinous light. Nishida characterizes this as the experience in which the self is impelled to move, being filled with the power of creative intuition arising from the *basho* vis-á-vis absolutely nothing. The self will be filled with the creative power descending from the transcendent, metaphysical dimension, and become one with the world. That is, it becomes an authentic "self" by sharing in the so-called "self-determination of the expressive world."

The world in its authenticity is the field in which the transcendent expresses itself. Disclosing the true profile of the being of such a world is the self's passive experience of creative intuition. This thought pattern in Nishida, we might say, is an inheritance of the traditional Japanese approach, which Kūkai took to be the power of "the disclosure of realization in wonderment," in which the transcendent descends from the metaphysical dimension to the phenomenal dimension. Kūkai characterizes such an ultimate state of *satori* as:

I am thus the Dharma world (heaven and earth).
I am thus the Dharma body (the absolute).
I am thus Mahāvairocana.
I am thus Vajrasattva.
I am thus all the buddhas.
I am thus all the bodhisattvas
 . . . that is, I am a heavenly dragon, *devas,* and the eight groups of deities.[37]

It is the state, we might say, in which *I*, the *absolute*, and the *universe* all exist inseparably connected with each other. This is the essential mode of the authentic self.

Incidentally, how is the body transformed in the metamorphosis from the everyday, inauthentic dimension to the authentic dimension? The fourth line of the verse quoted from *Sokushinjōbutsugi* reads: "This very body is the so-called 'jeweled net' (nonobstruction)." This net hangs over Indra's palace with numerous radiating jewels. This metaphor was used in the Chinese Buddhist Hua-yen (Kegon) school to explain the theory of the dependent relatedness of beings (*pratītya-samutpāda*). That is, each being does not essentially exist as an individual thing with a discrete, immutable nature of its own, but in a state we may call "the synthetic unity of functions" in which everything is interrelated with every other being. So the laws of identity and contradiction, the fundamental principles of thinking in the dimension of ordinary experience, are resolutely denied. Kūkai contends that the true meaning of "this very body" lies in such a synthetic unity of functions:

> This body is my body, the Buddha body, and the bodies of all sentient beings. They are all named the "body." . . . *This* body is, no doubt, *that* body. *That* body is, no doubt, *this* body. The Buddha body is no doubt the bodies of all sentient beings, and the bodies of all sentient beings are no doubt the Buddha body. They are different, but yet identical. They are not different, but yet different.[38]

In *satori,* there is no distinction between the body of oneself and others, between the body of a person and the Buddha. The body is changed into, as it were, a metaphysical body, and it loses all its objective characteristics found in the everyday dimension.

Cultivation has turned out to be a project of overcoming and rejecting the standpoint of consciousness in the dimension of the everyday. To put it differently, it means to break through the characteristics of being a *subject* (*shutai*), which the mind possesses in its ordinary dimension. The everyday self as a being-in-the-world does not stop being a subject that grasps things in the world by objectifying them. Cultivation, however, overcomes this subjectivity so that the self becomes no longer a subject (*shutai*). When the mind thoroughly rejects the subjectivity of the self, the body in turn goes beyond its being an object. No longer a being in the everyday life-space, the body will no longer be an *object*. The distinction between one's own and others' bodies, between being a self and the being of others, completely disappears. Every being is changed to a perfectly coherent radiance made transparent through the illumination of the transcendent. In this respect, Kūkai's philosophy may be characterized as a metaphysics or, in our new terminology, *metapsychics,* which has a theory of the body as its pivotal point.

EDITOR'S SUMMARY

PART THREE

Having examined some ways in which personal religious cultivation is explained in the East in Part II, Part III once again brings in the West, this time to see whether objective Western studies can shed any further light on the body-mind system within Eastern thought. Yuasa examines, in particular, the standpoints of modern Continental philosophy (Bergson, Merleau-Ponty, Sartre), neurophysiology, and psychoanalysis. Unlike the Eastern accounts examined in Part II, which were primarily developed as guides for people undergoing the cultivation practices, these Western disciplines all attempt to approach the mind-body relation in positivistic, empirical, or in some other scientific way. Can these Western approaches in any sense supplement Eastern understanding of the mind-body relationship? Yuasa believes so. In fact, he finds a useful complementarity between the Eastern and Western theories. As the Eastern theories helped us understand the techniques for personal development, the Western theories will help us understand the mechanics of that development.

Chapter eight discusses how both Bergson and Merleau-Ponty rejected the sharp Cartesian dualism between mind and body, positing a critical third term that underlies them both (for Bergson the sensory-motor scheme; for Merleau-Ponty the "habitual body"). In both cases, this third term is the realm where perception and action or sensation and movement come together. Yuasa explores some of the similarities and differences with Nishida's acting intuition. In his discussion, Yuasa also notes Merleau-Ponty's interest in the emotions, a topic also explored by Jean-Paul Satre. As we saw in the discussion of eroticism in Chapter seven, the emotions seem to be a bridge between the mental and the somatic. Yuasa suggests that this topic be pursued further in light of Eastern cultivation techniques and such resultant affective states as "bliss."

Perhaps Bergson and Merleau-Ponty saw the importance of the third term because of their knowledge of anatomy and, in the case of Merleau-Ponty, neurophysiology. Their work attempted to bridge, in a clearly limited sense, the distance between the scientific and the phenomenological study of experience. In chapter nine Yuasa looks more closely at the status of such empirical studies. Yuasa briefly outlines the basic physiological structure of thinking, internal perception (the splanchnic or visceral sensations of the internal organs), motor activity, and emotions. This leads him to differentiate physiological structure in a manner similar in function to his theory of the bright and dark consciousnesses. Specifically, the bright consciousness corresponds roughly to the "surface structure of the mind-body relation"—the thinking function, external perceptions, and motor sensations as they pass through the cortex. The dark consciousness, on the other hand, corresponds more to the "base structure of the mind-body relation"—the autonomic nervous system, the visceral sensations, and the emotional functions (as in the autonomic nervous system's internal sensations of primary disease). The base structure maintains the fundamental life functions, and the surface structure the functions of conscious life.

But how do these two interrelate, as we know they do through our study of Eastern cultivation? Is there a physiological version of the third term sought by Bergson and Merleau-Ponty? Here Yuasa describes some of the research into the conditioned reflex. The old cortex, for example, seems to be a location where the extroceptive sensory nerves ("the centripetal circuit") and the motor nerves ("the centrifugal circuit") interact in a way reminiscent of Nishida's acting intuition. It seems, then, that the empirical study of meditation techniques may be helpful in our getting a clearer picture of the mind-body system and the mechanisms of its enhancement or evolution toward greater integration. This is the point of Yuasa's last chapter.

In Chapter ten Yuasa shows how the mind-body problem (in the expansive sense developed in this book) is becoming a point of convergence for several fields: psychosomatic medicine, the neurophysiological research into meditation, the holistic health movement, psychotherapy, and the renewed study of traditional Indian and Chinese medicine. There are still fundamental methodological differences among these fields—some are more empirically oriented than others, some more interested in the movement from the abnormal to the normal rather than the normal to the exemplary, and so forth. Yuasa's final appeal is for us to understand the cultural and historical roots of these differences so that they will not inhibit progress beneficial to all. As we penetrate more deeply into the meaning of the mind-body system, we ultimately come to understand ourselves better—both what we are and what we are capable of becoming.

Part III

The Contemporary Significance of Eastern Body-Mind Theories

Consciousness and the brain are not the synthetic center of the mind.
W. G. Penfield

Chapter Eight

Contemporary Philosophical Mind-Body Theories

We have investigated in the last two parts traditional thinking patterns in the East, especially those of Japan, with regard to their body-mind theories. Along the way, we have examined how these relate to, and differ from, Western philosophical approaches. In this third part of our study we shall investigate afresh the significance of these traditional Eastern theories for the contemporary scene.

The theories of Bergson and Merleau-Ponty are among the best-known. Shedding new light on the correlation between the mind and the body, Bergson opened the way to overcoming the Cartesian mind–body dualism. To use Bergson's metaphor from *Matter and Memory*, the worlds of the mind and of the body are not two tracks intersecting at right angles, resisting exchange at all points; rather, they are two tracks connected to each other by curved lines moving smoothly from the one to the other. Bergson says that although he has not completely dissolved the duality of the mind and the body, he has attempted to replace the strictly dualistic opposition with the loose duality.

Following a phenomenological method, Merleau-Ponty noted the subject–object ambiguity exhibited by the body, connecting a Heideggerian existential ontology with a mind-body theory founded on the body's ambiguity. As a being-in-the-world, the self was seen as taking root deeply within the objective, connected network of the Being of beings discovered in the world of ordinary experience; this occurs because the self has the body for its fundamental delimitation. A human subject (*shutai*) is a being-for-itself incarnated in the world as objective (in-itself) connectedness. Merleau-Ponty says that the fundamental mode of the human subject is discovered in the fact that it extends its body towards the world, carrying an incarnated destiny for its fundamental delimitation so as to go beyond that destiny.

In more concrete terms, then, what do Bergson and Merleau-Ponty offer to our understanding of the mind-body relationship? What kinds of problems do they run into?

Bergson's Motor Scheme:

Beneath the permeation of perception and memory

Modern Western epistemology saw the cognizing subject as fundamentally capable of understanding and sensibility. Specifically, "understanding" is a judgmental function utilizing thinking, and "sensibility" a perceptual function utilizing the sense organs. Modern philosophical epistemology took these two functions of the subject to be conscious capacities that completely excluded bodily modes from cognition. At the very least, however, it is impossible to eliminate perceptual sense intuition from the function of the body. Bergson reopened the question of the mind-body mechanism by taking this cue from perception. Let us first summarize his contention, as stated in *Matter and Memory*.

Our actual perception has, according to Bergson, a time span or temporal thickness, as it were. We could say that perception is a *movement.* One might think that perception does not invoke temporality, since it is fundamentally spatial. But a perception without any movement, like a still picture, is not a lived perception. Therefore, along with its being a spatial perception, an actual perception also must be a perception of temporal movement. If we call a limiting perception that lacks any temporal movement a "sheer perception" (*perception pure*), we must say that such a sheer perception perceives an instantaneous point, spatially present without any memory of a past, without any anticipation of a future. For example, it would be a perception lacking the continuity needed to count the soundings of a bell. We might find such an instantaneous perception in a lower animal, the vivisectional response of a coelenteron or an amoeba to an instantaneous spatial stimulus, for example.

Still, we cannot deny that they retain some sense of the past in their perception insofar as they are also endowed with life. We know today that even lower animals like planaria have memory. If there is a perception that grasps only the spatial situation within an immovable present without retaining any past, it belongs to inanimate objects, responding by mechanistic causal relationships; that is, it belongs to the world of physical causality. Thus, Bergson's hypothesis of the sheer perception came to be criticized as a theoretical problem in his mind-body theory, but we need say no more about that here.

More important, Bergson maintained that a human's spatial perception is always permeated with temporal duration (*durée*), that is, it is a perception with temporal movement. What does this mean? It is a perception permeated with a memory-image (*souvenir-image*). For example, a perceptual image that "a streetcar is going down the street over there" is a perception that still retains in memory a spatial location that a streetcar occupied in an instantaneous past. Bergson analyzes in detail the operation of this permeation between memory-image and perception, using as a guide the phenomenon of "automatic recognition" in terms of acquired remembering (*souvenir-appris*). Acquired remembering is memory's automatic association or instantaneous recognition in a common, everyday experience such as listening to someone speak or reading a book. When we speak in our native language, we understand the meaning of a sentence as soon as we hear it spoken; in reading, we understand the meaning of each word as soon as we see it. Each word's meaning, however, was originally memorized in childhood. Thus, to understand a sentence, the memories emerge spontaneously and instantaneously as the need arises. Bergson cites such examples as the finger movement of a well-trained typist or pianist. These persons recollect immediately that a certain key is an "A" key or a "C" key within the very sensation of touching the key with a finger. How are the memory and perception related here?

Perception is usually considered to be passively receiving sensory stimuli from the external world, but the very fact that duration permeates perception implies that in perception the active function of the consciousness or mind is already there. Learned through the relationship with one's past life-space, the various verbal meanings are preserved in a deep layer of memory. Perception functions not simply as a passive physiological stimulus but also as recognition of recollected meaning. Permeating it is the subject's (*shutai*) will; attempting to recollect, perception selects from the preserved "memory store of concepts" a meaning corresponding to the present need. This is a *lived* perception, retaining memory's temporal duration. In this respect, a lived perception has a dual structure: It is active as well as passive.

We might say, alternatively, that in attempting to recollect instantaneously while selecting a "meaning" or "concept" required by the present situation, the will is the function that actively bestows a "meaning" on passive perception in the life-space. In the mutual permeation of perception and memory, the dual relationships of passivitiy and activity is established between the self and the world.

Common sense may seem to run counter to this idea. In reading a book or hearing someone speak, we are obviously already prepared to bestow meanings on what is to be perceived by selecting needed concepts from the store of memories; in such instances we already have the will beforehand to relate ourselves caringly or actively to the world. But what about cases where we do not assume such an active attitude? For example, when the sounds of a bell from afar are heard, this would seem to be a purely passive function. We do not bestow any meaning at all on it, do we? According to Bergson, we do. The sounds of the bell are not simply heard but rather we listen to them. To be more exact, we hear them as the sounds of a bell, we hear them while actively bestowing upon them the meaning "the sounds of a bell." Insofar as a subject (*shutai*) exists as a being-in-the-world, he or she is always prepared, without self-reflection, to project a meaning within that life-world onto the passive outside stimulus. One's potential intentionality of acting towards the external world makes the sense-impression, upon its passive reception, into the "perception endowed with meaning." This meaning-filled perception is what we have already discussed as a perception that retains a past, a perception permeated with duration.

What is this potential intentionality of action? Bergson calls it "life utility." The mechanism of automatic recognition works on a perception from within the memory store as required by present needs. This means, broadly speaking, that the body is essentially a sensory-motor apparatus (*les appareils sensori-moteurs*) made habitual and organized to aim at life utility.[1] The body is equipped to respond to the sensory stimulus from the external world. With its physiological system the body links the sensory stimulus to its own active movement toward the external world. Physiologically speaking, there is a linkage between the centripetal circuit of sensory nerves and the centrifugal circuit of somatic (motor) nerves. These centripetal and centrifugal circuits are linked in the brain (that is, in the sensory, motor, and association areas of the cerebral cortex). Memory's recollective function, entering into the center of this linkage, actively endows a particular meaning to the passive, centripetal, perceptual content and gives order to the centrifugal motor circuit.

From the physiological perspective, this is all very evident, but Bergson means something other than a physiological mechanism. As long as we look at it from a physiological viewpoint, the sensory-motor apparatus seems to start functioning only upon the passive reception of a sensory stimulus from the external world. Bergson contends, however, that consciousness's active, meaning-bestowing function, the subject's (*shutai*) bodily preparation towards action, makes the perception itself (that is, the lived perception) possible. He says, "We proceed, not from perception to concept, but from concept to perception, and the characteristic process of recognition is not centripetal but centrifugal."[2] In short, Bergson maintains that perception, in essence, illuminates the possibility of action toward the world. Here we find a mind-body theory that is completely different from the one generated out of a positivistic psychophysiology.

Brain function and the body's motor-scheme

Obviously, the perceptual content, arising from the sensory organs, and the concept recollected from the memory store meet in the brain, or more specifically, in the cerebral cortex. Physiologically, the cortex is the sensory, as well as the motor, center. It is also the seat of the judgmental function connecting the centripetal circuit (the sensory nerves) with the centrifugal circuit (the somatic nerves). What becomes problematic here is the relationship between the acquired remembering and the brain, that is, whether or not the brain is the organ that preserves the memory. We may be naive in hypothesizing that memory is stored somehow in the brain cells. The theories of cerebral memory localization and associationism, hypothesized by Bergson's contemporaries in psychophysiology, are, to a certain extent, a systematized form of such a naive approach. Opposing these hypotheses, Bergson believed the brain to be, not the organ *preserving* memory, but simply the *selecting* organ. In other words, the brain selects a needed memory from the standpoint of its life utility; the brain bestows a "meaning" on the particular perception. The brain is a passageway by way of which each perception is a perception of recognition: it plays the role of a filter.

Where, then, is the total memory content previous to this selection? If the memory store, that is, the place where the memory content exists, is called the "unconscious," this implies that it exists indepenently of the brain somewhere, yet paradoxically has no spatial determination. Organized to serve life utility, the *acquired* remembering is relegated by Bergson to the shallow layer of the unconsciousness.

He believes *spontaneous* remembering (*souvenir spontané*) to exist at a deeper layer. This spontaneous remembering may also be called the "historical memory," recollected with feeling and a definite date. Such memory has no practical bearing on life utility. (Although the distinction between acquired and spontaneous remembering somewhat resembles the Freudian distinction between the preconscious and the unconscious, Freud's work was little known when Bergson was studying the mind-body issue). It is not clear how far Bergson believed the spatially indeterminate deep layer of spontaneous remembering extends, but he does call it "sheer remembering" (*souvenir pur*). He says, "Of course, by rights, it exists independently."[3] In other words, it exists fundamentally independent of the body's physiological processes. Yet there is a link between the brain and the unconscious process—the brain, in selecting the needed acquired memory (or concept) from the viewpoint of its life utility, plays a role in directing the memory to the surface of consciousness.

We can paraphrase Bergson's position as follows. As the central nervous system, the brain does not have a special function essentially different from that of the peripheral nerves represented by the sensory and motor nerves. The brain is, in essence, not the organ to *cognize* but like the peripheral nerves the organ to *live*. That is, it is the organ through which we relate ourselves behaviorally to the world. A pure cognizing or thinking that does not accompany behavior is just the state in which behavior is, as it were, temporally suspended. The essential function of the brain is not this. In a positive psychophysiology, one first analyzes the mechanism of the body as a closed system, bifurcating the correlative aspect of being a body from the conditions of the external world; then one proceeds to think anew the relationship between the conditions of the external world and the bodily mechanism. One should not, however, think about the bodily mechanism (and consequently the brain) as being, from the outset, separate from its relating itself to the world. As already noted, Bergson defines the body as the sensory-motor apparatus that is habitualized towards life utility. Taking this to be the body's essential characteristic, the brain, as a part of the body, is regarded not as the organ to preserve memory, but as the organ to select it.

In the Japanese language, such expressions as "learning with the body" and "the body learns" are often used with regard to the skills and techniques acquired through repetitious training from childhood. These expressions are appropriate in referring to the artist's or craftperson's skills and techniques. The "body" that "learns" a skill or technique in this sense may also be understood as Bergson's "sensory-motor apparatus habitualized towards life utility." In this connection, Bergson postulates the existence of a "motor scheme" (*le scheme moteur*) habitualizing the body's psychophysiological mechanism in a definite direction with respect to perception.[4] The motor scheme grounds the psychophysiological mechanism that we study in anatomy. It might also be characterized as the invisible function that establishes, and is intended for, the behavioral relationship with the world.

The body's physiological mechanism cannot become a lived body until activated by such a motor scheme or embedded system. This is what Bergson attempted to verify through reference to aphasia, apraxia, and other special symptoms.[5] Let us just cite one simple example from his numerous illustrations. Mental blindness (optic agnosia) is being unable to recognize present scenes through visual memory; the patient is incapable of recognizing in the present a past visual memory, even though there is no disorder in the physiological function of sight. For example, when such patients are brought back to the town where they once lived, they do not recall it, even though they have the visual memory itself; that is, the patients can mentally recollect the conditions of the town in which they used to live; but even though the visual memories themselves are preserved, they cannot *re-cognize* the conditions of the town by connecting them with their present perceptions of actually being there.

Noting the loss of a sense of direction in such patients, Bergson believes that this symptom is due to a disorder in the capacity that directs the visual perception via bodily movements. In short, he says, "it certainly seems that a phenomenon of motor order (*un phénomène d'ordre moteur*) exists in the foundation of recognition."[6] If we were to approach this issue from positivistic physiological psychology, this is questionable, since the Bergsonian motor scheme is difficult to grasp directly at the anatomical and physiological levels. Nevertheless, we must admit his approach opens up a new direction for understanding the mind-body relationship.

What Bergson was trying to overcome is the Cartesian mind–matter dualism or parallelism that accommodates common sense. The opposition between idealism and realism, when seen from the theory of the body, is also an attempt to reduce either matter to mind, or vice versa, while still recognizing the parallel relationship between mental and material phenomena. For Bergson, though, the relationship between mind and matter cannot be so envisioned. Analogically, it is like the relationship of clothes to a hanger. Even though there is certainly some relationship, we perhaps have trouble finding the parallel, or corresponding, relation between them. At one end is the world of pure matter or space as discovered in the extreme condition of "sheer perception," and at the other end is the world of pure mind or time as discovered in "sheer remembering." In the lived world, these two permeate each other in a loose manner, conjoined within the body. The human body-mind is, as it were, a point on which these two giant spheres touch each other tangentially. Later philosophers have been unwilling to accept Bergson's "loose dualism," but his project of overcoming the common sense view of the mind and the body supported by positivistic, physiological psychology, is carried over into phenomenology or ontology, where it is developed in a different form.

Merleau-Ponty's Somatic Scheme:

The sensory motor-circuit and the somatic scheme

I do not intend to discuss phenomenology in detail. On the issues with which we are concerned here, Husserl's project is roughly similar to

Bergson's. In his early work, *Ideas,* Husserl strongly emphasized that the active bestowal of meaning operates within the stream of perception. In fact, to a certain extent, we have already used Husserlian expressions in explicating Bergson. Bergson's contention that the memory-image is permeated with a lived perception, for example, is roughly the same as Husserl's point that the active function of bestowing meaning is discovered in perception, since the memory-image of which Bergson speaks is nothing other than the "concept" (*idée*). Furthermore, Bergson thought any concept is organized and learned in accordance with its life utility. Verbal meaning is a case in point. Reinterpreting Husserl from this standpoint, the noematic "meaning" Husserl thought was found within perception at the extremity of noetic intentionality may be understood as the human "meaning" of various events in the life-space. In *Ideas,* Husserl seems to have attempted to grasp this "meaning" at the logical land abstract level; only later did he see phenomenology as the science of the "lived world."

Husserl did not consider the human body in *Ideas.* In his middle period, he developed the idea of a so-called "genetic phenomenology," and he came to think that there is a passive synthetic function underlying the active bestowal of meaning. In addition, he seems to have reached the idea that beneath the apodicticity of the bright *cogito* is a dark *cogito,* which is closely related to the status of the body. Since his thinking during this period is twisted and very unclear, however, it is too difficult to briefly summarize it here.[7] What we will next treat, then, is Merleau-Ponty's theory of the body, a new development in the analysis of the mind-body relation, incorporating the ideas of Husserl, Heidegger, and Bergson.

In his *Phenomenology of Perception,* Merleau-Ponty first considers the active function of meaning-bestowal in perception. In this work he concretizes the subject's meaning-bestowing function (something Husserl only grasped abstractly) by incorporating Gestalt psychology's concern for figure (*figure*) and background (*fond*). The visual meaning for which perception strives is nothing other than the structured interconnection between figure and ground. It resembles the grammatical relationship between figure and ground. The issue is: what supports the active character of the perception's meaning-bestowing function?

Here it seems Merleau-Ponty is greatly influenced by Bergson, even though he praises Husserl so highly. Although Merleau-Ponty is often critical of Bergson, this is out of methodological considerations about the phenomenological attitude. When it comes to the concrete analysis of the mind–body relation, however, it seems that Merleau-Ponty found Bergson most suggestive. For example, while Merleau-Ponty recognizes the importance of Bergson's taking the body to be the sensory-motor process (*processus sensori-moteur*) and its "unity of perception and behavior," he criticizes Bergson for maintaining this to be the "objective body," which is inadequate to account for consciousness's participation in the world.[8] Merleau-Ponty is also critical of Bergson's bipolar contrast between sheer memory and sheer perception, that is, the contrast between the world of the "mind," in which there is no spatial extension, and the world of "matter," in which there is no temporal duration. It was for this reason that Bergson took the body (the brain) to be the convergence of these two worlds. For Merleau-Ponty the important issue was not finding some compromise for mind–matter dualism, but clarifying the condition in which the for-itself (*pour soi*) is incarnated in the bodily in-itself (*en-soi*), that is, clarifying the concrete mechanism of a human subject's existence as a being-in-the-world.

In simpler terms, his focus is how consciousness as a subject (mind) fundamentally takes root in the world of beings, the objective interconnectedness (matter). If we regard a subject as "mind" and the objectified body as "matter," the duality of mind and body is a fatal delimitation for being a human subject as a being-in-the-world. Merleau-Ponty considers the problem to lie in the ambiguity in the body's subjective-objective being. Accordingly, he disregards all the Bergsonian problems of memory and the unconscious.* Yet he still takes the body to be a "sensory-motor circuit" (*un circuit sensori-moteur*),[9] an expression reminiscent of Bergson's habitual "sensory motor apparatus." Furthermore, Merleau-Ponty hypothesizes that, beneath the sensory motor circuit (a physiological mechanism, "the actual body"—*le corps actuel*), is the body's second layer, "the habitual body" (*le corps habituel*). This habitual body is the fundamental layer making the body a lived body, active underneath the centripetal-centrifugal, sensory-motor mechanism in the physiological body. The hypothesized habitual body, we might note, is almost identical with the "motor scheme" postulated by Bergson to be the basis of the physiological sensory-motor apparatus. Merleau-Ponty thinks that the bodily scheme (*le scheme corporéal*) functions in the layer of this habitual body, the layer at the base of the actual body.[10]

The concept of the bodily scheme, according to a footnote by a Japanese interpreter, is derived from Henry Head, probably referring to his intrinsic receptive perception of ecriptic sensations, that is, the sensation of the body's location in space.[11] Indeed, Merleau-Ponty's postulating the bodily scheme in the habitual body is based on the sensation of

---

*Merleau-Ponty's criticisms of Bergson are purely methodological and posed in terms of Husserl's phenomenology. I have some doubts about these criticisms, since Husserl himself neglects the issues of the unconscious. See below. [author's note]

locating our bodies in space, but its essential meaning is rather closer to
Bergson's "motor apparatus" than to Head's idea. For, in contrast with
Head, where we find simply the sensation of the body's spatial location
restricted to the interior of the living body, Merleau-Ponty's bodily
scheme, we can say, is the system of intentionality's potential functions,
by which the body's function is related to the external world; it lurks
potentially at the base layer of the physiological "actual body." Merleau-
Ponty also expresses this as the existential "intential arc" (*l'arc inten-
tionel*).[12]

Internal perception

Merleau-Ponty goes beyond Bergson in noting the body's significance
with respect to its internal perception. When modern epistemologists
(Locke and Berkeley, for example) dealt with the problem of perception,
they treated it only in terms of external perception. Bergson included internal perception to a certain extent: he took perceptual content to be an
"image," recognizing that there is an image of one's body in front of the
image of the external perception, the former being "known through an
inner feeling."[13] Phenomenologically, he eliminated the difference between the body's external and internal perception by using the same expression, "image," for both. Although this notion generated considerable dispute at the time, Bergson's intention was to criticize both
epistemological idealism and realism for dealing only with external perception, and for taking it to be the entire content of perception and to be
immediately related to the judgmental function of consciousness (the
brain). Still, Bergson took the idea of internal perception no further than
this. When he treated recognition as the permeation of perception by
memory, he considered only external perception.

As observed earlier, Merleau-Ponty criticized Bergson for reducing
the body to the "object-body." Why? Because the body's internal perception, to put it simply, is a feeling from the interior concerning, say, the
condition of one's hand or foot in contact with the external world.
Physiologically speaking, this refers to internal sensations about the condition of the motor organs. These sensations are transmitted from the
peripheral nerve endings to the central nerves by means of the so-called
introceptors (the muscle spindles and Golge's tendon organ) attached to
the muscles, tendons, and joints in the four limbs and regulated by the
somatic nervous system. In physiology, this is called the "deep sensitivity" located beneath the surface sensitivity of the skin (the tactile,
thermal, pain-receptive sensations and so on).[14] These internal perceptions in the somatic nervous system are located beneath the skin's surface

sensitivity in contact with the external world. After all, the internal perception is, in a broad sense, a part of one's consciousness.

To cite an everyday example, as the train approaches my destination and I stand up from my seat, I experience the jerking and lurching of the car as it slows down; I am at that moment somewhere conscious (in myself) of the muscular tension in my feet set so firmly on the floor. In such a state, the intellectual, judgmental function about the meaning of "destination," together with the perception of that destination in the external world, are clearly evident on the surface, of bright consciousness. But it could also be said that the body's internal perception just peeks through the bottom of the conscious function emerging on the surface. Merleau-Ponty seeks the phenomenologically essential foundation of the body's existential modality in this internal perception, understanding it as a continuum of the external perception. Just as Bergson eliminated the difference between internal and external perception by use of the concept of "image," Merleau-Ponty takes the body to be what is visible (*le visible*) to the self, as the perceiver (*le voyant*).[15]

Obviously, in this sense, "the visible" includes not only my body but all the things in the world. In other words, my body is the closest thing visible, yet insofar as it is "the visible," my own body and the things in the external world appear phenomenologically, in the immediate apodicticity of the same perceptual flow. It becomes apparent that at this point, that which sees (the subject, or the self as a being-for-itself) is deeply incarnated within the visible. We can find here the ontological interconnection with beings in the world, the totality of objects, that is, a being-for-itself connected with the being-in-itself. This implies at the same time, however, that the world is grasped as being constructed by "perspectivism" (*perspectisme*), with "my" body as its pivot. In this connection, Merleau-Ponty says "[my body] holds things in a circle around itself. Things are an annex or prolongation of the body; they are incrusted on its flesh. They are part of its definition";[16] that is, he thinks that the self's bodily incarnation in the objective interconnection with Being indicates in turn this ambiguity: Being's objective interconnections can be made subjective in their entirety. "Space is not the environment (either real or logical) in which things are located, but is the means through which the position of things is possible."[17]

The existential intentional arc in the habitual body

Merleau-Ponty's basic line of thought is as we have just stated. The issue, however, is whether he can maintain his position by taking internal perception as a cue. Therefore, we should examine Bergson's motor scheme hypothesis and Merleau-Ponty's bodily scheme hypothesis in light of the relationship between internal and external perception.

Although internal perception in the body is recognized as belonging to consciousness, this "consciousness" cannot be clearly classified within the Cartesian mind–body dualism, since it occupies a certain position in physical space even though it is consciousness. My consciousness of my feet, for example, is closely linked to the interiority of spatial points such as "here" and "there." For Merleau-Ponty, the body's internal perception is incarnated within physical space. In perceiving the external world, it might be possible to reduce the content of perception to "consciousness" as a "representation" within subjectivity—having no spatial determination and being separated from things-in-themselves as they exist in the external world. The internal perception, however, cannot be separated from the spatial position occupied by the body. The issue here is what can be further discovered beneath the ground of this physiological internal perception.

What Bergson and Merleau-Ponty attempted through the former's motor scheme and the latter's bodily scheme was to solve the puzzle of what lurks beneath the layer of bodily sensations. Merleau-Ponty recognizes that the notion of a bodily scheme within the habitual body is ambiguous, "like all concepts appearing at curves in science."[18] He sees it as an existential arc, potentially bridging the body's motor-oriented internal perception (somatic sensation) and the spatial, external world. He also refers to the mode of such bodily existence as "the third term (le troisième terme) between the psychological and the physiological, between the for-itself and the in-itself."[19] The mode of a "bodily scheme," throwing a net of potential actions toward the external world—linking it to the physiological bodily system, while incorporating within it a placement in the external world—can be grasped neither by an analysis of psychological functions experienced immediately in consciousness nor by an analysis of positivistic physiological functions.

Merleau-Ponty thinks it impossible to explain the function of Gestalt meanings and intentionality without postulating at the base of the physiological body such an intermediate mode of being that is neither "body" nor "mind." Only because this bodily scheme grasps the situation of the external world in advance, can we immediately read off a perceptual meaning whenever we perceive a situation in the external world. Physiologically, perception is considered to be a merely passive function responsive to stimuli from the external world. This view cannot, however, explain the experiential fact that we discover definite meanings in the perceived contents of our life-space. The habitual body grasps the external situation potentially and actively, in advance of the passive perceptual function in the actual (physiological) body. Only by this hypothesis can we explain how a lived perception can read off the interconnected Gestalt structure of figure and ground.

Merleau-Ponty attempts to verify this hypothesis by means of the well-known Schneider case.[20] Due to damage in the optical area of the occipital lobe in the cortex, Schneider suffered from optic agnosia. For example, he could not find where his nose was when he was asked to point to his nose with his finger, but if he were allowed to hold his nose, he could recognize its position. Why is it that he could know the position of his nose when allowed to hold it, but did not know it when asked to point to it? The problem here was relating "holding" (*saisir, Greifen*) to "pointing" (*montrer, Zeigen*).

Merleau-Ponty believes that "holding" something means to have a grasp of its goal from the outset. Various points on the body appear originally as points to be held, but not as points that are pointed to. Accordingly, the bodily space, that is, space as the extension of the body, appears as a meaningful interconnection in the case of holding, but not necessarily in the case of cognition. That is, the subject's space is the ground for action and is not seen as a neutral, objective environment for a subject. When one moves on command, one first puts oneself in the total emotive situation; when motivated by an emotion, one's movement starts of itself. At this point, the body would already have reached *in potentia* the destination of the command. The cognitive function of "pointing to" becomes possible only after the active, potential "holding" has taken place.

So, Schneider could feel his relation to the world by holding, even though he could not point. Moreover, in the case of being moved passively, he could not understand either the nature of movement or its direction. But he could understand them from his own active movement. When touching a part of a rectangular or oblong figure drawn on paper, for example, he could not recognize it as a figure. If allowed to trace it with his finger, however, he could recognize it to be a figure. This indicates that an actual perception becomes possible by virtue of the fact that the existential arc first grasps its goal potentially by means of the bodily scheme.

Merleau-Ponty notes the relationship between the Schneider case and a cerebellar disorder. Since the cerebellum is the organ controlling motor sensations, a patient with a cerebellar disorder does not have a problem with his or her vision, although the motor function is impaired. Such a patient, nonetheless, exemplifies the same pointing disorder found in the case of optic agnosia. Since the pointing in this case is not impaired by damage to the visual function, we must assume that the visual

stimulus can generate only an imperfect response because of the incapacitated holding (*Greifen*) by the motor function.[21]

To cogently explain optic agnosia as well as the cognitive malfunc-
tion derived from cerebellar disorder, Merleau-Ponty maintains that we
must refrain from explaining the relationship between bodily movement
and visual perception only from the perspective of the psychophysiological mechanisms in the actual body. Consequently, Merleau-Ponty argues,
we must postulate in the background, or at the base, of the actual body a
habitual body, and we must hypothesize that the potential relational
structure between self and world is established in advance (existentially)
by virtue of the bodily scheme operating there. Disorder occurs in a sick
person when this intentional arc is disturbed.

General assessment of Merleau-Ponty's theory of the body

As interesting as Merleau-Ponty's bodily scheme notion may be, it seems
to have no immediate bearing on the positivistic research in physiological
psychology. Merleau-Ponty himself took a basically critical attitude
toward such research in general because its fundamental attitude is not
phenomenological. My own viewpoint diverges from Merleau-Ponty's on
this matter, but since I will not delve into the phenomenological or scientific methodology, I shall not explain this any further. Merleau-Ponty's
hypothesis of the bodily scheme, though, should go beyond mere
philosophical speculation and might possibly be relevant to positivistic,
physiological psychology. If this were not even theoretically possible, his
hypothesis would be meaningless. I shall return to this point later.

Merleau-Ponty's major impact on philosophy, incidentally, was not
his hypothesis of the bodily scheme per se but, rather, its bearing on
phenomenological ontology. Following Heidegger, he called the mode of
the human subject "being-in-the-world" (*être au monde*), attempting to elucidate its concrete characteristics in light of corporeality. In terms of its
body, the human subject is incarnated in the network of interconnections
of the in-itself, or the Being of beings. Metaphorically speaking, its subjectivity is in its upper body whereas the lower body is buried in the objective
world. A human subject must necessarily exist as a being-in-the-world, in
other words, one cannot transcend the world in the manner of modern
rationalism's "consciousness."

The inevitable delimitation of human being, we might say, was more
concretely expressed in Merleau-Ponty than in Heidegger. Thus, for
Merleau-Ponty, the body's mode of space-consciousness comes to bear a
more fundamental importance than the subject's time-consciousness, the
latter being what Heidegger took to be the fundamental structure for
Dasein's mode of being. Since Merleau-Ponty's analyses of space-

consciousness and time-consciousness are somewhat diffuse, we need not try to elucidate them here. In Part I, by comparing Nishida's acting intuition with Heidegger's *Dasein* analysis, we concluded that there should be a relational active-passive space within the body at the foundation of the temporal structure which Heidegger calls the subject's "thrown project." The *thrownness* of a human subject means that, in the objectivity of its body, the subject is thrown into, is incarnated in, the objective interconnections of the Being of beings within the world-space. *Project* means that the being-for-itself, as a conscious subject with a body, bears the essential destiny such that one must cast an existential arc toward the world, relating oneself to it behaviorally. If we still accept this interpretation, then Merleau-Ponty's theory of the body pushes the issue of being-in-the-world into a deeper layer than does Heidegger's *Dasein* analysis. Accordingly, the quest for the meaning of the Being of beings came to be more closely tied to the human being's fundamental structure as a being-in-the-world. This observation is somewhat aside from our main concern here, however.

Emotions:

The base of the sensory-motor circuit

The first thing we notice in Bergson's and Merleau-Ponty's theories of the body is that their analyses focus on the interrelationship between the body and the external world, specifically the connection between perception and action or between sensation and movement. This is probably due to the fact that modern psychophysiology developed out of research into perception and learning behavior. In any case, in neither Bergson nor Husserl nor Merleau-Ponty do we find an adequate theory of the somatic function of the emotions or feelings.

Of course, this issue is not entirely ignored in their work. In Bergson, for example, emotions are discussed as a form of spontaneous (or historical) memory, a memory recollected with a definite historical dating and with a subjective flare of feeling. It is thought to exist in a layer of unconsciousness deeper than that of the acquired remembering that is automatically recollected for life utility. The deeper memory is not recognized automatically in perception but can be recollected only in the "attentive recognition" (*la reconnaissance attentive*) that accompanies effort.

In *Phenomenology of Perception,* on the other hand, after his studies of perception and behavior, Merleau-Ponty examines the "body in its sexual Being." He takes note of the fact that *eros* exists at the base of corporeality.[22] Schneider, for example, lacked sexual discrimination in his perception; the body of any woman gave him an indiscriminate impression. Even with close bodily contact, he generated only "the idea of something indeterminate." That is, both temporally and spatially, his perceptions lost all erotic structure (la structure érotique). From this phenomenon, Merleau-Ponty argues that eros or libido vivifies perception in the normal person's relating to the world. In fact, our life-space appears to us with a sexual meaning or value.

Lacking any analysis of how the activation of the erotic structure within the life-space is related to a person's physiological system, however, Merleau-Ponty's investigation lacks the necessary concreteness to be a full-fledged theory of the body. In the analysis of optic agnosia, we saw Merleau-Ponty emphasize the bodily scheme (and Bergson, the motor scheme) as activating the sensory-motor scheme circuit, but how does the emotive function relate to these schemes? This, I believe, is a critical issue which neither Merleau-Ponty nor Bergson discuss even though it is one of the most problematic points for a contemporary theory of the body.

As a psychological function, the emotions are difficult to define clearly. Analogous terms like "feeling," "sentiment," and "appetite," and "passion" have their own subtle nuances. For our purposes, we can define them as follows. "Feeling" refers to a comparatively simple and discrete process such as sorrow or anger. "Emotion" refers to a process with a stronger feeling limited to a brief duration. In contrast, "sentiment" is a definite feeling with a vague, uniform state, prolonged over a period of time.[23] "Appetite" is an emotion appearing in conjunction with a physiological and instinctive desire. "Passion" may have a meaning similar to emotion, but is employed here with a nuance approximating it to appetite. I shall use "emotion" as a general term, following the convention of physiological psychology.

How is emotion related to the mind-body mechanisms developed by Bergson and Merleau-Ponty? As already noted, the central issue of their analyses is the mind-body relationship in perception and behavior. Accordingly, the body is regarded as an instance of the habitual sensory-motor circuit or process. Physiologically, this circuit first recognizes passively a situation in the external world by means of the sensory organs, and sends an informational impulse to the central nerves (the cerebral cortex) via the centripetal circuit (sensory nerves). Consciousness makes a judgment based on this information and the body actively relates itself to the external world by virtue of the central nervous system's impulse to generate bodily movement via the centrifugal circuit (motor nerves). Consequently, the sensory-motor circuit relates the self to the world by forming a passive-active circuit between the self and world. Bergson and

Merleau-Ponty hypothesized that there exists a "motor" or "bodily scheme" transcending the psychophysiological dimension, a system embedded in the physiological (actual) body as a sensory-motor circuit. They also believed that the physiological circuit begins to function only when guided by the activating function of these intangible schemes.

Incidentally, we can say for the time being that the emotive function is basically generated through this sensory-motor circuit. Jean-Paul Sartre, in *Sketch for a Theory of the Emotions,* cites such examples as Janet's patient who burst into a tearful, hysterical convulsion because she did not want to confide her secret, and people's fainting from fear upon the sudden appearance of a wild animal. When all means are closed to us, Sartre says, we still must act somehow. In such circumstances, we attempt to change the world in a single stroke; that is, we attempt to live not by changing the state of affairs in the world through a "determining process," reasoning out the interconnection with the Being of a definite being, but as if that interconnection were determined magically. To faint is to obliterate consciousness itself so as to eliminate the world's being an object of consciousness. Sartre claims that emotion is generated when consciousness abruptly falls into such a magical comprehension of the world.[24]

In fact, from a phenomenological standpoint, Sartre contends that emotion is a way for a human being to comprehend the world, but our main concern is that the strong emotions such as hysterical convulsions or fainting in fear arise when a person cannot make an appropriate response to his or her situation. That is, an intense, emotional instability occurs when an appropriate bodily movement via the centrifugal circuit does not occur in response to an external situation, perceived and recognized via the centripetal circuit. Emotion is generated through a faulty connection between the centripetal and centrifugal circuits. So I feel pain when a needle is inserted into my arm and the pain incites the bodily movement of pulling back my arm. If this movement is impossible, however, a feeling of pain is generated from the base of the sensation. This is because the centripetal sensory circuit is not smoothly linked to the centifugal motor circuit.

From the standpoint of a positivistic physiological psychology, emotion is defined as "a function of the mind to feel clearly whether or not a desire is well satisfied, and which brings this to the surface [of consciousness]."[25] Accordingly, emotion is related to the "motivation" for behavior.[26] In our daily experience, an emotion makes us aware of our desires, and it decides a direction for our behavior. In short, an emotion fundamentally restricts the function of the sensory-motor circuit, influencing that bodily mechanism from its ground.

Bergson and Merleau-Ponty theorized a bodily (or motor) scheme at the base of the sensory-motor circuit, a scheme activating this circuit and enabling it to function for a lived body. How is this scheme related to emotions? Even though this relationship may not be evident at first glance, our considerations imply that to clarify the holistic structure of the mind-body relation, we must analyze the psychophysiological mechanism of the emotions and proceed to investigate its relationship with the sensory-motor circuit. The hypothesis of the bodily or motor scheme, it would seem, should be examined after the discussion of that holistic structure.

Two directions in emotion

The mechanism by which emotion influences the body has been researched by clinical psychology since Janet and Freud, and by positivistic studies in depth psychology and psychiatry. Bergson's investigation preceded Freudianism, and Merleau-Ponty did not delve into it much either. In contrast, as noted in Part I, many scholars interested in Eastern thought are in the fields of depth psychology and psychiatry. This suggests that the traditional Eastern mind-body theory has been concerned mainly with the function of emotion, or philosophically, with the problem of *pathos* and *eros*. Accordingly, in investigating the contemporary significance of the Eastern body-mind theories, we should also examine psychophysiological research on emotion.

For this investigation, we observe the following points. The actual cases manifesting the function of the emotions—the hysterical convulsions or fainting from fear cited by Sartre above, as well as the neurotic instability often used as clinical examples in depth psychology—may be defined from our standpoint as the abnormal instability of emotions arising from faulty connection between the centripetal and centrifugal circuits. In contrast, when a person is adjusted normally to his or her environment, such an emotional function does not appear so obviously on the surface of consciousness, since the bodily mechanism of the habitual sensory-motor circuit is functioning smoothly. Consequently, in our consideration of emotion we tend to examine the emotional instability with which depth psychology deals. It is not always the case, however, that we recognize the emotions only in their unstable, negative aspects. For example, the ecstatic state of pure experience, or the creative intuition in the (authentic) self vis-à-vis *basho* (with which we dealt in discussing Nishida's theory of acting intuition) appear concretely in various forms of revelatory experience—from the inspiration of a religious genius to the creative act of the artist's brush "moving itself." Such an emotive mode is different from the normal, everyday emotional state, but it also differs from pathological instability. We might say such a person is in a stable yet exalted state.

If we tentatively set neurotic instability at the negative pole, using the normal, ordinary emotions for the central parameter, an exalted emotional state would be at the positive pole. This positive emotion, the state higher than normal, cannot be a subject of clinical therapy. Since it is rarely found in our experience, it can seldom be an object for investigation. It has, at best, been generally studied psychopathologically—as the abnormality of the genius or madman, for example. (The studies by William James and Ernst Kretschmer, for instance, fit into this category.[27]) In order to clarify the traditional Eastern body-mind theories, however, we must examine the exalted mode of emotions from the body-mind standpoint, even though this mode is an extraordinary state. Eastern meditation, an aspect of personal cultivation, can be viewed as the pursuit of this higher-level, emotional ecstacy.

Chapter Nine

Dual Structure of the Mind-Body Relationship

Surface and Base Structures:

Dual psychophysiological structures of body and mind

In their traditional modes of thinking, the Eastern and Western mind-body views differ widely, so we cannot clarify their differences and problematics as long as we continue to employ the general notions "mind" and "body." Therefore, we will investigate the mind-body mechanisms in more concrete terms.

We begin with a relatively simplistic account aimed at the reader with little background in physiological psychology. (A somewhat more technical exposition is given in the footnotes.) First, we can divide the body into two functional systems: the organs of movement (that is, the four limbs) and the internal organs (such as the lungs, heart, stomach and intestines—all that are located within the thoracic and abdominal cavities). The latter group of organs perform the basic functions for maintaining life: we breathe air into the lungs, the heart pumps blood throughout the body, and the stomach and intestines digest food. If these organs fail, we die.

In ordinary terms, the rationale for the twofold division is this: we can willfully move our hands and feet, but cannot freely command the functions of the internal organs. For a normal, healthy person, grasping with the hand and walking on the feet are subject to the will, but the pulsation of the heart, for example, is independent of the will. When food is ingested into the stomach, it initiates its digestive activity through no decision or judgment on our part. Breathing can be freely controlled to a limited extent, but only for a short period of time. While we sleep, our lungs continue to inhale and exhale independently of the will.

We can distinguish these two bodily functions because of a difference in the nerve functions controlling the two systems. The four limbs are moved by the motor nerves, or, to use physiological terminology, by the motor nerves as the centrifugal circuit of the "somatic nervous system." This nervous system is centered in the motor area of the brain's cerebral cortex and is dispatched through the spinal cord to the limbs. In our attempting to move a hand or foot, an impulse issues from the center and the limb moves by virtue of the fact that the impulse travels to the effectors at the end of the motor nerves, that is, through the centrifugal circuit.

What about the internal organs? The autonomic nervous sytem runs the internal organs. "Autonomic" means, of course, that it functions on its own without recourse to the will. Although this nervous system is also distributed from the brain to the internal organs, its center is not in the cerebral cortex, but in the brain stem that runs from the diencephalon (between-brain) to the medulla oblongata. The section connecting the cortex and the diencephalon is the limbic system, commonly called the "old cortex." Anatomically and physiologically, this differs in function and organization from the cerebral cortex (the neocortex).[1] For our purposes, we shall refer to the limbic system and the brain stem together as the "center beneath the cortex."

When the foregoing is schematized, we get the following dual structure of the body:

DUAL STRUCTURE OF THE BODY

Center	Peripheral Nervous System	Organs	Commanded by Will
cerebral cortex	somatic nerves	limbs	yes
center beneath cortex	autonomic nerves	internal organs	no

Now let us consider the functions of the mind. First, one set of functions within consciousness is the *sensations* (of the external world): visual, auditory, olfactory, tasting, and tactile. Ordinarily, we think of sensations (a figure seen by the eyes or a sound heard by the ears, for example) as indicating conditions in the external world, but when we take them to be representations, we can consider them contents of consciousness. These sensing functions are physiologically connected to the sensory area of the cerebral cortex. The optic nerves receiving visual sensations, for example, have their center in the visual area of the cerebral cortex's occipital lobe. What we previously called the "centripetal circuit" is the general term for the sensory nervous system connecting the various sensory areas of the cerebral cortex with the appropriate sense organs, the extroceptors such as the eyeball, at the end of this nervous system.

A second function of consciousness is *thinking*. Although its center is difficult to specify, the frontal lobe and various associative areas of the cerebral cortex are important. The third part of consciousness is *feeling* or *emotion*. Although there is a center in the underlying part of the frontal lobe in the cortex, the area originating feeling is not apparently in the cerebral cortex itself, but in the limbic system. Furthermore, the center for expressing emotions is in the hypothalamus of the diencephalon. Thus, the limbic system is sometimes called the "brain of the emotions," and the diencephalon the "center of emotions."

One might add the *will* to this list of consciousness's functions, since we ordinarily speak collectively of knowing, feeling, and willing, but it is difficult to define the will as being psychophysiologically independent of other functions. It is customary to use in psychology the word "need" instead of "will," since the latter term in ordinary discourse refers to the notion that the totality of conscious functions guides the body in a certain direction; that is, its concrete content cannot be defined separately from thinking and feeling. In the history of philosophy, there are many arguments as to whether the freedom of the human will implies a "will to good" or a "will to evil," but when we look at the issue from the physiological psychologist's viewpoint, this dispute arises out of a lack of clarity concerning the concept of will itself.

Schematizing the above, we may represent consciousness as follows:

FIG. VI: RELATION BETWEEN EXTERNAL WORLD & MIND-BODY

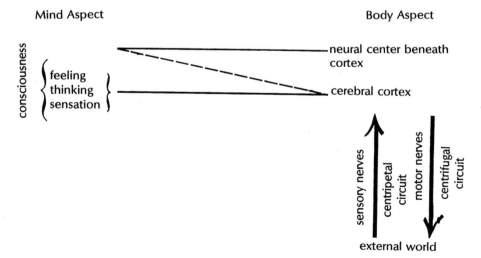

Note: The structure of Nishida's acting-intuition shown in Diagram I (chapter 1) represents basically the same structure, albeit in a less explicit form.

We should also mention a body's internal perception as a special form of consciousness. With regard to this, we can distinguish between the *motor* sensations of the limbs, that is, the internal perception of the somatic nervous system, and the *splanchnic* sensations of the internal organs, that is, the autonomic nervous system's internal perception. Unlike thinking, feeling, and externally directed perceptions (representations), the internal perceptions are inseparable from the body's spatial position. Thus, it is difficult to classify them within the Cartesian mind-body dichotomy. As already noted, these internal perceptions are a deep sensitivity distinct from any perceiving of the external world. The motor sensation of the limbs is transmitted via the centripetal sensory nervous system to the cortex from the introceptors attached to the muscles, joints, and tendons. This is the basic sensation in being aware of the body's spatial conditions. Merleau-Ponty's contention about the body's ambiguity derives from this motor sensation of the limbs, that is, the somatic nervous system's internal perceptions. Obviously, the motor sensations form the bodily consciousness in the operations of the "sensory-motor circuit," consisting of the sensory nerves' relating to the external world and to the motor nerves. Psychophysiologically, this internal perception has some relation to the functions of outer perception and thinking operative in the cortex.

On the other hand, the sensations of the internal organs, another form of internal perception, appear in consciousness when an impulse is transmitted to the cortex through the visceral afferent nerves, the introceptors distributed among the heart and other organs. Compared with the motor sensations, the impulses of the visceral afferent nerves are only vaguely felt and lack any distinct sense of location. For example, we can feel the different positions of the thumb and index finger with respect to the sensations of the hand, but internally we cannot feel clearly and distinctly the different positions of the heart and stomach, at least not without the aid of an external, tactile sensation. This is because the space in the cortex correlated with splanchnic sensations of the thoracic and abdominal cavities is very small. In light of his classifications of tactile sensations, Head distinguished between sensations with a clear sense of location (epicritic sensations) and those lacking such differentiation (protopathic sensations). This distinction also applies to internal perception. According to this distinction, the motor sensations of the limbs discussed by Merleau-Ponty are epicritic, and the splanchnic sensations of the internal organs are protopathic.

Ivan Mikhailovich Sechenov, the father of Soviet physiology, directs our attention to the point that "there is a dark and indefinite sensation originating from the internal organs in the thoracic and abdominal cavities, although this is not generally considered to be a phenomenon of self-consciousness." He says it exists at the base of the organized sensations (the motor sensations as epicritic), accompanying the influence of movement. It is a "dark and vague sensation" forming a "general ground."[2] Since the time of Pavlov, a disciple of Sechenov, research into the conditioned reflex may be seen as an attempt to investigate the physiological mechanism hidden at the base of this dim consciousness of "dark and vague" protopathic sensations.

According to contemporary physiological psychology, the splanchnic sensations of the internal organs, that is, the internal perceptions of the autonomic nerves, are vague because, among the centripetal impulses originating from the introceptors, direct connections to the cortex are limited. Although an impulse via the visceral afferent nerves can reach the cortex, we know of two other routes by which the nervous system is informed of the condition of the internal organs. One, discovered by H. W. Magoun, is an impulse passing through the reticular activity system in the brain stem.[3] The other is the so-called viscero-cutaneous reflex, wherein the impulse goes beneath the cortex by means of the centripetal nerve fibers contained in the autonomic nerves.[4] These impulses do not reach the cortex per se, but are indirectly, or in a diffused form, sent to the cortex from below via the limbic system. For this reason, a splanchnic sensation from the internal organs lacks any clear sense of location and only reaches consciousness dimly.

What we should observe from the psychological viewpoint is that the internal organs' splanchnic sensations are closely related to the function of the emotions. As already noted, since the central nervous system beneath the cortex, represented by the diencephalon and the limbic system, is the center for the autonomic nerves' functions as well as for emotional functions, it is natural for the internal organs' splanchnic sensations to be interrelated with the emotions. It was discovered in depth psychology, based on its clinical knowledge of such phenomena as hysterical convulsions and anxiety neuroses, that an abnormal splanchnic sensation appears in conjunction with emotional instability. We might say, then, that recent progress in physiological psychology has verified the findings of earlier, depth-psychological research.

Now we can establish the unconscious regions underlying the various functions of consciousness with which we have dealt so far, taking into consideration the discoveries of depth psychology. Most important in this regard is the function of feelings or emotions. An individual mental pattern lurking in the unconscious region is usually referred to as a "complex," an abbreviation for "emotionally colored complex." This is the not sufficiently conscious accumulation of emotions, passions, appetites, and so on. As noted in the last chapter, emotion cannot be as clearly defined as the other functions of consciousness, but this is because the feeling that surfaces in consciousness is only a small segment of it, the deeply rooted aspects being hidden and connected with a past memory. Even though the Freudian postulation of the unconscious region underlying consciousness has been criticized as an arbitrary speculation, the physiological distinction between the cortex and the limbic system has opened the way to a physiological study of the distinction between the conscious and unconscious.[5]

This psychological distinction between the conscious and unconscious should not be regarded as absolute, but rather, as two mutually permeating regions. Thus, there are cases in which thinking or sensation functions in the areas belonging to the unconscious processes. While dreaming, for example, we may think of something or hear an external sound such as an alarm clock, taking it to be the departure bell of a train. Still, the main character of the unconscious process is emotional. We shall consider this distinction between the conscious and the unconscious to be the dual structure of the *mind*.

We can now attempt a statement about the dual structure of the whole mind-body relation by conjoining the dual structures of the body earlier mentioned with those of the mind. First, we have the body part (the limbs), the so-called sensory-motor circuit which makes the cerebral cortex its center, and the main parts of consciousness tied to that circuit— the thinking function as well as the external perceptions and motor sensations (the somatic nervous system's internal perceptions). Collectively, we call this "the surface structure of the mind-body relation." It relates the self to the world through the bright consciousness accompanying the sensory-motor circuit. Philosophically, it forms the surface of the human being as a being-in-the-world within the field of ordinary experience. Bergson's, Merleau-Ponty's, and Husserl's views of the body are all conceived in terms of this surface structure.

We now also postulate that underlying that surface structure is "the base structure of the mind-body relation." This refers both to the interconnection among the various organs controlled by the autonomic nervous system, and the splanchnic sensations of the internal organs, as well as to the conjoined emotions (the autonomic nervous system's internal perception as protopathic sensation). Psychologically, this base structure appears in part as conscious feeling (through the stimulation of the cortex), but most of its function lurks in the unconscious region, resisting any clear differentiation. It forms the dark consciousness hidden beneath the bright consciousness.

Physiologically, this section maintains the life functions. Philosophically, it does not arise as a mode of ordinary experience's being-in-the-world, since the latter implies the human immersion in a caring relation with things and a conviction that consciousness is free, that is, that the mind ordinarily controls the body in everyday experience. A being-in-the-world is regulated through the relationship between the self and the life-world by means of the bright, discriminating consciousness. When the dark, primitive consciousness lurking at the base of the bright consciousness surfaces, it is within such events as dreaming, sleeping, neuroses, or various mental disorders. To this extent, it appears only in "abnormal" boundary situations, that is, in extraordinary experiences. Moreover, thrusting into the dark, primitive consciousness, the creative intuition of a genius may also seem endowed with a sense of "abnormality."

Psychophysiological research and Eastern thought

To evaluate the contemporary significance of Eastern mind-body theories, we must pursue the dual mind-body structure just discussed. Early modern Western epistemology, for example, British empiricism, dealt only with the relationship between external perception and judgments. Independent of philosophy since Wundt, modern psychology has concentrated on positivistic research into perception and learning behavior. Contemporary philosophical mind-body theories, represented by such figures as Bergson and Merleau-Ponty, introduced cognition and behavior into the field of the mind-body problem, while taking into account positivistic findings about the mechanism operating between perception and physical movement. In short, in the modern period, both philosophy and psychology have stopped at the analysis of the surface structure in the mind-body relation. Among philosophers, only the early Sartre paid at least some attention to psychoanalysis and Cannon's physiology of emotion. In contrast, in the Eastern traditions of the mind-body problem the base structure of the mind-body relation has always been regarded as fundamental. As mentioned repeatedly, many Western thinkers with an interest in Eastern thought belong to offshoots of Freudianism, since the problems of interest to them are identical with the questions asked in the Eastern body-mind theories.

Incidentally, before going on, we should first outline recent trends in physiological psychology, since its investigations into the base structure of the mind-body relation have undergone various developments. The first historical step in this research into emotion is the so-called James-Lange theory: "One does not cry because one is sad, but one is sad because one cries." That is, emotions are understood to be determined by a stimulus, the excitement of the peripheral receptors; thus, it was also called emotive peripheralism. The functional center of emotion was not well understood in James's time, but, based on animal experiments, W. B. Cannon, an American physiologist, argued during the 1920s and 1930s that the center of emotion is in the thalamus of the brain stem.

Cannon also examined the relationship between emotion and the autonomic nervous system, clarifying the function of the autonomic nerves as smoothly maintained by the balance between the sympathetic and parasympathetic nerves. He also discovered that the sympathetic nerves control mainly emergency reactions. For example, when one gets nervous, the pulse rate increases, as does the rate of blood flow. This stems from the excitement of the sympathetic nerves, and the nerves are restored from their excitement by the parasympathetic nerves. Cannon used the term "homeostasis" for the organism's mechanism of response to environmental change through the mutual functions of the sympathetic and the parasympathetic nerves. Unlike James, he thought that the activated state of the body's organs is not the cause producing emotion but is the effect of emotion, and that the cerebral cortex has the function of suppressing the expression of emotions in the activities beneath the cortex. His research generally holds up even today. Cannon related emotion to the central nervous system and, consequently, revolutionalized thinking about the relationship between emotions and the functioning of the autonomic nerves, bringing a more holistic view of the various functions of the body and mind. This research was formally called "psychophysiology," but it stagnated for a time after Cannon.

We should mention as another development of the 1930s, the stress theory of H. Selyé, a Canadian physiologist.[6] His research focused on the endocrine gland, rather than the nervous system. Since the hormones secreted from the endocrine gland intensify the function of the autonomic nerves, they have a strong bearing on neurophysiology. Today the term "stress" has become a part of everyday speech; it originally meant a strain in the body's functions. Such a strain is stimulated by a stressor, of which there are two kinds: mental and physical. The scholarly significance of Seylé's stress theory lies, in spite of the different kinds of stressors, in the idea of the "non-specific response" or the "general adaptation syndrome" appearing as a definite response pattern. But from our viewpoint, its significance lies in its being a clue for exploring the interconnection between emotions and the body via research into the endocrine system.

Since the 1950s psychophysiological research has shown rapid development. Since recent research in both qualitatively and quantitatively overwhelming to us nonspecialists, we will only note here that there has been remarkable progress in our understanding of the functional relationship between the cortex and the autonomic nervous system, owing to research into the "old cortex" of the cerebral limbic system. This gives a positivistic clue as to how the surface and base structures of the mind-body relation are interconnected.

What is interesting from our standpoint is that psychophysiological research has started to merge with the offshoots of Freudianism. Psychosomatic medicine derives from this convergence. (Incidentally, it is sometimes said that psychosomatic medicine was originally developed in Germany, but it actually developed in the United States in the 1940s, although today, of course, it is a worldwide phenomenon.) In psychosomatic medicine, the "mind" and "body" are mainly viewed as the emotions and the autonomic nervous system, respectively. The reason for the confluence of Freudianism and psychophysiology is that the clinical knowledge of the depth psychologists harmonized with the later, independent results of psychophysiological research; the latter has thus given theoretical support to the former.

Another relevant new development is the interrelation established between psychosomatic medicine and Pavlovian studies of the conditioned reflex, so-called nervism. Pavlov's conditioned reflex originally opened the door to elucidating the correlative functions of the cortex and the autonomic nerves. In the well-known dog experiments, the conditioned reflex of the dog's salivating upon the intake of food is, physiologically speaking, the result of the function of the autonomic nerves (in this case, mainly the parasympathetic nerves). A reflex independent of the cerebral cortex's function, as in the case of salivation responses, is called the "unconditioned reflex." In contrast, the sound of a bell is a "conditioned stimulus." Naturally, the mere sound of a bell does not produce salivation, but, when trained so that the presence of food is associated with the sound of the bell, a dog soon comes to salivate merely at the sound of the bell. This is the "conditioned reflex." For a conditioned reflex to develop, then, there must first be an unconditioned reflex. Since hearing the bell is a sensation from the external world affecting the cortex as its nervous center, a conditioned reflex means that the functions of the cortex and the autonomic nerves establish a temporary connection through training and habit.

In Pavlov's work, the function of the autonomic nerves was limited to salivation, but Bykov and other students proved a conditioned reflex can be established with respect to the functions of the various internal organs.[7] Expert clinicians had observed that the activities of the stomach and heart were influenced by psychological responses to situations in the external world, and this was known, to a certain extent, in both psychophysiology and Freudianism. Research by Bykov and others made it clear, however, that a conditioned reflex can also be established in the

organs that seemed, at first glance, to have a bearing on the mind's function: kidneys, liver, pancreas, heart, respiratory organs, digestive organs,
thermal metabolism, and introceptor response (when an outside stimulus
for an internal organ causes a response, as in the stomach's response to
the intake of water, for example). Bykov claims that the autonomic nervous system is only relatively autonomic; its complex mechanism is holistically regulated in connection with the central nervous system in the cortex. Thus, the absolute demarcation between the so-called "animal and
vegetable processes" in the body would tend to disappear. Like both
depth psychology and psychophysiology, the study of conditioned reflexes has examined the effects of an emotional stimulus from the external world on the function of the autonomic nervous system.

For our present investigation into the base structure of the mind-
body relation, it is philosophically interesting to observe how the offshoots of nervism and Freudianism are subtly approaching each other.
The study of the conditioned reflex is considered to be a brilliant, mon-
umental cornerstone of materialistic medicine. It calls human mental activities the "higher nervous activity," attempting to explain them in light
of conditioned reflexes. In humans, conditioned reflexes are established
not only by means of the primary signal system, such as the sounds of the
bell, but also by means of language, the secondary signal system. Consequently, the Pavlovian school believed that the higher mental functions
can be explained physiologically or materialistically. From this standpoint, Freudianism was taken to incorporate an idealist principle incompatible with materialism. It is said that Pavlov prohibited his students
from using the word "mind" under any circumstances. In return, there
were depth psychologists who were critical of the convictions of materialistic medicine. In the present situation, however, wherein psychosomatic
research aims at elucidating the ground of the mind-body relation, the
ideological opposition is gradually fading away.

The research into the conditioned reflex originally had the psychological significance of elucidating the physiological foundation for
protopathic sensations within the splanchnic sensations of the internal
organs, what Sechenov called the "vague and dark sensations" forming
the general ground for self-consciousness. Bykov said that "the old problem of the splanchnic sensations of the internal organs became a research
object for physiological analysis in its multiple aspects."[8] Freudianism
has pursued the same problem from a psychological aspect. Consequently, if we disregard the ideologically defined goals, both have pursued, in
essence, the same issue.

Orientals cannot fail to observe that interest in traditional Eastern
thought has arisen in recent years together with these new movements in

psychosomatic research, especially the offshoots of Freudianism involved with the practical development of psychotherapeutic techniques, such as Jungianism. But Jung's points were not sufficiently understood by psychologists and physicians, because of the difficulty of his theories and his philosophical tendencies. The source of the spread of serious interest in Eastern thought arises from the realization that meditation is an intimate part of it, a point having relevance to psychotherapeutic technique in clinical situations.

For example, the "autogenic training" newly disseminated in Japan was developed by Schultz, a German, using yogic techniques. First introduced into the United States, it has now spread worldwide.[9] Furthermore, psychophysiological research into Zen and Yoga meditation have flourished in recent years. Originally a technique by which to attain religious experience, yoga can be used in such a way that one's own body-mind becomes a vehicle for experiential, practical research. To this extent, it overlaps with medicine and physiology in some of its implications. Hatha Yoga, especially, has tended to be used in this way.

Since it does not have the same psychotherapeutic significance, Chinese acupunctural medicine does not clearly fall within the realm of present psychosomatic research. Generally speaking, the traditional Chinese (acupuncture) and Indian *Ayurveda* systems of medicine are not readily interrelated with the theories of modern Western medicine, but perhaps it is only a matter of time before fruitful comparisons can be developed. From our standpoint, the key issue is that experiential, practical research into mind-body mechanisms has been conducted from ancient times under the name of personal cultivation; in the Eastern traditions, religious and medical problems have always been inseparable. At any rate, it is fascinating that both idealism and materialism as well as Western and Eastern thought seem about to converge in the arena of mind-body theory. This seems to symbolize the development and tendency of our present historical period.

Philosophical significance of body-mind research

Given this summary of the attempts to elucidate the base structure of the mind-body relation, what are the implications for philosophy? By delving into such psychopathological cases as aphasia and optic agnosia, Bergson and Merleau-Ponty wrote in light of cerebral physiology. The fields of psychopathology and brain physiology have not been fully accepted by those who view modern medicine as a natural science. Their objection is that only the body's physiological functions can be objectively described, and one should not be compelled to treat mental functions, something requiring subjective description. Yet, many medical researchers, psychologists, and philosophers have entered into the dialogue and, conversely, many medical researchers have tended towards philosophical investigations. Seen from the standpoint of medicine as a natural science, this is understood as simply an area for further research: The subjective descriptions must be overcome by new developments in positivistic knowledge. Naturally, this is the goal of nervism.

The exchange between contemporary philosophy and psychopathology is not strictly limited to Bergson and Merleau-Ponty. Heidegger's *Dasein* analysis, for example, influenced Ludwig Binswanger and Medard Boss. Unlike most philosophers, these physicians were interested in Freudianism as well. From the philosophical side, against the continuous assault of those advocating medicine as a natural science, philosophy retained its interest in the fields of psychopathology and brain physiology. This was the situation through 1945, when Merleau-Ponty published his *Phenomenology of Perception.*

Since the end of the Second World War, psychosomatic medicine has opened up new vistas. Although psychopathology and brain physiology up to then had treated the surface structure of the mind-body relation, the cutting edge of this new study has been directed to the base structure: mind-body research moved in one stroke from the defensive margins to the clinically central field of internal medicine.[10] The philosophical psychopathology of Binswanger and others argues that psychiatry follow a phenomenological method in attempting to understand internally the mode of being a "sick person" (*Kranke*) as a human subject, without analyzing "illness" (*Krankheit*) as an objective phenomenon. Although this approach challenged modern medicine's view of disease as separate from the ill person, it has now become almost a slogan in psychosomatic medicine.[11]

In philosophical terms, the present research into the mind-body mechanism has returned to Descartes' ideas in *The Passions of the Soul.* From a contemporary viewpoint, his theory of the emotions or passions does not distinguish between the functions of the cortex and those of the autonomic nervous system. Descartes concentrated on the functional relationships between the emotions and the internal, autonomic organs. For Descartes, passion is the passive function of the soul (*passion de l'âme*). The act of the soul's passions is the will unified with the act of thinking, and it has no spatial extension whatsoever. In the passive acts of the soul are included such external sensations like colors and sounds, as well as internal perceptions like hunger, thirst, and pain. Since the sensations relate to external objects or to the position of the body in space, they have the sense of being a kind of extension. Since passions, on the other hand, have no extension even though they are received from objects, Descartes says that they belong to the spirit, not the body.

Descartes mentions six basic passions: wonder, love, hatred, desire, joy, and sadness. Descartes notes that these passions are related to conditions in the various internal organs.[12] For example, when love is dominant, he maintains that the heartbeat is uniform and loud, the heart is warm, and the digestion good. When hatred rules, the heartbeat is supposedly irregular, quiet, and rapid; one feels in the chest a sensation of cold mixed with piercing heat; the digestive power of the stomach is weakened, leading to nausea. Descartes thought these functions linking the passions to the organs of the autonomic nerves were the result of the animal spirit (*spiritus animalis*) first hypothesized by Galen. The animal spirit is a form of life-matter flowing together with the blood, and is the vital source activating the autonomic organs and the somatic muscular movements. When the notion of this animal spirit was rejected by modern medicine, so was Descartes' *Passions of the Soul.*

Still, from our present standpoint, we might say Descartes' attempted correlation between the emotions and the various autonomic organs was a forerunner of the psychosomatic medicine born of the synthesis of depth psychology, neurophysiology, and the study of the conditioned reflex. As Princess Elizabeth of Bohemia pointed out in Descartes' time, there is a logical inconsistency between Descartes' mind–matter dualism, the departure point of his philosophy, and his theory of the emotions. The ideas in *The Passions* reflect Descartes' own *bon sens* and its recognition of mind-body unity. Perhaps we could say it has taken three hundred years for modern medicine, beginning with Descartes' dualism, to return to the *bon sens* behind his theory.

Let us sort out more precisely this ambivalence in Descartes' theories. In his *Principles of Philosophy,* the mind–body dualism is based on the surface structure of the mind-body relation connected with the bright consciousness, that is, the bright *cogito;* the union of the mind and body in *The Passions* is related to the base structure of the mind-body relation associated with primitive consciousness, that is, the dark *cogito.* Any contemporary philosophical theory of the mind-body relation should give this issue a fresh perusal.

Reversing Our Ordinary Understanding of the Mind-Body Relation:

Reevaluation of Bergson

Our distinction between the surface and base structures of the mind-body relation is derived from our knowledge of physiological psychology, but we did make a small revision in our characterization. According to physiological psychology, the nervous system is divided into the central nervous system (the brain and spinal cord) and the peripheral nervous system, the latter being further divided into the somatic and the autonomic nervous systems. The somatic nervous system has, for its centrifugal circuit, the motor nerves running from the cortex to the four limbs and, for its centripetal circuit, the motor sensation nerves in the introceptors attached to the four limbs. The nerves (such as the optic nerve) connected to the extroceptive sensory organs (the eyes, nose, and ears) govern the perception of the external world and can, broadly speaking, be included in the somatic nervous system. Since they originate immediately from the brain without passing through the spinal cord, however, they are classified as the cerebral nerves, and are distinguished from the ordinary somatic nervous system governing the motor organs.

Following the philosophers, we have called the extroceptive sensory nerves governing the perceptions of the external world, the "centripetal circuit," and the corresponding motor nerves, the "centrifugal circuit." In light of their distinction, Merleau-Ponty's motor circuit can be regarded as the function of the somatic nervous system. For him, the motor sensation in the four limbs, namely, the internal perception via the somatic nervous system, indicates the subject's self-consciousness with regard to the sensory-motor circuit. According to the common division in physiology, the centripetal and the centrifugal circuits in the somatic nervous system correspond to the relationship between the introceptive motor sensation nerves and the motor nerves themselves. But we postulated the centripetal and centrifugal circuits as corresponding to the extroceptive sensory nerves of the external world and the motor nerves. (Physiologists also recognize the viability of viewing them this way.[13]) The physiological classification is natural in view of anatomical structures, but the body in this case is treated as a closed system, separated from the external world enveloping it. In contrast, our classification locates the body in a relational field including both the world and the psychological function through which the subject is conscious of the body's function in this world-field.

As we saw above, Bergson's and Merleau-Ponty's investigations into the mind-body relation dealt with the mechanism of the sensory-motor circuit; in dealing with psychopathological cases like aphasia and optic agnosia, they hypothesized that a function, which they called the "bodily motor scheme" or "existential arc," is potentially operative at the base of the sensory-motor circuit. In psychopathology proper, cases of aphasia can be treated merely by either explaining the symptoms descriptively or by classifying the kinds of aphasia so as to locate the corresponding region of the cortex. Bergson and Merleau-Ponty go a step further by attempting to think in terms of a fundamental intangible mechanism within the body as lived, one producing such symptoms of disorder. They thought in this case that an opposite physiological function might be at the base of the operation of the sensory-motor circuit.

Let us start with Bergson's view on this reverse function. Memory, the recollecting of an idea based on some past experience, always permeates the passive, lived perception given via the sensory-motor circuit. This memory ascends from the sheer memory, the unconscious region, to the surface of consciousness, and it permeates the contents of perception, endowing it with a definite meaning connected to life utility. For example, as soon as the train arrives at my home station, I recognize the scenery as "the town in which I live." Bergson thought that, in the process of memory's ascension from the unconscious to surface consciousness, the brain selects the ideational content, indicating only the memories necessary for the present situation. This selection process and the ascent of the memory means that the body at its unconscious level prepares itself to act towards the world. Bergson calls this the "motor scheme." The body mediates the motor scheme, already initiating behavior on the unconscious level through its preceding, potential act; thereby, a perception becomes a lived perception endowed with a definite meaning. Thus, the potential, active selecting behavior is what makes passive perception possible; as a physiological lfunction it is the reverse of that of the sensory-motor circuit in which a passive perception is transferred to actualized behavior.

Now let us consider Merleau-Ponty's hypothesis. At the base of the motor circuit within the physiological (actual) body, there is the layer of the habitual body. Equipped with the bodily motor scheme, the habitual body latently forms an existential arc towards targeted things in the external world. At the outset, the bodily scheme's existential arc already potentially reaches the action's aim and, thereby, an actual (physiological) perception becomes a "phenomenological" perception endowed with a definite meaning. Merleau-Ponty interprets Schneider's symptoms to be a disorder in this intangible bodily scheme.

Insofar as the above discussion is concerned, Merleau-Ponty fundamentally agrees with Bergson, but he is critical of Bergson's "gentle dualism," which connects the material and mental worlds by a single convergence point in the brain (the cerebral cortex). Thus, matter and spirit permeate each other through the whole body, as it were. Merleau-Ponty maintains that the body is an indivisible ambiguity between subjectivity and objectivity. Merleau-Ponty's criticism of Bergson arises from his own going one step further, taking into consideration the internal perception of the body, that is, the motor-sensations, which Bergson did not sufficiently take into account. Still, Merleau-Ponty is wrong in believing he completely eliminated the relationship with the unconscious as postulated by Bergson. Even if we adopt Merleau-Ponty's view of the body's ambiguity, Bergson's hypothesis is still significant: the motor scheme's function lies in the brain's selection of memory-content arising from the unconscious region and its direction of the memories to the field of consciousness illuminating the matter at hand. This is how the perception becomes a *lived* one. If we were to follow Merleau-Ponty in understanding the internal perception as a bright epicritic sensation, we would lose the key to verifying physiopsychologically his own hypothesis that the bodily scheme is at the base of the sensory-motor circuit. I think that his hypothesis of the bodily scheme might be verified by experimental research into the region of the dark protopathic sensations, rooted in the unconsciousness.

As already noted, the relationship between the conscious and the unconscious in Freudianism has been substituted, through the development of neurophysiology, with the relationship between the cerebral cortex and the limbic system. Bergson obviously was too early to take advantage of these physiological insights and even Merleau-Ponty did not take into consideration developments after about 1950. (*The Phenomenology of Perception* appeared in 1945, but up to his death in 1961, Merleau-Ponty changed his theory of the body very little.) Consequently, in dealing with the brain as the body's central function, Bergson and Merleau-Ponty limited their discussion to the cerebral cortex. Today, however, we can reexamine their hypotheses in light of the nervous system beneath the cortex. It would seem that Bergson's mechanism for the memory can again be supported by the more recent knowledge achieved by neurophysiology.

Since the 1950s, some of the most celebrated neurophysiological research on memory has been carried out by a Canadian neurosurgeon, W. Penfield, and his associates.[14] In performing epilepsy operations, he discovered that when one applies a stimulating electrode to the temporal lobe of a patient's cerebral cortex, a perfect chain of memories is often produced, almost like the reproduction in a photographic memory. (Since memory in the temporal lobe is often related more to auditory perceptions, we should perhaps call it a "tape recorder memory.") For example, a formerly forgotten childhood memory came alive for one patient, including the recollection of a man's and woman's voices calling each other at a river bank and of carnival scenes. (Visual memories can be produced when certain areas of the temporal lobes are stimulated.)

This does not imply that the temporal lobes themselves preserve the memory, however. Old memories were not lost to the patient when the two temporal lobes were removed in a lobotomy. Only recent memories and the recollecting process were impaired. Hence, it seems the temporal lobes are only the entrance to where memories are stored, and older memories arise upon the stimulation of the lobes. That is, the temporal lobes reproduce memories and are conscious of them. We may conjecture that the storehouse of the memories is the limbic system, its center at the hippocampus contiguous to the inside of the temporal lobes.

Research into the hippocampus has shown it to be probable, however, that there are *two* kinds of memory. When a hippocampus is damaged, relatively recently obtained information will be lost, but an old memory, such as one from childhood, will be retained. We are consequently led to think there are two processes of memory: one to preserve recently acquired information for a short time, and the other to retain other information for a long duration.

Let us first consider the short-term retention. Researchers like Isaacson believe that the incapacity resulting from the elimination of the hippocampus should be understood as a "deficiency in learning how and when to respond to a stimulus" and that failure to acquire new information itself is not the essence of this deficiency.[15] When the hippocampus was stimulated in animal experiments, the subject became attentive, making a groping gesture as though looking for something. Moreover, when Krüber removed a monkey's "old cortex" (the hippocampus and amygdaloid nucleus) and temporal lobes, the animal lost its ability to discriminate among things and started to touch everything within its sight, even approaching nonchalantly a formerly feared snake and dog. This experiment indicates that the mechanism linking the hippocampus to the temporal lobes joins the motor process and the memory. If so, the first process of memory can be thought to be a mechanism preserving and systematizing acquired memories (Bergson's "learned memory"), directing the organism's response to the stimulus from the external world.

The second process of memory, with its long-term retention, has nothing to do with the hippocampus and the limbic system, nor the temporal lobes either. The temporal lobes and the hippocampus are simply a switch for recalling the old memories. The process of preserving old memories is still not sufficiently clear, but it is noteworthy that an old memory preserved deep in the unconscious region is connected, as shown by Penfield's research, with the memory of an emotive function from childhood such as being afraid, having fun, or having a sense of longing. The neurons of the brain cells are not fully interrelated with each other in a child, and, as one grows, the dendrites and netlike synapses are further developed.[16] This implies that the cortex is immaturely developed in childhood and that the functions of the old cortex and the nervous system beneath the cortex are strongly vivified, having a close relationship with the emotions. That is, a child lives within a dreamlike, semi-unconscious world of emotions; the function of the cortex's rational suppression is still weak. This is probably why fluctuating emotional responses are so common in children, responses like the sudden reversals between crying and smiling.

In short, old memories have been recorded together with emotional impressions; this process is totally unrelated to the link between the hippocampus and the cortex. According to recent research, the thalamus and the medulla oblongata beneath the cortex are apparently connected with the preservation of memory. They are the center of the autonomic nervous system and are related to various internal organs. Accordingly, if I may venture a bold hypothesis, the preservation of old memories may be related even to the lungs and heart. In light of his physiological study of the relationship between reproducing old memories and the nervous mechanism, Penfield maintains that the synthesizing center of the mind is not in the region of the cortex, related to the functions of consciousness, but is in the area of the upper brain stem beneath the cortex. This means, from the psychological standpoint, that the synthesizing center of the mind is not in the consciousness but in the base of the uncoonscious region. Penfield says that the mind exists, metaphorically speaking, like a ghost, essentially independent of the existence of the bodily organs. As the synthesizing center of the mind, the upper brain stem is merely the passage through which the mind interrelates with the body.

This neurophysiological model has something in common with Bergson's analysis of memory. Bergson held that there are two kinds of memory: the learned memory organized towards life utility, and the historical (spontaneous) memory accompanied by specific dates and emotions. This is the same distinction we have just described on the physiological level. Moreover, since the cortex (the temporal lobes) is a switching center for reproducing memory in accordance with the situation, Bergson was right to say that the brain (cortex) is not the organ that preserves memory but the organ that selects it.

That Bergson's hypothesis about memory is supported by research into the region beneath the cortex leads us to the following conclusion: If there is some truth to Bergson's and Merleau-Ponty's notion of the motor scheme functioning at the base of the sensory-motor circuit, its mechanism cannot be clarified merely through an analysis of the cerebral cortex; instead, it should be reexamined in light of the base structure of the mind-body relation connected with the nervous system beneath the cortex. In this respect, we must say that Merleau-Ponty went too far in rejecting Bergson's hypothesis about the existence of an unconscious, the region of sheer memory.

Intuition and the unconscious

Physiological psychology is not yet sufficiently able today to elucidate the mechanism of the mind-body relation found within Eastern meditation. We have entered into a hypothetical region where the darkness of the unknown still enshrouds us.

In Part I, we began with an interpretation of Nishida's theory of the acting intuition. To the extent his account clarifies the mechanism at the base of the lived experience in Zen, we can use it as a guide in probing into the base structure of the mind-body relation. Although Nishida's investigation of the mind-body theory is clearly inadequate for us, his acting intuition, according to our interpretation, has the dual surface and base structure. The surface is the acting intuition grounded in the so-called "*basho* vis-à-vis being." This shows a relational structure by which the self (self-consciousness) relates itself actively in the field of ordinary experience to the various entities in the world. At this level, the self cognizes the Being of those beings through a *passive* sense intuition (or perception); based on this cognition, the self *actively* directs itself toward the target object (being). From a psychophysiological standpoint, this structure matches the centripetal and centrifugal structures of the sensory-motor circuit, asserted by Bergson and Merleau-Ponty to exist within the body's structure. The sensory-motor circuit is the mechanism by which the self acts directly towards the world through the centrifugal motor circuit, based on the information received passively via the centripetal perceptual circuit (sense intuition).

In contrast to this ordinary structure, Nishida also posits another level, the acting intuition of the *authentic* self, grounded in the "*basho* vis-à-vis nothing." We interpreted the process of descent from the *basho* vis-à-vis being to the *basho* vis-à-vis nothing as the process by which the self, forgetting itself, recedes and submerges into the dark region of the unconscious. When this dimension of the authentic self, hidden from the surface layer of the ordinary experience, gradually becomes visible through this submergence and descent, the acting intuition's structure begins to manifest a reverse function from that of the mechanisms of the sensory-motor circuit operative in ordinary experience. That is, the creative intuition springs forth from the base of the unconscious process, thrusting the self into motion. As inspiration, intuition acts out of the base layer of the body-mind. At this point, the self becomes an instrument or empty vessel receiving this intuition, that is, it simply acts as no-ego. The intuition potentially takes hold of a targeted action, and the bodily behavior, guided by this intuition, simply follows the path made visible.

In its everyday dimension, the self must grope to ascertain the character of each thing (its mode of being) through the complex physiological apparatus of the sensory organs. This procedure is not at all necessary in the authentic dimension, however, for the intuition here has already reached the act in a single stroke. For example, in a conversation with an Indian sage, Medard Boss referred to one of Mozart's letters:

> He [Mozart] reports that he sometimes has the experience of becoming aware of an entire musical piece from the beginning to end, transcending all temporal rules. It is always a joyful experience, incomparable to composing music in an ordinary, limited, spiritual attitude within a temporal mode.[17]

That the active (creative) intuition guides the bodily action in advance is parallel to Bergson's and Merleau-Ponty's motor scheme. The creative intuition stipulated by Nishida is not a common, everyday occurrence, obviously, but it is the function of the non-everyday dimension exemplified in the creative activity of a genius. Nonetheless, by training the body-mind continuously, it is possible for even an ordinary person to have a glimpse of this dimension. There is only the smallest gap between the movements of the body and mind on such occasions as a gymnast's performing his or her best techniques in a state of no-mind, or a master pianist's performing in total absorption, or an experienced actor's acting out his role on a stage, becoming the role itself. These people are, so to speak, in a state of "the oneness of body-mind" (shinjin ichinyo). A genius is, of course, a person with an innate, inherited, genetic character, but without training even a genius cannot manifest that character in practice. Thus, the mechanism of the authentic dimension by which the intuition guides action is a possibility at the base of each person's body-mind.

Intuition and action, in their everyday dimension, belong to the mechanisms of the physiological body: sense intuition is the function of the sense organs, and action the function of the motor organs. In contrast, in its authentic dimension, intuition at least does not belong to the surface structure of the body-mind relation associated with the cortex functions. It is an illuminating function, like a flash of light, breaking the darkness and issuing out of the nebulous region of the unconscious at the base of the bright consciousness. A genius can directly experience this function; in fact, everyone can approach this realization, to a certain extent, by training the body-mind, even though one may not become aware of it. This possibility implies that within the base structure of the mind-body relation is a mechanism that is the reverse of the ordinary operation. Here, the significance of the cultivation traditions in Eastern religions becomes clearer. Meditation investigates and makes manifest, in a practical way, this reverse mechanism hidden at the base of the mind-body relation. Meditation is the tool by which we recapture the Being of beings in the everyday world under the intuition's illumination shining forth from the darkness of the unconscious.

Chapter Ten

Eastern Meditation

Psychotherapy and Cultivation:

Disease and cure in psychosomatic medicine

As already mentioned several times, many clinical psychologists belonging to Freudian offshoots have taken an interest in traditional Eastern thought. Jung, Erich Fromm, and Medard Boss are three examples. As therapists, they have a practical concern with Eastern thought and a theoretical interest in Eastern views of humanity. Thus, yoga has attracted much psychological attention in recent years—in autogenic training for example—because it is considered to be effective as a clinical therapy.

Although Western philosophers tend to restrict themselves to theoretical problems, one characteristic of Eastern thought is that theoretical problems are always closely related to practical problems. In the East, there is the ancient conviction, born of experience, that meditative cultivation affects the well-being of the body and mind. Zen Master Hakuin's introspective meditative method (the so-called *nanso no hō*) is a well-known example.* MORITA Shōma's psychotherapy, recognized in the modern scholarly world, is another.† Since the rationalistic thinking of the natural sciences predominates in modernized Japan, this conviction about meditation has lived on most strongly only at the popular, folk level. But in the Yogic tradition of India, we find this way of thinking in its original form.

---

*Hakuin Ekaku (1686–1769) was a major figure in the development of contemporary Rinzai Zen Buddhism. A good translation of some of his most important works is Philip B. Yampolsky, trans., *Zen Master Hakuin* (N.Y.: Columbia University Press, 1971).—*Ed.*

† For a good account of the practice of Morita psychotherapy, see David K. Reynolds, *Morita Psychotherapy* (Berkeley and Los Angeles: University of California Press, 1976).—*Ed.*

As a cultivation tradition, yoga is generally a technical method for achieving extraordinary religious experience, as much as it is a physiological, hygienic method independent of sectarian religion. This juxtaposition of religion and medicine, or faith and therapy, may evoke suspicion or even seem superstitious when viewed from our modern, rationalistic world view. A closer examination, however, finds this relationship to be a universal phenomenon handed down in the original scriptures of world religions prior to their developing theoretical, ideological dogmas. The New Testament, for example, is filled with accounts of Jesus' curing the sick. We may now be in the age of rediscovering the significance of the traditional wisdom rejected by modern rationalism.

Merging with recent studies on the conditioned reflex and with physiological psychology, Freudianism has given rise to psychosomatic medicine. This medical field deals clinically with the base structure of the mind-body relation, so its conclusions might be helpful in our understanding the Eastern view of the mind and body.

Psychosomatic medicine today can be seen from either a narrow or a broad perspective. The former regards it as a new, special field among the various existing divisions of clinical medicine. From this standpoint, illnesses treated by psychosomatic medicine are generally referred to as "psychosomatic diseases." They are said to be organic diseases caused by emotional disorder, or diseases linking neuroses and organic disorders. In contrast, the broader perspective maintains that all diseases are open to both treatment by, and research procedures of, psychosomatic medicine. This outlook would apply, for example, even to an organic disease like cancer, one that does not, as yet, seem to have an identifiable psychogenic cause. This is still only a theoretical hypothesis without abundant practical applications, but in both clinical and theoretical contexts, one may believe that many organic diseases are, in some sense, related to psychological factors. If such a view develops, we will have to rethink the very nature of human disease. Holistic medicine is step in this direction.*

The following is one expert's definition of psychosomatic disease:

A disease of the mind-body correlation exhibiting either a prolonged, functional change in a specific organ or an organic change [developed from the former]. A normal physiological response to emotion, es-

---

*For a brief summary of the holistic medicine movement in North America and its potential impact on health care issues, see Sally Guttmacher, "Whole in Body, Mind and Spirit: Holistic Health and the Limits of Medicine," *Hastings Center Project,* vol. 9:2, April 1979, pp. 15–21.—*Ed.*

pecially one suppressed from surfacing in consciousness, is displayed in a chronic, as well as exaggerated, form.[1]

We note, first of all, that the issue of emotion is raised. Before dealing with this problem, however, we must touch upon the distinction between the functional change of an organ and an organic change. The *function* is the activity of a physical organ; a functional abnormality is an acceleration (excess) or decrease (paralysis) in the level of its activity. In contrast, an *organic change* is an abnormal alteration in the physiological system, observable with or without a microscope. That is, it is pathological. In the clinical distinction, for a neurosis, the psychological factors cause mainly functional changes, but, for a psychosomatic disease, there are mainly organic changes, although there may also occur some functional changes as well. This distinction is relative, however, and not theoretically essential.

In recent years, there has developed a tendency to distinguish also between psychosomatic disease and disorders of the autonomic nerves, as the disease units for a clinical standpoint. (The former displays more psychological factors, the latter more organic factors.) Again, this categorization arose from clinical necessity and is important in dealing with actual cases, but it is not necessary for us to go into details here. Now we consider how such a disease with a high mind-body correlation is explained, and what its therapy amounts to.

As already noted, neuroses and other diseases involving a marked mind-body interaction are, roughly speaking, triggered by the accumulation of emotional stimuli, and result in abnormal functioning of the bodily organs or in a pathological organic change. The organs displaying abnormality are mainly those governed by the autonomic nerves. The physiological study of the conditioned reflex has made this mechanism clearer: Bykov concluded that the autonomic nervous system is only relatively autonomic. This means that not all autonomic nerve functions are completely autonomic: They also have some bearing on the cortex functions. But such research did not sufficiently consider the fact, however, that the function connecting the cortex to the autonomic nerves is *emotion*. This insight belongs to the Freudians.

Let us first consider this point physiologically. Through the body's sensory-motor circuit, human beings (in fact, all living organisms) have an association with the external world in the life-space. Through this relationship, human beings receive information about general feelings as well as specific emotional stimuli. Physiologically, this is the so-called "temporary conjunction" of the conditioned reflex, connecting the cortex to the nervous center beneath it. (The mechanism of the conditioned reflex is "temporary" because it may later disappear.) Although the detailed physiological mechanism of the conditioned reflex is not fully clear,[2] it is at least certain that the temporary conjunctive passage is established because the internally generated emotional excitements are repeated with accompanying information from outside. An organism strengthens this temporary conjunction by the repeated reception of stimuli from the environment, eventually developing the conditioned-reflex mechanism.

The psychophysiological mechanisms of natural conditioned reflexes are the same as those of conditioned reflexes produced in the laboratory. All autonomic nervous system functions are, in fact, a systematized unity of unconditioned reflexes; the conditioned reflex mechanism is established over the unconditioned reflex system by virtue of the environmental stimuli imposed upon it. Consequently, a link is formed between the autonomic and the cerebral functions. Although there are naturally many instances in which the conditioned reflex is useful to the well-being of the mind and body, nevertheless we might say that a diseased correlation between the mind and body is an undesirable temporary conjunction, inducing an abnormal function or pathological change. (Apart from environmental conditions, temperamental factors also play a role in the emergence of disease, but since our present concern is not the analysis of disease itself, we will not consider these factors here.)

Next, how are we to deal with the psychological aspect? We begin with a Jungian account.[3] A psychic disorder occurs when the emotional energy of the unconscious region enters into the field of consciousness in an uncontrolled form. A patient then experiences "that which one cannot tell to anyone." Examples include the nervous anxiety of neurotics and the hallucinations and delusory thoughts of psychotics; that is, a patient experiences the psychological isolation of having an inner secret. This isolation brings about a state of "compensatory animation" (*Ersatzbelebung*), a way of filling the loss of spiritual communication with other people. As the activation of this compensatory animation, emotional instability can be understood in terms of an energy theory. A normal relationship with various objects in the environment is maintained by consuming a set amount of emotional energy. If this relationship with objects is eliminated, however, the emotional energy stagnates, producing a "compensatory image" (*Ersatzbildung*) corresponding to this quantity of energy. Delusions and hallucinations are produced in this way.

If this explains the emergence of psychosomatic disease, the rationale for therapy is evident. Physiologically, a repeated temporary conjunction that is causing either a functional abnormality or a pathological, organic change must be eliminated by therapy. Medication may serve, but our present concern is psychotherapy. Psychotherapy achieves its therapeutic effect by dissipating or extinguishing an unstable emotion accumulated below the consciousness. Psychotherapeutic techniques developed by post-Freudian clinical psychologists have such a general aim: the synthesis of the conscious functions with the power of the unconscious processes. The power accumulated in the unconscious region, that is, the "complex," remains in an infantile state, as it were; it is the source of childish tendencies and impulses. When this power is consciously experienced, it is recognized as having a strongly emotional impression reminiscent of an infantile period, but it dissolves when conjoined with adult consciousness.[4] In this respect, psychotherapy wants the self to enter into the depths of the unconscious.

Psychotherapy and meditative cultivation

Now our concern is the relationship between psychotherapy and personal cultivation. Since the cultivation methods of Eastern religions, such as Yoga and Zen, are not designed as therapies, they are modified when applied to psychotherapy. But why is it possible to apply them at all in the context of clinical medicine? For now, we will say it is because meditation dissolves emotional instability. Meditation brings to the surface the complexes and emotions sunk in the unconscious region, freeing them and ultimately dissolving them by slowing the conscious activities connected with the cerebral functions. This is the same principle behind techniques like hypnotism.

Although meditative cultivation and psychotherapy do overlap in such a way, they obviously are not identical. Generally speaking, therapy is designed to cure an illness and, in this respect, it guides the patient from a less-than-normal to a normal condition. The concepts *healthy* and *normal* are not strictly clear, however. The distinction between a normal and a sick person is, from the outset, relative. According to Fromm, many patients today are socially well-adapted and not sick in the traditional sense, but they visit analysts because of a disruption in their inner life which should be called a "sickness of the times."[5] American psychoanalysts seem to serve as consultants on personal problems, a role formally played by the clergy. To a greater or lesser degree, everyone experiences some psychological dissatisfaction about his or her living environment, and so states of emotional instability—such as sorrow, anger, and anxiety—are caused by environmental stimuli. In a highly mechanized society in which numerous stimuli abound, a great majority of people have probably lost their "normality" to some degree, as evidenced by the contemporary increase in psychosomatic disease. Still, this does not mean that the distinctions between healthy and sick, or normal and abnormal, is totally meaningless, for they serve a common sense function in everyday life. Ordinarily, we use these relative distinctions to judge the state of one's body and mind and of others'. In Heidegger's philosophical terms, the distinction between normal and abnormal or between healthy and sick is "ontical" but not "ontological."

At any rate, in our ordinary understanding, therapy is a process supposed to lead one from a sick to a healthy condition, from an abnormal to a normal state. In contrast, the cultivation techniques found in Eastern religions attempt to go beyond the standards of normality in its everyday (ontic) sense. As stated in Part Two, cultivation is necessarily a practical project, imposing upon oneself stricter constraints than those of the socially normal according to which average people in society live their lives; that is, cultivation means pursuing a way of life that is *more than* (*Leben mehr als*) the average way of life. To restate this, though still imprecisely, cultivation aims at enhancement and perfection of the personality by elevating various capacities of the body-mind from average normality to a supranormal standard.

But what is this supranormality? How can such a condition exist? As long as we remain within the perspective of clinical medicine as curing sickness, the expression "supranormal condition" is, indeed, meaningless; the goal of clinical medicine is reached upon the recovery of the healthy, normal state in our daily life. If we broaden our perspective to include the training and enhancing of the various abilities of the body-mind, the expression clearly does have a use, however. Normality here simply means the average, and we can certainly make a distinction between below and above above in reference to various physical and psychological abilities. We could, for example, obtain a regular IQ distribution and find the mean. Theoretically, one could do the same for all the capacities of the mind and body. Philosophically, however, we would have the following situation. As long as we stick to the ontical, ordinary understanding, normality or averageness is the judgmental criterion and all conditions deviating from it are indistinguishably "abnormal." Both the genius and the maniac are abnormal. This ordinary *ontic* view cannot achieve an *ontological* understanding of human nature. To accomplish the latter, we must probe into the ideal, ultimate conditions for body-mind capacities.

One characteristic of the Eastern cultivation theories is the holistic, unified grasp of the various mental and physical abilities, lending religious significance to the personality's nucleus as the center of that unity. In the theory of artistry, for example, the process of training and enhancing artistic creativity, that is, the learning (*keiko*) of the art, is considered to be cultivating human perfection. In the martial arts, also, the training in physical technique was considered a cultivation of that same perfection. Prior to the modern period, even scholarly research was regarded as cultivation. In all these cases, whatever path one may tread in cultivating oneself, the training and enhancing of mind-body capacities must lead to the nucleus of the personality. All these paths are related to the journey of perfecting the personality's core as the focal point in a holistic unity of mind and body. Training solely for technique without concern for the perfection and enhancement of the personality has usually been regarded as heretical in Eastern cultivation theories. No matter how one may excel in bodily skills or scholarship, one cannot win respect as long as there is a flaw in one's human sentiments. The preoccupation with technique alone is taken to be dangerous. That is, the Eastern tradition of religious cultivation is the central ideal unifying all forms of cultivation.

Our concerns have already taken us beyond the medical perspective. If there is some overlap between cultivation and psychotherapy, however, we can clarify the meaning of cultivation by applying or extending the investigations within physiological psychology. As we have seen, the surface and the base structures of the mind-body relationship are psychologically distinguished into the bright and dark consciousnesses; physiologically, as the functions of the cerebral and the autonomic nerves. Not completely separate from each other, the poles in each pair are connected through the emotions. Accordingly, we should be able to enter deeply into the base structure, controlling the emotional or sentimental capacity through training. But what is a sentimental capacity? Most ignored in the modern view of humanity may be the role of emotion. Other capacities— physical, intellectual, artistic, and financial—all produce some objective products by which they can be evaluated, but the emotional capacity does not directly produce any objective product at all. Jung writes:

> There is the talent of the heart as well as of the brain; it is equally important, though difficult to discern. For, among those possessing this talent [of the heart], the brain is often inferior to the heart. In addition, however, people with this talent are often more valuable and useful for the happiness of society than those who have other talents.

He also says:

> The talent of the heart is often not so clearly noticeable as intellectual and technical talents. Just as the latter naturally demands of the educator a specialist's knowledge, so the former demands that the educator be as good a human being as possible.[6]

As we see it, the talent of the heart is probably the capacity to bring peace of mind and harmony to human relationships as preached in the ancient religions in terms of love or compassion. Therein lie the issues touching on the nucleus of the personality.

The body-mind relation in Indian meditation

Meditative cultivation may be regarded as a process for controlling and overcoming unstable emotions generated in the unconscious. The condition into which humanity has fallen in ordinary life is expressed in early Buddhism by the term *kleśa* (desire). *Kleśa* literally means "delusory thought" or "the function troubling and bothering the body-mind of sentient beings."[7] Its most representative functions are the three poisons: desire (*rāga*), hatred (*dveṣa*), and ignorance (*moha*). *Rāga* is often translated into Japanese as *musabori* (craving), concretely it refers to instinctual drives such as sexual desire. *Dveṣa* is the angry mind; *moha* is said to be the dark, foolish mind. In contemporary terms, we can say *kleśa* is a dark, egocentric passion or emotion. In seeing the ordinary human mode as having an emotional modality for its foundation, we recognize the importance of the base structure in the mind-body relation for the Buddhist perspective on humanity and the body. The cultivation prescribed by the precepts and the meditative states is the controlling and overcoming of emotions operating at the base of the body-mind relation.

Cultivation's control of the emotions is different in principle from suppression. To suppress an emotion is, psychologically speaking, to push it into the depths of the unconscious. Since the rise of Puritanism, this approach has been found in the modern movements of ethical rigorism where, as in Kant, reason governs sensibility. (Generally speaking, since ethics by and large governs the dark consciousness by means of the ego's bright consciousness, it has a natural tendency to go in this direction.) According to the Freudian view, if the suppression of emotions is carried to the extreme, it has a negative effect on the mind-body relation, producing a distortion in the personality. Neurosis and hysteria are often the result of excessive suppression. Consequently, therapy has tried to free and extinguish the unstable emotions suppressed beneath consciousness.

In its initial stages, meditative cultivation has the same effect, but its final goal goes beyond liberation from unstable emotions: Eastern meditation, whether Buddhist or Yogic, asserts in various ways the idea that beyond the dark and unstable region of the emotions, there exists the dimension of the authentic self. *Samādhi,* a deep stage of meditation, is a psychologically stable, exalted, and transparent state of emotional ecstasy. Nishida understands the state of the genius's ecstatic pure experience, filled with creative inspiration, as the state of the "*basho* vis-à-vis nothing." According to our interpretation, this is the dimension wherein the authentic self exists beneath the "*basho* vis-à-vis being," beneath the field of the everyday self.

Given this interpretation of meditative cultivation, how can psychology and physiology understand this process? We shall take *yogic* cultivation for our example. In Yoga, cultivation is explained in eight stages, the so-called Eightfold Rule.[8]

1.	Yama	negative ethical code
2.	Niyama	positive ethical code
3.	Āsanas	sitting postures
4.	Prāna-yama	breathing exercises
5.	Pratyāhāra	withdrawal of the senses
6.	Dhārṇa	meditation
7.	Dhyāna	concentration
8.	Samādhi	stasis

The first and second stages correspond to the previously discussed Buddhist precepts, the first of the three components of Buddhist study. *Yama* means "restraint," specifically, the five ethical prohibitions against killing, lying, stealing, sexual dissipation, and greed. *Niyama* means "observance" or "resolution," that is, the virtues of cleanliness, serenity, asceticism, the study of yogic metaphysics, and the effort to make Iśvara (God) the goal of all one's actions. In short, by one's own initiative, one establishes regulations and constraints on one's everyday life.

The next five principles correspond to the Buddhist *samādhi*. Of these, stages three to five are collectively called *saṃyama*, meaning "to control" or "regulate." In actuality, these are the instructions for meditation. *Āsanas* are the various postures for sitting in meditation, the essential point being to achieve a stable, quiet body over a long duration. From a physiological viewpoint, it puts the activities of the four limbs, the motor organs, into a state of rest. Since the motor nerves are in the cortex and linked with conscious activities, a resting bodily state lowers the activity of the bright consciousness and its activating of the sensory-motor circuit. The eyes, one of the sensory organs that can be willfully moved, are half-closed, shutting off external stimuli.

The next stage, *prāna-yama*, is a general term for various breathing methods; the term literally means "to control" (*yama*) and *prāna*. *Prāna* is a philosophical term translated as *ki* (life-force) in Japanese. In Western philosophy, it approximates the meaning of the *pneuma* or *logos* in Greek thought. In other words, although breathing is physiologically only the inhalation of air, from the standpoint of Eastern philosophy it is simultaneously an act with philosophical significance, namely, to come into contact with the life-force belonging to an invisible, metaphysical dimension.

Eastern methods of meditation, whether Zen or Yoga, always begin with training respiration; this is important physiologically. The organs governed by both the cerebral and the autonomic nerves include only the respiratory organs and the sphincter muscles. Since the respiratory apparatus is under the control of voluntary muscles, it can be, to a certain degree, consciously regulated. At the same time, though, the center of the respiratory nerves located in the medulla oblongation function autonomically. Respiratory training, therefore, seems to produce a temporary conjunction, or conditioned reflex, between the conscious functions centered in the cortex and those of the region beneath the cortex. Yoga emphasizes *kumbhaka,* holding the breath for a long time. According to SAHODA Tsuruji, if, at the outset of training, one practices *kumbhaka* in its extreme form, one will lose one's eyesight.[9] So, one gradually increases it over a number of days. As one progresses, one will start to perspire, tremble, and feel an acute pain in the stomach. Passing through these stages, it is reported that one comes to a stable state, both of mind and body. These phenomena in the course of training, we may conjecture, indicate the establishment of a passage between the cortex and the autonomic nerve functions. Another yogic breathing is called *"bhastrika,"* literally, the skin bellows. This method is said to break through the three firm nodes in the *Suṣumnā nāḍis* along the spinal cord.[10] These three nodes probably correspond to the lower three wheels (*cakras*)—*mūlādhāra, svādiṣṭhāna,* and *maṇipūra*—mentioned in our discussion of Kuṇḍalinī Yoga in Part II. These three wheels are all related to sexual, emotional, and basal spiritual concerns.

According to research carried out by MOTOYAMA Hiroshi in India, the *bhastrika* method alternates rapid breathing with regular breathing twice each minute. A yogi whom he examined breathed about forty times in twelve seconds for the excessive breathing and the other eighteen seconds were spent in regular breathing. The yogi repeated this many times (see the graphs in Figure 7). Usually, people breathe about sixteen times a minute, taking almost four seconds per breath. In the *bhastrika* method, one breathes at more than three times that rate. If an ordinary person were to try to force this breathing method, he or she would experience headache, nausea, dizziness, and fainting. No matter how one may strain, it is impossible to breathe consciously in such a rapid rhythm. This being the case, it must be performed autonomically by giving a conscious stimulus to the respiratory nervous system beneath the cortex. This

Fig 7:

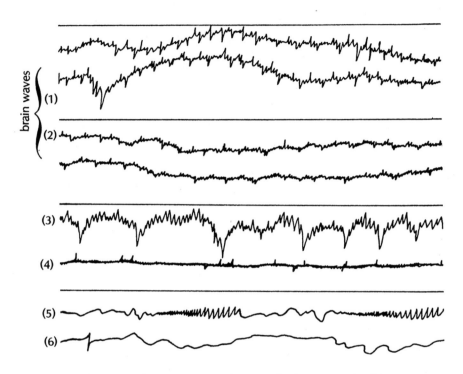

Reproduced with permission from MOTOYAMA Hiroshi, *Yoga to Chōshinri* [Yoga and Parapsychology] (Tokyo: Institute for Religious Psychology, 1972), p. 73ff.

Notes: The two sets of EEG printouts (1) (2) in Fig. 7 are readings from the left frontal and the back part of the head. Note that the amplitude of the wave during meditation (2) is rather small. The plethismograph shows the rhythm of the heart's circulatory system, measuring the flow of blood at the finger tip. You can see that the ECG blips in (4) correspond to the valleys in plethismograph readings (3). Respiration patterns (5) show a distinct difference between the *bhastrika* and normal breathing. The GSR (6), registering the activity of the autonomic nervous system, that is, emotional response, is very small. [Author]

(1) Electroencephalogram (EEG) at the time of Bastrika Prāna-yama
(2) Electroencephalogram (EEG) at the time of meditation
(3) Plethismograph
(4) Electrocardiogram (ECG)
(5) Respiration
(6) Galvanic Skin Response (GSR)

means, physiologically, that meditative training establishes a temporary conjunction in the form of a conditioned reflex between the cortex and the region beneath it. The possibility of consciously controlling the autonomic nervous functions is opened up through this temporary passage.

Pratyāhāra, the next stage of the breathing method, is mean to control the sensations. This has been explained as the withdrawal of the sensory organs' function inward away from their external objects.[11] For example, when absorbed single-mindedly in reading or thinking, we do not notice any external noises, and are not aware of seeing anything, even when looking at it. *Pratyāhāra* tries to produce such a state of mind in meditation. For example, in concentrating on a monotonous sound like the ticking of a clock, we enter into a mildly hypnotic state. Then, shifting our attention to other things, we do not hear the clock for a while. Training in this way, one can produce a state in which the sensory organs do not respond to outside stimuli. When the activity of the sensory-motor circuit is stopped, the bright consciousness that had been activating it lowers its functional level; the dark, primitive consciousness surfaces, and various unconscious powers manifest themselves. Henry Head says that there is vigilance in the conscious functions connected with the cortex.[12] Put simply, this is the level or degree of bright consciousness, its activity level fluctuating with the condition of the mind and body. When vigilance is high, the conscious activity is vigorous; when low, it approaches the unconscious level. In these terms, then, *pratyāhāra* voluntarily lowers the vigilance of the bright consciousness. The mental energy in turn activates the function of the unconscious process.

The sixth through the eighth stages, the deepening of meditation, are descriptive of the states of consciousness from the inner side of experience. These terms are widely used also in Buddhism. *Dhāraṇa* is translated as *sōji* (holding fast) in Japanese Buddhism, and it means the mental concentration on one object through a conscious effort. Its object may be, for example, a part of one's body (the space between the eyebrows, the tip of the nose, or the lower abdomen) or it can be a conceptual object (a buddha, a bodhisattva, or the notion of emptiness). Mandalas and pictures depicting a Buddha's descent, for example, were originally meditative tools in the tantric Buddhist practices of the Heian period.

From the depth-psychological view, it is interesting that when a person enters this state, a phenomenon analogous to psychosomatic disease occurs. As noted earlier, a patient with a neurosis becomes psychologically isolated from the outside world, falling into a state that Jung calls compensatory animation. The emotional energy, denied any contact with the external world, is blocked, producing a compensatory image.

Meditation guides one into a state of psychological isolation by voluntarily arresting the activity of the sensory-motor circuit. Consequently, the emotional energy issuing from the unconscious loses its means of dissipation, gets blocked up, and produces compensatory images. At the initial state of meditation, a cultivator often experiences emotional instability, physical abnormalities, and hallucinations. Those who take these images naively are prone to think of them as having some religious significance, but they are really more like the states induced by drugs like LSD. In Yoga handbooks, there are descriptions of what kinds of hallucinatory experiences may occur. The Tendai Buddhist meditation tradition, *shikan,* calls this the state of *"majikyo"* (the demonic realm) and it warns us not to confuse it with a true *satori.* The Zen-sickness discussed by Zen Buddhism is probably also the same. To use an analogy, meditation is immunization therapy: one elevates the soul to a higher state by producing voluntarily a stage of slight sickness.

The next stage, *dhyāna,* is transliterated in Japanese Buddhism as *zenna,* the etymological source of the term, *Zen.* It is a state in which the unconscious, unstable emotions are gradually eliminated: the mind rests quietly and stably on a single place without any conscious effort. The last stage, *samādhi,* is one in which ego-consciousness is eliminated, that is, one achieves the "self without a self" in which the distinction between the ego and its object is eliminated.

Needless to say, these Yogic categories are not simply intellectual speculations, but arise from the experience of cultivation. Physiological research into Yoga and Zen has been in vogue recently, but it is difficult for nonspecialists to understand it without having any knowledge of electronic, physiological measuring techniques like polygraphy. Here, we shall avoid the technical details, simply stating the general tendencies. This research studies the physiological effects that meditative cultivation has on the mind-body relation or on psychosomatic functions. Its immediate concern is meditation's influence on the function of the autonomic nerves.

This research development should have been anticipated. The reason that psychotherapy and cultivation overlap is that both have noted the influence of the emotions on the mind-body relation. Since the emotions are closely related to the function of the autonomic nerves, and if the psychological aspect of cultivation is to control and overcome emotions, meditation should naturally have a physiological impact on the function of the autonomic nervous system.

As mentioned earlier, the meditative training of respiration establishes a temporary conjunction in the conditioned reflex between the cortex and the region below it. Thus, one becomes capable of controlling the autonomic nervous system's functions. For example, it is reported that some well-trained yogins can slow their pulse rates.[13] Since it is of some relevance, I shall mention here the disease called "specific esophagostenos." Caused by a disorder of the parasympathetic nerves, it is a disease in which food is difficult to swallow because the esophagus expands. Whatever is eaten stops at the cardiac orifice. Some cultivators, however, can willfully expand the esophagus temporarily, and swallowing a gold fish with water, they can bring back the gold fish alive. If the fish were to enter the stomach, the gastric acid would kill it, but by expanding the esophagus and letting the fish swim therein, one can swallow it without killing it.[14]

Generally speaking, there is always some interchange between the surface and base structures of the mind-body relation through the emotions. In diseases with which psychosomatic medicine is concerned, the personality's base structure is distorted by a dark, unstable emotion. Ego-consciousness, the central subject of the ordinary life-world, is shaken by the distortion in the base structure. Thus, the person in such a condition finds it difficult to adjust socially and is driven into a state of psychological isolation. In contrast, in the case of meditative cultivation, the self roots itself deeply in the base structure by controlling and overcoming emotions. In terms of Nishida's philosophy, we can say that the self approaches the authentic self grounded in the *basho* vis-à-vis nothing. This power, springing forth from such a center of the personality, is the function that produces the mental harmony and solidarity in human relationships known as love or compassion.

Metaphysics and the Mind-Body Theory:

Body-mind and Eastern metaphysics (metapsychics)

In our methodological discussion of Eastern thought in Chapter Three, we touched on some fundamental differences between metaphysics in the East and West. In considering metaphysics, we must note how the passage through which we seek the metaphysical dimension and its proper foundation, the physical, is understood. Generally speaking, the mainline Western tradition sought the most fundamental mode of being within the physical, that is, within nature as the material universe. Aristotle's *Metaphysics* is the historical departure point for this tradition. In contrast, in the Eastern tradition, although this, too, is a rough generalization, the fundamental mode of physical being has been sought in the true character of human being.

Within the wide diversity of Eastern thought, we can, for the present, consider the mainstreams to be Buddhism and Hinduism, originating in India, as well as Chinese Confucianism and Taoism. Of these four, Confucian thought finds the true character of being human in social aspects such as morality and politics, that is, in the field of ethics. In contrast, Buddhism, Hinduism, and Taoism have found it in the mode of one's own body-mind understood as something existentially prior to such social aspects. At the foundation of this way of thinking, cultivation is presupposed in some form. That is, they sought the basis of human nature by investigating practically (experientially) one's own body-mind as transformed in the lived experience of cultivation. After this investigation, they went on to question the significance of human "being-in-the-world." It is after this stage that cosmology entered their philosophical speculations. Accordingly, even if we might call these Eastern philosophies *metaphysics,* they are really more like *metapsychics* or *metapsychophysics,* that is, the metatheory of the body-mind. In contemporary terms, their mind-body theory is the fundamental science, the entrance into metaphysics.

In traditional Eastern metaphysics, there is, then, no sharp demarcation between the metaphysical and physical dimensions. They are two mutually permeating regions in a continuum; cultivation is a process in which one's soul progresses gradually from the physical to the metaphysical dimension. We can find a somewhat similar "Eastern" sense of metaphysics even in Western intellectual history, especially among the theologies of the Eastern Church and of gnosticism as derived from Platonism. But ever since the cosmogonic view of God's creating the world out of nothing (*creatio ex nihilo*) came to dominate the theology of the Western Church, the former ideas came to be regarded as heretical, since God, as a metaphysical Being, became separate from the dimension of physical, created things.

In the modern period, using the notions of transcendental subjectivity or absolute spirit, Western philosophy has tended to replace God with human rationality as a metaphysical, transcendental being, the regulator governing all experiential phenomena. If we restrict our purview to Western intellectual history, the shift in the modern period from God's to man's dominance may be called a Copernican Revolution in its pattern of thought. But when we contrast it with the Eastern tradition, Western intellectual history is still a single, coherent development. For example, in recent times, the Western philosophical tradition (represented by Husserl, for example) has emphasized the difference between the methodologies of the empirical sciences and of philosophy. But this would seem to be a secularized inheritance of the premodern pattern in which the physical and the metaphysical, that is, the experiential and the transcendental orders, were taken to be discontinuous. In contrast, the experiential investigation of the mind-body relationship in traditional Eastern metaphysics should be regarded as a stepping stone leading to metaphysical concerns. Eastern thought does not methodologically recognize any essential difference between philosophy and empirical science.

In our interpretation, the central issue in Eastern mind-body theories is to pursue practically the basal mechanism of the mind-body relation. Although, as we have seen, a similar interest has recently arisen among clinical psychologists and medical doctors, I would like to argue as well for the scholarly or intellectual significance of this idea. Resistance to my argument might be formulated as follows.

Scientific progress occurs by denying and overcoming its own former theories, so ancient Eastern thought or philosophy can have no bearing on contemporary science. That is, since the ancient ideas were obviously established by the social and historical restrictions of each period, it is inconceivable for them to be resurrected in our contemporary period. Still, if we limit our discussion to the mind-body relation, there is a different issue that cannot be explained away by this general argument.

Jung has pointed out that human thought at the conscious level is constantly changing. The logic and world views of a hundred or a thousand years ago are completely different from ours. Yet, as is evident in dreams, experiences on the unconscious level of a thousand years ago are no different from those of today. For example, just as Chuang-tzu dreamt of being turned into a butterfly, contemporary people dream of flying or of turning into animals.

> We are confronted with the depth of man's soul (*Seele*), different from consciousness, which hardly changed over the centuries. Here, a truth of two thousand years ago is still a truth today. In other words, it is still alive and working. Herein we discover the basic facts of the soul that have existed for the past thousand years without change and that will continue to exist for a thousand years in the future.[15]

From this perspective, we might say that an Eastern body-mind theory, having its foundation in the lived experience of cultivation, pursues in a practical way, the external region transcending the flow of time, if we may allow hyperbole. If there exists an unchanging mechanism of the soul at the base of the mind-body relation, independent of consciousness's theoretical thinking and of historical changes in world views, and, furthermore, if an Eastern body-mind theory is based on the practical or experiential investigation of this mechanism, it is possible to find a truth in it that can have a meaning for contemporary science and philosophy. In light of this hypothesis, I will now make a few comments about future tasks and directions, although I fear that what I say might be criticized as a philosopher's folly.

The body in Indian and Chinese medicine

In examining views of the body in Eastern historical materials, we find a radically different view from that of modern science. If we call Yoga's psychophysiological aspects "Indian medicine," then both Indian and Chinese medicine agree in postulating, at the base of the physiological body recognized by the senses, the existence of a body with another ontological form.

First of all, in Yogic theory, the body has three dimensions: gross, subtle, and causal. The "gross body" (*stūla-śarīra*) is the corporate body grasped by the senses. The second is the "subtle body" (*sūkṣma-śarīra*). The dictionary meaning of *sūkṣma* is "small, delicate, thin, intangible, inaudible, and atom-like." The third, "causal body" (*kārana-śarīra*), is the ultimate body that constitutes (*kāra*) the so-called transcendent, divine body. For our present purposes, the first two dimensions are of most interest. The subtle body has a delicate (*sūkṣma*) mode of existence that a personal cultivator can perceive during meditation. It might also be called, then, the depth-psychological body, the "third term," that which is neither body nor mind. According to Yogic teachings, this subtle body consists of numerous *nāḍīs* (rivers, veins, tubes). According to the *Haṭha Yoga Pradīpikā*, there are 72,000 *nāḍīs* in the body,[16] but other sources say as few as one thousand or as many as 350,000. In any case, there are fourteen major *nāḍīs*. Among Indian doctors, some say this is a nervous or vascular system, while others reject this interpretation. We will here follow the classical interpretation, considering it to be the system of a quasi-bodily system, something of a different dimension from the physiological body.

Interestingly enough, we find in Chinese medicine an understanding of the body similar to this Indian view. In Chinese medicine there is a kind of artery system in the body known as the "meridians" (*keiraku,* in Japanese). The acupuncture points, in fact, are determined by the location of the meridians. Tradition states there are twelve regular and eight irregular meridians. Although Chinese medicine, including acupuncture, has been the focus of much interest lately, it is difficult for it to affect modern medicine because its view of the body is completely incompatible with the accepted principles of physiology. Anatomically, there is no artery system corresponding to meridians. What is especially annoying is that Chinese medicine completely ignores the distinction between the somatic and autonomic nervous systems. The somatic nerves, centered in the cortex, are distributed to the four limbs, and the autonomic nerves, centered below the cortex are distributed to the internal organs. The latter branch out from the spinal cord horizontally inside the thoracic and abdominal cavities, going slightly downward. The meridians, however, are said to start from the fingertips (*seiketsu*), running vertically so as to end at the tip of each toe. This system cannot, of course, be anatomically recognized, and present physiological notions cannot explain its efficacy. When Western medicine was introduced in Japan in the late nineteenth century, the Meiji government ordered the acupuncturists to renounce the existence of the meridian system. (How strange to see a governmental power decide on the body's form of existence.) Still, we cannot deny that the meridians have therapeutic significance.

Although this mystery has not been solved, work on it continues. Among specialists, it is studied from the perspective of physiological functions on the one hand, and from the aspect of internal perception, on the other. Physiologically, for example, it is known that the areas of skin corresponding to meridian points have a weaker electric resistance than other areas. We can locate the meridian system by measuring and tracing the places where an electric current is most easily conducted. (See NAKATANI Yoshio's research into skin conductivity circuits, for example). There are also numerous studies from the aspect of tissue fluid, but we shall not delve into them here. We might mention, as another line of research, NAGAHAMA Yoshio's study of the system in terms of inner perception. He treated a patient with atrophy of the optic nerves, who was sensitive to needle stimuli. It is reported that this patient, when a needle was inserted into the meridian point, could feel clearly the speed and direction of its sensation running along the meridian. Then Nagahama examined the line of these sensations from various meridian points; the result, contrary to Nagahama's expectation, accorded with illustrations and explanations from ancient medical books.[17] This discovery is psychophysiologically intriguing, for it permits us to surmise that the meridian points are, in some sense, related to deep sensitivity. It could be that when the deep sensitivity is acute for some reason, one might be able to respond to stimuli, sensing the location of the meridian points. If so, I wonder if it might be possible to regard the body's meridian system as a depth-psychological body, differing in ontological dimension and function from the physiological body. Or could it be a quasi-body, the third term between the mind and body?

From the modern medical viewpoint, the theory just presented is ludicrous. Modern medicine proceeds by understanding the body first as a collective system of anatomical organs, and then it studies the functions of these organs from a physiological standpoint. Consideration of psychological functions comes next. Following this procedure, it is natural for psychopathology and brain physiology to be regarded as illegitimate offspring or as fields of undeveloped research. After all, these disciplines have to deal with the mind, something that cannot be dissected, and whose functions cannot be measured by sensations. According to the modern view of the body, disease is, first of all, a pathological change in the organ, creating an abnormal condition. From this physiological standpoint, neurosis, in fact, had to be regarded simply as a state in which nothing is wrong. If, however, we develop the principles of philosophical psychopathology and psychosomatic medicine, "the problem is not to analyze sickness (*Krankheit*) but to understand the sick person (*Kranke*)."

Taking this approach, we can grasp the body's modality in a way opposite to the traditional view of modern medicine. That is, our starting point for understanding the body's mode is the *mind,* the way the body is grasped internally and subjectively. Thus, the physiological functions correlated with the psychological functions will be regarded, as it were, as the field out of which the psychological functions emerge. The body's organs, moreover, will be understood as an expressive form of this correlated mind and body. We must note, in this case that the "mind" here is not simply the surface structure of the mind-body relation associated with consciousness, but the mental totality, including the unconscious region as well. It would seem that Eastern medicine's traditional view of the body takes the body's mode in the opposite direction from modern medicine's procedure of anatomy first, then physiology, and only finally psychology. Our investigations have thus given us the rationale for positing a quasi-body at the base of the psychophysiological dimension.

Historically, the meridian system in Chinese medicine takes its inspiration from the *yin-yang* and five-agent theories of the *I Ching* [Book of changes], a common source for both Taoism and Confucianism. It would seem that the theory of the five agents had a bearing on the cultivation method of Taoism when seen in view of our study of the mind-body relation. For example, the *T'ai-chi-t'u-shuo* [Explanation of the diagram of the supreme ultimate], written by Chou Tun-yi in the Sung period, and which discusses philosophically the five agents, is considered to be based upon Taoist cultivation methods.* There are also Taoist meditation methods influenced by Buddhism, as well as physical training techniques later associated with the Chinese martial arts. (The so-called *t'ai-hsi* and *tao-yin,* for example. *T'ai-hsi* is a breathing and sitting method, while *tao-yin* is a related physical training and hygienic method.) Chinese medicine's

---

*For the diagram itself and a brief discussion, see Fung Yu-lan, *History of Chinese Philosophy,* Vol. 2, chap. 11 (Princeton, N.J.: Princeton University Press, 1953).—*Ed.*

theory of the body apparently arose from the experience of Taoist cultivation methods. Here is an experiential background similar to the one we found behind Indian medicine.

In short, for both the Chinese and Indian traditions, the quasi-body belongs to two different dimensions from the physiological body. They think of the quasi-body as the field of power operative at the base layer of the physiological body, while recognizing the correlation between the mind and body, a mechanical relation having its domain in the physiological body. The quasi-body's existence must be inferred indirectly but experientially from its curative effects, the change of mental and physical functions. Another way to recognize its existence is on one's own, to experience the unconscious region in meditation.

Incidentally, such a depth-psychological body, according to the classical interpretation, is a system exchanging energy with the external world in a dimension transcending the senses. As mentioned earlier in reference to *yoga,* the subtle body as the system of *nāḍīs* is assumed to be beneath the physiological body (the gross body). It is an artery system where *prāṇa* (the life-energy, *ki* in Japanese, *pneuma* in Western terms) is the invisible yet abundant inflowing and outflowing energy of the external world. (As noted earlier, *prāṇa-yama* in *yoga* means to control the breathing while referring to *prāṇa,* the invisible life energy.) Jung says it is futile to try to understand *prāṇa* intellectually. *Prāṇa* cannot be known rationally but only experientially—along with the functions of the heart, belly, and blood—in one's own meditation.[18] In this context, philosophy and experimental psychology come together.

Moreover, according to the Chinese view, the meridians are an invisible artery system by which the life-force of *yin* and *yang* in the external world enters and leaves the person; that is, Chinese medicine distinguishes the two ontological levels of the mind-body relation. The first is the psychophysiological interconnection between the mind and body that can be directly seen or experienced. In this dimension, the distinction between the external world and the self as an living organism is recognized by consciousness and the senses. At the base of this level, however, is the dimension that cannot be recognized by the senses, where the mind-body exists in a stricter unity (that is, as a system of functions that is neither mind nor body) and there is no clear ontological distinction between the contours of self and things in the external world. They exist in a state of permeated interpenetration.

If this is indeed a fair representation of Eastern medicine's view of the body, it is interestingly commensurate, although coincidentally so, with the ideas of Bergson and Merleau-Ponty. As we have seen earlier in Part III, Merleau-Ponty believed "the habitual body" to be at the base of the physiological body. In this habitual body, the function of "the bodily scheme" is activated in order to form an existential and intentional arc, invisible and potential, towards the external world. Only when activated by the bodily scheme, does the physiological body function as a lived body with its mind-body correlation. Merleau-Ponty believed that an abnormal function of the mind-body mechanism occurs in a sick person because the intentional arc's function slackens at the layer of the habitual body. He attempted to verify this by reference to special psychopathological cases such as Schneider's.

But I wonder if we cannot reexamine his idea from the broader perspective of today's psychosomatic medicine. Recognizing his notion of the habitual body to be ambiguous, appearing in a transitional period of scientific theory, Merleau-Ponty wondered whether his mind-body perspective might eventually present the possibility of a new ontology, that is, a metaphysics serving as a mind-body metatheory. With our new understanding of Eastern medicine, we might well raise the same question.

Intuition and humanness

Next, we consider intuition. Philosophically, the everyday self, as a being-in-the-world, is caringly related to things in the world. From the standpoint of our body-mind theory, this is the surface structure of the mind-body relation, governed by the bright self-consciousness. At the base of such a self is a mind-body relational structure covered by the dark consciousness.

Eastern meditation attempts to investigate the inner mechanism hidden in this base structure. We have called this the region of the "authentic self," in contrast to the experiential region of ordinary consciousness. Unlike the everyday self, the authentic self cannot be experienced by everyone. Moreover, the authentic self cannot be fixed conceptually; it is simply an ideal. The Eastern traditions have grasped it in various ways. For example, such metaphysical concepts as *puruṣa* in Yoga, *ātman* in Vedānta, *śūnyatā* and the buddha-nature in Buddhism, and Tao in Taoism, may all be said to refer, from our standpoint, to the region of the authentic self.

If we limit our perspective to Japanese thought, it would seem that there has been a strong tendency in the Japanese philosophical tradition to graph the authentic self as a creative, productive "function" (*hataraki*), or "field" (*ba*) of life-energy. Consequently, the authentic self is felt and acquired through some sort of life-energy emanating downward from the metaphysical dimension; its field of acquisition and feeling is one's body-mind within meditative cultivation. Although this pattern is discernible throughout the history of Japanese Buddhism,[19] in my opinion, it was Kūkai's philosophy that first established this interpretation, and it ultimately flowed into Nishida's modern philosophy. Nishida's acting intuition means to act as a self without being a self, to be guided by creative intuition while receiving its power springing from the *basho* vis-à-vis nothing, the region of the authentic self.

Incidentally, unless also a theologian or philosopher, the psychologist does not deal with this higher intuition. Since philosophers attempt to reach the ultimate in a single stroke, riding on the wings of speculation, it is natural that empirical investigations cannot catch up with them. But this only blocks our progress. So, instead, we will turn to Jung, as a modern analytical psychologist, to be our guide in dealing with the issue of intuition.

Jung divides the human psychological functions into thinking, feeling, sensation, and intuition. The motivation behind this distinction is to develop a classification of personality types, but this is not our concern here.[20] Jung depicts these four functions as follows. (See Figure 8.)

The two polar functions of "sensation" and "intuition" are called "irrational," but this term is used in a special sense: it simply means that one cannot give any (psychological) explanation for its acts. That is, both sensation and intuition are felt to be facts of experience, but one cannot question why one senses in a certain way. Moreover, intuition and sensation often accompany each other. When a genius intuits something, he or she usually intuits through a sensation of something. For example, Newton intuited the law of gravitation upon seeing an apple fall. (Unfortunately, however, this sort of intuition does not occur in us ordinary persons.) In such a case, there is no direct logical relationship between the apple and the law of gravitation; the apple could have been a pear or a stone, for that matter. The sensate stimulus simply triggered, or was an opportunity for, the function of intuition. This sort of experience psychologically resembles the case of a Zen monk, after long cultivation, suddenly attaining *satori* upon hearing the cracking of a bamboo.

Secondly, Jung calls the other two bipolar functions, "thinking" and "feeling," together the "rational" function. It is natural that thinking should be considered rational, but why is feeling included as well? As used here, "rational" designates the function of passing a (psychological) judgment, or giving a reason. Thinking's judgment is of the form, "This is such and such" or "We should be such and such." In contrast, feeling, accompanied by the function of thinking, passes value judgments, such as, "I want to do such and such" or "I like such and such." If we separate out

Figure 8: Four Psychological Functions

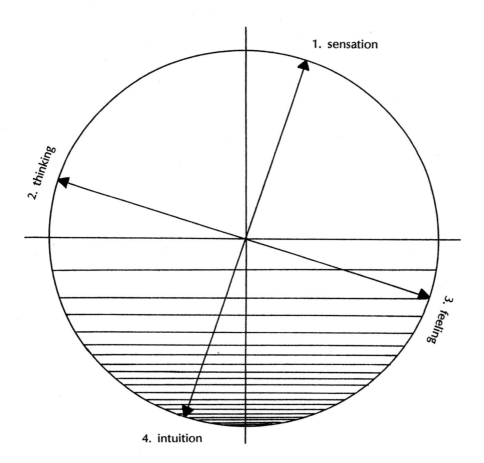

the function of feeling in this case, it is not a judgment per se, but simply the mind's choosing directively between alternatives, that is, making the distinction between liking something, or not. In contrast to sensation and intuition, feeling makes a dual act of discrimination, setting out the positive and the negative values for oneself. In the case of thinking, this discrimination takes a logical form, making a judgment of existence ("Is it such, or not?") or of fact ("Is it true or false?"). Thinking's logical judgments and feeling's value judgments are indeed very different, but, psychologically considered, insofar as they discriminate between two alternatives, they share a common element.

Moreover, in the actual workings of human psychology, the thinking and feeling functions tend to act hand in hand. For example, in attempting to convince people, on many occasions, one may give an orderly, well-argued presentation, but the people's warped emotions may be strongly at work on a lower level. The delusions of a psychotic or neurotic are extreme examples, but there is a similar tendency even in a normal person. Jung says, sarcastically, how interesting it would be to study professors' private lives. "If you want to know in detail how intellectuals behave at home, their wives know very well." People with a developed capacity for intellectual thinking are skillful in giving rationales for their feelings, but an excessive tendency towards logical coherence is an expression of emotional instability. To take an example from mass psychology, an ideological political explanation may define an opposing group as "the enemy of people," or "the enemy of freedom," and the view may be supported by a coherent logic deduced from one's fundamental principles. But, in reality, the effectiveness of such an explanation is more the collective function of feelings and emotions. At any rate, thinking and feeling always tend to accompany each other, and together they are regarded as the rational, unified, complementary functions performing their dual discriminations.

In what forms do these four functions appear in the field of ordinary experience? First, sensation recognizes things in the world: "There is. . . . "[21] It teaches us what exists through seeing and hearing. Second, thinking makes a judgment about the experience: "It is . . . " Third, feeling discriminates values, as to whether "one likes such and such, or not." These three functions fulfill the needs of everyday life. The fourth, intuition, is unnecessary for that. Why then must we consider it as one of the four primary functions? Jung says that intuition gives us a sense of temporality. Insofar as we relate ourselves to the things of the everyday life-world, human life can be exhausted by the following three functions: "There is . . . ," "It is . . . ," and "I like (or don't like) this or that." These indicate only our relating ourselves to spatial things, however, and introduce no element of time.

How is time related to ordinary experience and to the issue of intuition? According to Jung, time is the issue of whence (woher) the self comes and whither (wohin) it goes. To take an example, if we were lost in an African jungle, we would be helpless with only the previous three functions. In such circumstances, we have to rely on intuition to decide in what direction to go. In an ordinary situation, the question of whence and whither can be answered through the functions of sensation, feeling, and thinking, but in boundary situations with which these functions cannot deal, we must respond with intuition. This indicates that the question of whence and whither essentially pertains to the region of intuition. Philosophically stated, intuition is the function of judging *the place of one's being* by grasping holistically and synthetically the ontological relationship between self and world. This appears in ordinary experience as a mode of time-consciousness, the mode of pondering how one should act towards the future and how one was acting in the past. To use Heidegger's terminology, intuition is the subject's time-consciousness as a "thrown project," found in everyday caring.

From the standpoint of depth psychology, this function is the interiority of one's own self. What is concealed at the base of the everyday self's caring mode? Heidegger calls it an "existential anxiety," the anxiety over the self's existing here and now in the world, the anxiety that we are unable to know the meaning and ground of the self's being. From the standpoint of Jung's depth psychology, this is the question of *who (wer)*.[22] That is, to ask about whence and whither is to ask about the self's mode as a being-in-the-world. When these questions are directed to the base of the everyday self's mode of being, however, they change into questions like, "Who is it who comes whence and goes whither?", and, "*Who* is my self?" When people, like amnesiacs, are in a psychopathological boundary situation, they are tortured by this kind of question. How then does the mind-body theory respond to these questions?

Jung barely explained the relationship between the four psychological functions and the body, but he does state that the emotions are identical with certain bodily states, and that they are deeply rooted in the primal part of the body. He also points out the correlative relationship between the emotions and the sympathetic nerves.[23] Jung devised the diagram of the four functions (Figure 8) to classify people's psychological types. In different individuals, different functions become dominant.

According to our interpretation, though, the diagram can also be seen as a general indication of the relationship between the bright and dark consciousness, that is, between the surface and base structures of the mind-body relation. In our view, the bright section of the upper part of the diagram corresponds to the surface structure of the mind-body relation. It is usually in sensation that the bright consciousness is most vigorously active in the field of ordinary experience. In Jung's terms, sensation is the dominant function that is most directly developed, and thinking is its complement. (We can add, as another element of bright consciousness, the internal perception of the somatic nerves.) In contrast, the dark section of the lower part indicates the undeveloped functions deep in the unconscious region. From our standpoint, this corresponds to the base region of the mind-body relation. Intuition is usually deep beneath this shadowy region, as subordinate function. Feeling, as the complementary function, connects the bright and dark regions. (The internal protopathic perception of the autonomic nerves is associated with this connection.)

Jung says that intuition functions through the unconscious:

> I regard intuition as a basic psychological *function*. . . . It is the function mediating perception in *an unconscious* way. Everything, whether outer or inner objects or their relationships, can be the focus of this perception. The peculiarity of intuition is that it is neither sense perception nor feeling, nor intellectual inference, although it may also appear in these forms. In intuition, a content presents itself wholly and completely, without our being able to explain or discover how this content came into existence. Intuition is a kind of instinctive apprehension no matter what the content may be.[24]

What sorts of actual experiences did Jung have so as to be capable of giving such a full explication? Clinically, he recognized over a long period of time the phenomenon in a few of his patients. In addition, in living with Pueblo Indians and with African natives, he observed that "primitive," or "uncivilized" people relied more on intuition than did "civilized" peoples. Furthermore, Jung extensively researched the nature of knowledge achieved through extrasensory perception. In a lecture addressed to physicians and psychologists, Jung said:

> I have tried to describe that function as well as I can, but perhaps it is not very good. I say that intuition is a sort of perception which does not go exactly by the senses, but it goes via the unconscious, and at that I leave it and say, "I don't know how it works." I do not know what is happening when a man knows something he definitely should not know. I do not know how he has come by it, but he has it all right and he can act on it. For instance, anticipatory dreams, telepathic phenomena, and all that kind of thing are intuitions. I have seen plenty of them, and I am convinced that they do exist. You can see these things also with primitives. You can see them everywhere if you pay attention to these perceptions that somehow work through subliminal data, such as sense-perceptions so feeble that our consciousness simply cannot take them in.[25]

The study of such phenomena as dream prophesy and telepathy is today called parapsychology. In the circles of modern scholarship, this area has been regarded as superstitious; it is, as it were, taboo as an academic research discipline. Even today, this cautious attitude is widespread. When people recently discussed parapsychological phenomena as part of the occultism boom in Japan, they were criticized as misleading the people in the street. If we can better study the function of intuition positivistically by examining parapsychological phenomena, however, the field can be recognized as a subject of objective scholarly investigation. Moreover, it would seem that there lies a possibility of discovering more about the true character of the human being.

Paranormal knowledge

In this section, we deal with a few examples of scholarly work related to parapsychology, and give some thought to future directions of research that might be relevant to our own topic. In his dream studies as well as his clinical experiences, Medard Boss examined many documented reports of clairvoyant, prophetic, and telepathic dreams. He recognized in these dreams, in this unconscious process, the activity of extrasensory perception as a way of participating in the world.[26] "Today, it has become unnecessary to deny *prima facie* the existence of telepathic phenomena." Numerous instances of extrasensory or parapsychological phenomena have been handed down from ancient times as descriptive reports, but because they were regarded as abnormal experiences, and because the experiencers themselves could not explain the phenomena, they were either believed half-heartedly or obfuscated through exaggeration. Thus, in the modern period, these phenomena have been regarded as belonging either to superstition or to psychopathological, abnormal psychology.

As mentioned earlier, from his youth Jung was convinced of the significance of these phenomena. In fact, his doctoral dissertation concerned occult phenomena in a young woman. Jung's autobiography informs us that he himself was endowed with extrasensory abilities and experienced various parapsychological events. In the schism with Freud, one reason was their disagreement over the existence of parapsychological phenomena.[27] (Freud was apparently interested in these phenomena in his later years, but he did not make his opinions public for fear of the response from scholarly circles.) At any rate, anyone dealing with parapsychological phenomena had to be prepared to take public criticism. Moreover, since research in this area had to rely on descriptive reports or speculative explanation, it was barely acknowledged by most scholars. Jung's unified view is found in *Interpretation of Nature and the Psyche* (written in collaboration with W. Pauli, a physicist), but his explanations remained speculative.[28]

It was J. B. Rhine, in the United States, who moved these studies out of their speculative and descriptive stage into experimental research.[29] He devised specific experimental apparatuses (such as cards with special symbols) and quantified his data according to statistical methods. His research was first made public in the 1930s. The report of the American Psychological Association recognized Rhine's methodology as unimpeachable from a scholarly viewpoint, but the general response from scholarly circles was severe and there were only a handful of supporters for parapsychology before World War II. There were even psychologists who preferred to ignore the phenomena even if they *did* exist. From the 1950s on, however, support increased. It was Rhine who called cognition unmediated by the senses "extra-sensory perception," or ESP. In addition, he performed experiments on the phenomenon called "psychokinesis" (PK), the apparent ability of concentrated thought to bring about physical effects on such laboratory paraphernalia as dice or, in recent years, electric current and elemental particles. Proof for the existence of ESP is today taken to be complete, bu some specialists still regard the evidence of PK as insufficient. Rhine's study was the first step in parapsychological research as an academic discipline.

The next question is: in what body-mind mechanism are such psychological functions generated? Rhine's study provides no clue; his point was simply that the existence of such phenomena cannot be denied from a statistical standpoint. Although Rhine recognized that this psychological ability is activated in the unconscious, he concluded that it is impossible to control this function. Since the 1960s new investigations have been conducted on these two problems: the mechanism of parapsychological phenomena and the possibility of its control. For example, there has been research in connection with the experimental methods of physiological psychology, hypnotism, and psychopathology. As issues have become increasingly complex, the experimental apparatus has become more elaborate and the researchers have included not only psychologists, but also physiologists, physicians, and physicists. Investigators in the United States, the Soviet Union, Europe, and India are actively pursuing this research.

In Japan, only a few researchers, such as MOTOYAMA Hiroshi, are involved. Motoyama maintains parapsychological phenomena are correlated with the autonomic nervous system. His theory arises from experiments with the viscero-cutaneous reflex and other mechanisms. Again, we will omit the technical details, as his research is understandable only to those knowledgeable in physiology, especially the measurement techniques of electrophysiology.[30]

To mention just one of his conclusions, though, he has found a correlation between greater activity of organs governed by the autonomic nervous system and high scores on ESP tests; subjects also display different patterns of such organ activity. Moreover, it is known that among people who have high ESP scores the capacity of their autonomic functions—the tense–lax amplitude between their sympathetic and parasympathetic nerves—is greater than that of the average person. To have this greater capacity would be regarded as a pathologically unstable condition in an ordinary person, but it is normal for people who can consciously control their parapsychological or *psi* capacity. (Incidentally, part of this research has been introduced to the world community through the UNESCO headquarters in Paris.)[31] The correlation between autonomic nerve functions and extrasensory phenomena might have been anticipated if the *psi* capacity is indeed related to the deep layer of the unconscious. This is an important step in experimenting with, and verifying, these phenomena through physiological measurement. Perhaps we are now able to obtain a clue to the objective difference between parapsychological and psychopathological phenomena, and we will be able to control such phenomena.

At any rate, it is a future task to achieve an accurate, academic evaluation of this research. Yet we must note that such issues have been considered an important part in traditional Eastern theories of the body-mind as a lived experience in personal meditative cultivation. In Yoga, it is considered experientially evident that parapsychological abilities arise in the process of meditation. This is usually referred to as *siddhi*. In the Chinese translation of Buddhist *sūtras*, it is transliterated as *hsi-ti* and translated as "fulfillment." It refers to the completion or results of cultivation. Since various spiritual and paranormal powers accompany the completion of personal cultivation, *siddhi* can also be translated as "spiritual ability" or "passage to the divine." (The term *ṛddhi* is mainly used in Buddhism in a similar sense.)[32] In short, in Eastern body-mind theories, these abilities are understood to be potential in every person, and if one investigates the deep region of the soul through meditative cultivation, these phenomena will always be experienced.

Jung considered parapsychological phenomena to be an intuition emerging from the deep region of unconsciousness. If this is right, is it not possible to investigate the secrets concealed in the true character of being human by taking parapsychological research as a clue? Consider the miracles in various ancient religions, admittedly reported with perhaps some exaggeration and superstition. Research into these events may present a means for objective, academic examination.

There is a modern intellectual tendency, even among some religious figures, to consider parapsychological phenomena and miracles to be mere superstition. Perhaps this is one reason why the secularized religions have lost their popular support. What truly moves people's minds is not speculative logic, whether sound or invalid, but the charismatic power radiating from within the personality. Various world religions bloomed by first taking root in a "superstitious" base of the people's "magic garden."

Obviously, issues such as the nature of faith and the perfection of human personality in accord with the divine are different in character from the investigation of these facts, but, unless we have an accurate assessment of the concrete aspects in the various religious experiences transmitted to us from ancient times, the ultimate essence of religion can never be clarified.

Author's Conclusion to the English Edition

Although this study is only tentative, I shall conclude with some thoughts about cooperative relationships between philosophy and science in the future. As represented by Newtonian physics, modern European scholarship began with the renovation of natural science. Furthermore, by using a methodology so successful in physics as a causal analysis for living phenomena, science gave birth to anatomy, physiology, biology, and so on. This movement also developed the system of modern medicine in which the structure and function of living organisms are separated from their mental modes. This mechanistic investigation was further applied to mental phenomena themselves. Modern orthodox psychology started with Wundt's psychophysics, analyzing how the subject learns and behaves in its environment. Thus, by objectifying the external world, the thrust of modern science has been to clarify the causal mechanisms determining the way beings exist.

In contrast, in the modern period, philosophy has been gradually diminished in its coverage, retreating in proportion to the development of science. Although Descartes was a physicist as well as a philosopher, Kant was not. Today, scientists have snatched away from philosophers the study of biological and psychological, not to mention physical, phenomena. The domain left to philosophy is reduced roughly to logic and problems in existential thought. In short, the history of modern scholarship in Europe is mainly marked by the constant development of science and the gradual retreat of philosophy.

We may be compelled today to inaugurate a new perspective transcending the difference in methodological attitudes between philosophy and science. Historically, it was only in the Age of Enlightenment in the eighteenth century that the methodologies of philosophy and science started to drift apart. Moreover, in light of Kant's critique of knowledge through reflectively examining the methodological presuppositions of the physical sciences, philosophy saw its position as higher than science. Kant insisted that philosophy is a methodological science superior to the other sciences, that it is "the science of all sciences." Kant's view is a secularized return to the European Christian tradition in which theology was regarded as "the queen of all sciences," which dominates all other sciences.

Accordingly, by deifying and absolutizing human reason, Hegel established a philosophy of the "absolute spirit." He attempted to subject natural, along with historical and cultural, phenomena to the dominance of philosophy. In spite of his failure, the Western philosophers' belief in the methodological superiority of philosophy over the sciences has survived. The neo-Kantian school attempted to place philosophy above all other scholarly activities by clarifying the methodological presuppositions, not only of the natural sciences, but also of the humanities and social sciences. Even though Husserl's phenomenology established a new method that goes beyond the limitations of Neo-Kantianism, his notion of science was basically inherited from the Kantian critique of knowledge. Husserl contrasted the "physicalistic objectivism" of modern science since Galileo with the "transcendental subjectivism" originating with Kant. He maintained that his own position was inherited from the latter tradition.[1] Together with this, Husserl shifted his perspective to the immediate experience of consciousness in the everyday life-world, where he discovered the ultimate foundation on which phenomenology could stand. By laying his foundation in the everyday life-world, he argued that the objectivistic attitude of the empirical sciences—the positive sciences' attitude of objectification in grasping the human, subjective experience— took a course that isolated analysis from the human, subjective life.

In his scholarly distinction between the ontical and the ontological dimensions, Heidegger argued for the methodological superiority of philosophy over science. This attitude leads in the same direction as Husserl. Merleau-Ponty also insisted on the superiority of philosophy over science. He declared that the objectivistic attitude of the empirical sciences is incompatible with the attitude of phenomenological investigation, although, admittedly, he did broadly incorporate the positivistic results of Gestalt psychology and physiological psychology.

Wittgenstein, whose concerns were completely different from those of phenomenology, also reached a similar conclusion regarding the relationship between philosophy and science. He says, "Philosophy is not one of the natural sciences. The word, 'philosophy,' must mean something whose place is above or below the natural sciences, not beside them."[2] He says this is so because the causal relationships presupposed by the natural sciences are a "superstition"; the belief that the sun will rise tomorrow, for example, is only a hypothesis. Wittgenstein says that today's world view regards natural laws in the way God and fate were once viewed, that is, as something that should not be defied. People today think that is all there is to it.[3]

In the present situation, philosophy and science are separate from, in opposition to, and critical of, each other. The psychological anxiety of contemporary people is rooted in this gap between the philosophical and scientific world views. Such emphasis on the differences in methodological attitudes between philosophy and science seems to be the result of European scholarship in the modern period. (Figure 9 depicts the issue.)

The starting point for the objectivistic attitude of modern science is established by the research methods of physics. Modern medicine and biology extend this attitude from the study of physical to living phenomena. Moreover, orthodox psychology, which began with behaviorism, attempts to grasp mental phenomena by objectifying and quantifying the mechanisms regulating mental phenomena. Such a scientific method assumes that physical phenomena exist at the foundation of all phenomena, that the life-phenomena rests on that physical foundation. In addition, we are led to believe that mental phenomena exist only thanks to a biological foundation. An ascension (at the left of Figure 9), from the natural world, through the biological world, to the mental world, indicates the world view presupposed by scientific research methods.

By that analysis, a discontinuity is found at the boundary between life-phenomena and mental phenomena (at A and B in Figure 9). What

the diagram 9

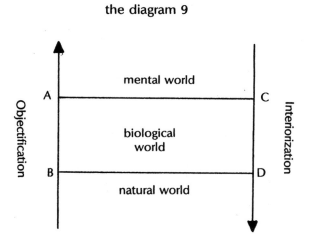

dominates physical phenomena is the mechanistic causal pattern. (We can interpret "probable contingency" to be an extension of causality.) Living phenomena, however, have a teleological character that contradicts mechanistic causality. Also, the mechanisms dominating living phenomena in the biological world is found in both animals and humans, but human beings are endowed with language and other higher intellectual mental faculties that animals do not possess.

Philosophers have noted these discontinuities and argued that the objectivistic attitude of modern science is limited. In other words, they have thought that insofar as we accept the possibility of the teleological world view and of the existence of human reason, the attitude of the prevailing scientism and objectivism has to be denied. The attempt to extend philosophical speculation by pointing out the limitations of science, however, is evidence that philosophy is incapable of shaking itself free from the European tradition in which philosophy and science are separated from and opposed to each other. For example, today's biophysics and genetics have eliminated, in principle, the barrier (point A on Figure 9) separating physical from living phenomena. Moreover, the study of the conditioned reflex interprets the sense stimulus given to living organisms as the primary sign system. Stimulus by means of language is considered, therefore, a secondary sign system.

But research has shown that the mechanism of the conditioned reflex can also be formed by language. Although it is questionable whether or not the study of the conditioned reflex has eliminated the barrier separating living phenomena from mental phenomena (point B), we must at least acknowledge that such an attempt is reasonable. Insofar as we do not restrict ourselves to the standpoint of traditional philosophy, we do not have any reason to oppose such an attempt.

Contemporary philosophy has confined itself to logic and existential issues, areas free from the influence of the positivistic research of science. Philosophy has turned its back on the development of science. Now we must reverse the path that modern philosophy has taken since Descartes. Taking self-consciousness for its ground, modern philosophy has investigated the meaning of the subject's existence with respect to experiencing the world. But contrary to the path of modern philosophy, we must move into the interiority of self-consciousness, stepping into the region concealed at its base. This fundamental direction is found in interiorization, reversing the causal direction of positivistic science indicated by the descending arrow on the right of Figure 9).

In Part I, we relied on Jung's depth psychology to show that the Eastern philosophical tradition has developed parallels to clinical psychological practice. Depth psychology took the first step toward enabling a new cooperative relationship between philosophy and science. Although Freud always approached academic philosophy with cold indifference, he did not reject all philosophy. In fact, for him, psychoanalysis was a path leading to true philosophy. In two letters addressed to Wilhelm Fliess in 1896, Freud wrote:

> Far beyond these considerations [on psychopathology] lurks my ideal and problem child, *metapsychology*.
>   I see that you are reaching, by the circuitous path of medicine, your first ideal, that of understanding human beings as a physiologist, just as I cherish the hope of arriving, by the same route, at my original goal of *philosophy*. For that was my earliest aim, when I did not know what I was in the world for.[4]

For Freud, true philosophy should be metapsychology. Following Jones's analysis, since psychoanalysis deeply illuminates human nature from a completely new angle, it makes a decisive contribution to all studies pertaining to human nature: anthropology, mythology, education, arts, marriage, law, religion, and social science, for example. Thus, Freud welcomed the positivistic research of nonmedical fields so that this research could develop a closer relationship with psychoanalysis. If psychoanalysis becomes part of medical psychiatry, such a great opportunity will be lost. In short, the path blazed by psychoanalysis, Freud believed, should guide and direct all the empirical sciences having a bearing on human nature and on the policies of social practice. In this sense, psychoanalysis would methodologically dominate all the sciences, standing above them as philosophy did in the past. According to Freud, academic philosophy in the contemporary period is simply a formless area that can no longer play a leading role.

Jung's attitude toward philosophy is much clearer. As mentioned in Part I, he accepted the fact that academic philosophy is recognized as "philosophy" in the scholarly world, but he maintained that psychotherapy is a *new* philosophy. He says that depth psychology is essentially a natural science studying the laws of psychic energy. Unlike the existing natural sciences, however, it requires collaboration with philosophy, literature, and history. As Freud anticipated, depth psychology also has the character of philosophy in that it can have a wide scholarly influence on religion, the arts, humanities, and the social sciences.

Jung adopted this view at the same time he discovered in it elements commensurate with the traditional character of Eastern philosophy. As noted in Part I, he contrasted Eastern and Western philosophy, saying that there has always been a tendency in the Western traditions to separate metaphysics from psychology, whereas the Eastern traditions have always taken them to be inseparable. Psychology, or depth psychology in its broader sense, is various empirical studies pertaining to human nature. Insofar as depth psychology examines human nature from a new angle, it may have a broad scholarly influence on the research of the empirical sciences related to the study of human nature. Consequently, Jung's remark about this relationship between metaphysics and psychology, if generalized, can also state the relationship between philosophy and science. That is, in the Western tradition philosophy and science tend to be opposed to each other. In contrast, in Eastern thought the two have always been inseparable. Given this background, the Eastern traditions' theories of the body assume a new significance in our own period.

The new perspective pioneered by depth psychology may bring about closer cooperation between philosophy and science. Philosophy should not, as existing academic philosophy has done, criticize negatively the objectivism of empirical sciences, or the inhuman aspects of technical society. On the contrary, its role lies in questioning the meaning of human experience in the *opposite direction* than that taken by the scientific enterprise, while incorporating gradually within it the positivistic findings acquired by empirical science. Depth psychology is positioned between the mental and the biological world (in Figure 9, at point C). It delves into the region of the unconscious at the base of human self-consciousness, in cooperation with physiology. It attempts to clarify the mechanism of the correlative relationship between the mind and the body established through the emotions in that deeper region. This is the present situation in psychosomatic medicine: starting from the mental phenomena, the relationship between the mental and the biological will be understood by delving into the interior of mental phenomena. If we continue to investigate this region further, we will naturally break through (from within) the barrier separating living from physical phenomena (point D).

The development of parapsychology mentioned at the end of Part III may be regarded as a positive challenge for this enterprise. Such paranormal phenomena as clairvoyance, telepathy, and psychokinesis indicate that a psychological experience within the subject is not simply a subjective hallucinatory experience, but that there can be some correspondence between subjective experience and physical phenomena in the external world. Although we can hardly say that a scholarly evaluation of parapsychology has been established, we can assert that the existence of paranormal phenomena itself is proven by Rhine's methods of experimental control and quantification. In this connection, both Freud and Jung knew that the path opened by depth psychology leads to the paranormal. There is, though, a difference in their attitude. Freud ap-

proached this issue with caution and skepticism, whereas Jung positively
supported parapsychology.

A further development of parapsychology will probably be made in
cooperation with medical psychology. The psychosomatic research into
yoga, examples of which were mentioned in Part III, indicates there is a
definite correlation between the development of the autonomic nervous
functions in *yoga* and paranormal experiences. In short, starting with the
subject's inner experience and investigating the mechanism of the deep
region at the base of self-consciousness, we will remove the barrier
separating mental phenomena from living (biological) phenomena as
well as the barrier separating living from nonliving phenomena. This is
the reverse of the tendency in modern science. The meanings of human
rationality and the teleological world view will be understood anew
through investigation of the human's inner world.

As long as contemporary phenomenology and existentialism attempt to clarify the meaning of life in view of the human subject's inner
experience, they follow the same path as depth psychology. Still, they do
not shake themselves free of the modern European view of scholarship,
emphasizing the methodological differences between philosophy and
science. Since Husserl's phenomenology arose from the analysis of self-
consciousness's stream of the experienced, it does not have the creden-
tials to analyze unconscious phenomena.

Jung says, "In my world view, there is a vast outer region as well as a
vast inner region, and man stands in the middle of the two."[5] Human
consciousness is, as it were, a tangential point where two vast spheres of
the outer and the inner worlds meet. Consciousness is usually capable of
observing the outer world, but the inner world is concealed in darkness.
The analysis of dreams and hallucinations illumines this dark region and
discovers the meaning of phenomena lost in the inner world.

Here we probably need a new philosophy that may be called a
"phenomenology of the inner world" or a "phenomenology of the deep
layer of consciousness." It will not be a phenomenology in the sense of
discovering the apodicticity of self-consciousness, but it will discover the
true meaning of human experience in the modality of the authentic self
concealed in the depth of the unconsciousness. The tradition of Eastern
philosophy, as represented by Buddhism, leads us to this new sense of
phenomenology, which should mean our passage into a new kind of
metaphysics.

Part I contrasted Western philosophy with Eastern philosophy in
terms of "metaphysics" and "metapsychics." As represented by Aristotle's philosophy, metaphysics assumes an objectivistic attitude in ascending gradually from physical to human being, while objectively ob-

serving outer nature. It further postulates a transcendent being beyond the human dimension. In contrast, Eastern philosophy can be called "metapsychics" because it starts with a reflective attitude toward the human soul (psyche), the inner nature. It seeks a transcendent region beyond the inner psyche. As indicated by the previous diagram, this path is the reverse of that of modern science, and it advances through one's inner experience toward nature, that which forms the fundamental delimitation of possibilities for human being.

Unlike the way of modern science, this route is open to everyone. So far, only a few fortunate people, as well as those who have suffered unfortunate destiny, have been aware of the existence of this closed, mysterious path lurking at the base of the human soul. Moreover, if, unlike modern philosophy, this route can be opened up in cooperation with science, it will allow us to approach the mystery of nature. From there, a new sense of metaphysics, different from the traditional, will emerge; that is, it will be a metaphysics transcending the interiority of the mind toward nature as the fundamental limit for human beings. Here, metaphysics and metapsychics, in the new senses of the terms, become identical. This is probably the path to a new philosophy, one that would reconcile religion and science.

Notes

Author's Introduction to the English Edition

1   WATSUJI Tetsurō, *Fūdo: ningengakuteki na kōsatsu* (Tokyo: Iwanami Shoten, 1935). English translation: *Climate and Culture: A Philosophical Study,* trans. J. Bownas (Tokyo: Hokuseidō Press, for UNESCO Japan, 1971).
2   Gino K. Piōvesana, "Watsuji Tetsurō" in Paul Edwards, ed., *The Encyclopedia of Philosophy* (New York: Collier MacMillan Publishers, 1967), vol. 8, p. 280.
3   WATSUJI Tetsurō, *Watsuji Tetsurō zenshū* [The complete works of WATSUJI Tetsurō] (Tokyo: Iwanami shoten, 2nd ed., 1978), vol. 10, pp. 336ff.

Chapter 1: WATSUJI Tetsurō's View of the Body

1   DOI Takeo, *Amae no kōzō* [Anatomy of dependence] (Tokyo: Kōbundō, 1967); KIMURA Bin, *Hito to hito to no aida: seishin-byōrigakuteki Nihonron* [Between person and person: a psychopathological theory of Japan] (Tokyo: Kōbundō, 1972); SAKABE Megumi, *Kamen no kaishakugaku* [Hermeneutics of masks] (Tokyo: Tokyo University Press, 1976); especially Sakabe's essay, "*Araware to copula*" ["Appearance and the copula"]. References to Watsuji are found in the last two books.
2   WATSUJI Tetsurō, *Watsuji Tetsurō Zenshū* [The complete works of WATSUJI Tetsurō] (Tokyo: Iwanami shoten, 2nd ed. 1978), vol. 8, pp. 1–2.
3   Ibid., p. 11.
4   Saint Augustine, *On the Trinity,* trans. NAKAZAWA Hiroki (Tokyo: Tokyo University Press, 1975): see pp. 242ff and p. 510n regarding the relationship between love (*amor*) and desire (*cupiditas*); also see pp. 292ff. regarding the relationships among memory (*memoria*), intelligence (*intelligentia*), and will (*voluntas*). A detailed explanation of the transition of these functions from exteriority to interiority is found in ch. 14. Regarding the theory of time in *Confessions,* see Augustine, *Confessions,* trans. YAMADA Akira, *Sekai no meicho,* vol.

14 (Tokyo: Chūō kōronsha, 1968). For a technical treatment of this subject, see TAKAHASHI Wataru, "Sei augasuchinusu no sanmi-ittairon niokeru Imago Dei" ["Imago Dei in St. Augustine's theory of the Trinity"] in *Sei augasuchinsu kenkyū* [Study of St. Augustine] (Tokyo: Sōbunsha, for Sophia University, 1955).

5 Immanuel Kant, *Kritik der reinen Vernunft,* B.135.
6 Watsuji, *Zenshū,* vol. 3, pp. 242, 257.
7 Ibid., vol. 10, pp. 65–70.

Chapter 2: NISHIDA Kitarō's View of the Body

1 NISHIDA Kitarō, *Nishida Kitarō Zenshū* [Complete works of NISHIDA Kitarō] (Tokyo: Iwanami shoten, 3rd ed., 1979), vol. 8, p. 277.
2 Ibid., p. 326.
3 Ibid., p. 328.
4 M. Merleau-Ponty, *Me to seishin* [*L'oeil et l'esprit,* Gallimard, Paris, 1953], trans. TAKIURA Shizuo and KIDA Gen (Tokyo: Misuzu shobō, 1966), pp. 257ff.
5 Nishida, *Zenshū.* p. 283.
6 Martin Heidegger, *Sein und Zeit,* (Tübingen: Niemayer, 1953) S. 134.
7 Nishida, *Zenshū,* vol. 4, p. 245.
8 NISHIDA Kitarō, *Zen no kenkyū* [Study of Good] (Tokyo: Iwanami bunkō, 1950), p. 69.
9 KŌSAKA Masaaki, *Nishida tetsugaku* [Nishida Philosophy], in *KŌSAKA Masaaki chosaku shū* [Works of KOSAKA Masaaki] (Tokyo: Risōsha, 1965), vol. 8, pp. 108ff.
10 Nishida, *Zenshū,* vol. 5, p. 8.
11 Ibid., vol. 4, p. 234.
12 Nishida, *Zen no kenkyū,* p. 15, n. 8.
13 Ibid., p. 64.
14 Ibid., p. 18.
15 Ibid., p. 47.
16 Immanuel Kant, *Kritik der reinen Vernunft,* B. 74ff.
17 Nishida, *Zen no kenkyū,* pp. 47–48.
18 Nishida, *Zenshū,* vol. 8, pp. 324–25.

Chapter 3: Method and Attitude in Studying Eastern Thought

1 KAWADA Kumatarō, "Taishō shōwa niokeru shōpenhauā" [Schopenhauer in the Taishō (1912–26) and Shōwa (1926–   ) periods], *Jitsuzonshūgi* [Existentialism], vol. 76, June 1976 (Tokyo: Ibunsha); WATSUJI Tetsurō, *Genshi bukkyō no jissentetsugaku* [Practical philosophy of early Buddhism] in vol. 5 of his *Zenshū.*

2   C. G. Jung, *Zur Psychologie westlicher und östlicher Religion* in *Gessamelte Werke,* (hereafter *Werke*), (Zurich: Rascher, 1973), Bd. 11. and *Psychology and Religion: East and West,* in *Collected Works* (hereafter *CW*), (Princeton, N.J.: Princeton University Press, 2nd ed., 1967), vol. 11.

3   Erich Fromm, *Psychoanalysis and Religion* (New Haven: Yale University Press, 1950); "Psychoanalysis and Zen Buddhism," in Erich Fromm et al., *Zen Buddhism and Psychoanalysis* (N.Y.: Harper & Row, 1960).

4   Medard Boss, *Indianfahrt eines Psychiaters* (Pfüllingen: Gunther Neske, 1959). Medard Boss is a psychopathologist influenced by Heidegger and Binswanger, and is a follower of "Dasein Analysis." He is also influenced by Freud. See his *Psychoanalyse und Daseinsanalytik* (Bern: Mans Hüber, 1957).

5   See Rudolf Otto, *Mysticism East and West* (N.Y.: Living Age Books, 2nd ed., 1958). Originally published in German in 1929, this book compares Śankara and Eckhart. Otto also studied Zen Buddhism in cooperation with OKAZAMA Shūei.

6   We can note, for instance, Karl Jaspers' criticism of Freud; a detailed introduction is given by ODA Yukio, "Yasupāsu no seishin bunseki hihan" [Jaspers' criticism of psychoanalysis], *Jitsuzon shūgi,* vol. 45, Oct. 1968 (Tokyo: Ibunsha).

7   Jung, "Psychotherapy and a Philosophy of Life," in *CW,* vol. 16, p. 7.

8   Jung, *Psychological Commentary on the Tibetan Book of the Great Liberation,* in *CW,* vol. 11, pp. 475ff.; and *Commentary on the Secret of the Golden Flower,* in *Collected Works,* vol. 13, pp. 50ff.

9   YUASA Yasuo, *Yungu to kiristo-kyō* [Jung and Christianity] (Kyoto: Jimbun shoin, 1978), pp. 268ff. Also, YUASA Yasuo, *Yungu to yōroppa seishin* [Jung and the European spirit] (Kyoto: Jimbun shoin, 1979), pp. 227ff.

Chapter 4: What Is Cultivation?

1   NAKAMURA Hajime, *Bukkyōgo daijiten* [Dictionary of Buddhist terms] (Tokyo: Tōkyō shoseki, 1975), vol. 2, p. 1316.

2   WATSUJI, *Genshi bukkyō no jissentetsugaku, Zenshū,* vol. 5, p. 167.

3   Max Weber, *Gesammelte Aufsätze zur Religionssoziologie* (Tübingen: J. C. B. Mohr, 1971), Bd. 1, S. 260.

4   HIRAKAWA Akira, *Genshi bukkyō no kenkyū* [Study of early Buddhism] (Tokyo: Shunjūsha, 1964), p. 33.

5   Max Weber, Bd. 2, S. 142.

6   *Taishō shinshū daizōkyō* [The Tripitaka in Chinese], 2nd ed. TAKAKUSU J. and WATANABE K. rev. and ed. (Tokyo: Daizō shuppan, 1936), vol. 25, pp. 158ff.; (1934), vol. 23, p. 179.

7   Max Weber, Bd. 1, Ss. 311, 321.

8   KAMATA Shigeo, "Chūgoku Bukkyō no seiritsu" [Establishment of Chinese Buddhism] in *Chūgoku bunka sōsho* (Tokyo: Taishūkan, 1967), vol. 6 (Religion), pp. 76ff.

9 INOUE Mitsusada, *Nihon kodai no bukkyō to kokka* [The state and Buddhism in ancient Japan] (Tokyo: Iwanami shoten, 1971), pp. 33ff.

10 KIMURA Kiyotaka, "Bukkyō no oyako rinri to kō" [Filial devotion and the parent-child ethic in Buddhism], *Rinrigaku Nenpō* [Annals of Ethics], vol. 18 (Tokyo: Ibunsha, 1969).

11 SHIMADA Kenji, *Chūgoku ni okeru kindai shii no zasetsu* [The breakdown of modern thinking in China] (Tokyo: Chikuma shobō, 1970), pp. 39, 91ff.

12 Hirakawa quotes the *Ta-chih-tu-lun* [Great perfection of wisdom treatise, T. 1509], *Taishō*, vol. 25, p. 155:

> Some do not receive the precepts under a teacher's guidance, but live the vows personally on their own by saying, "Starting right now, I will not kill. . . . "

Here we find a method for taking on the self-vow precepts.

13 "*Upāsaka*" signifies the male secular laity in Buddhism. For the significance of the self-vow precepts before Saichō, see ISHIDA Mizumaro's *Nihon ni okeru kairitsu no kenkyū* [Study of *kairitsu* in Japan] (Tokyo: Zaika bukkyō kyōkai), pp. 32 ff.

14 Saichō, *Kenkairon* [Treatise on *śīla*] in *Nihon shisō taikei* [Outline of Japanese thought], vol. 4 (Saichō) (Tokyo: Iwanami shoten, 1974), pp. 86ff.

15 Ibid., p. 199.

Chapter 5: Theories of Artistry

1 *Karonshū Nōgakuronshū* [Theories of waka and nō drama] in *Nihon koten bungaku taikei* [Outline of Japanese literary classics], vol. 65 (Tokyo: Iwanami shoten, 1961), p. 137.

2 Ibid., p. 129.

3 Ibid., pp. 131–32.

4 *Shasekishū* [The Sand and Pebbles Collection] in *Nihon koten bungaku taikei,* vol. 85 (Tokyo: Iwanami shoten, 1966), pp. 222ff.

5 *Rengaronshu Haironshu* [Theories of renga and haiku] in *Nihon koten bungaku taikei,* vol. 66 (Tokyo: Iwanami shoten, 1961), pp. 182–83.

6 Ibid., p. 203.

7 *Zeami Zenchiku* in *Nihon shisō taikei*, vol. 24 (Tokyo: Iwanami shoten, 1974), pp. 36–37.

8 Ibid., p. 165. [From *Yuraku shūdō fūken*]

9 Ibid., p. 167.

Chapter 6: Dōgen

1 *Sōtōshū seiten* [Sacred books of the Sōtō sect] in *Kokuyaku daizōkyo* (Tokyo: Tōhō shoin, 1929), p. 13.

2 Ibid., p. 13.
3 *Dōgen* I, in *Nihon shisō taikei,* vol. 12 (Tokyo: Iwanami shoten, 1970), p. 35.
4 TAMAKI Kōshirō, trans. *Dōgen* in *Nihon no meicho,* vol. 7 (Tokyo: Chuō kōronsha, 1974), p. 121.
5 The term, "molting of body-mind" (*shinshin datsuraku*) is supposed to be suggested by the phrase "molting of the mind's dust" (*shinjin datsuraku*) found in Ju-ching's *Analects.* Cf. TAKASAKI Jikidō and UMEHARA Takeshi, *Kobutsu no manebi: Dōgen* [Imitation of ancient Buddhas] in *Bukkyō no shisō,* vol. 11 (Tokyo: Kadokawa shoten, 1969), pp. 49ff.
6 Tamaki, p. 332.
7 *Dōgen* I, vol. 12, p. 125.

Chapter 7: Kūkai

1 SAWA Ryūken, *Kūkai no kiseki* [Kūkai's trail] (Tokyo: Mainichi shinbunsha, 1973), pp. 170, 181ff.
2 FUKUDA, Gyōei, *Tendaigaku Gairon* [Outline of the study of Tendai Buddhism] (Tokyo: Sensei dō, 1954), pp. 95ff.
3 See the introductory essay in ARAMAKI Noritoshi, trans., *Jūchikyō* [Daśabhumika sūtra], in *Daijō butten* [Mahayana sūtras] (Tokyo: Chuō kōronsha, 1974), vol. 8.
4 TAMAKI Koshirō, *Nihon bukkyō shisōron* [Japanese Buddhist thought] (Kyoto: Heirakuji shoten, 1974), vol. 1, pp. 4, 14.
5 MATSUNAGA Yūkei, *Mikkyō no sōshōsha* [Inheritors of esoteric Buddhism] (Tokyo: Hyōronsha, 1973), p. 85.
6 Kūkai, *Seireishū* [Essays and letters of Kūkai] in KATSUMATA Shukyō, ed., *Kōbō daishi chosaku zenshū* [Works of Kōbō Daishi] (hereafter *Chosaku zenshū*) (Tokyo: Sankibō busshōrin, 1968–70), vol. 3, pp. 98–100.
7 SHIBA Ryōtarō, *Kūkai no fūkei* [Kūkai's landscape] (Tokyo: Chuō kōronsha, 1975), vol. 1, p. 66.
8 See the illustration of the arrangement of the halls of Mt. Kōya in Sawa, p. 175.
9 Kūkai, *Jūjūshinron* [Ten stages of mind] in *Nihon shisō taikei,* vol. 5: *Kūkai* (Tokyo: Iwanami shoten, 1975), p. 15.
10 Kūkai, *Sangō shiiki* [Indications of the goals of the three teachings] in *Chosaku zenshū,* vol. 3, p. 56.
11 Kūkai, *Goshōrai mokuroku* [Memorial presenting a list of newly imported *sūtras* and other items] in *Chosaku zenshū,* vol. 2, p. 30.
12 Plato, *Politeia,* 621. YAMAMOTO Mitsuo, trans., *Sekai no daishisō: Puraton* (Tokyo: Kawade shobō, 1965), vol. 10, p. 344. According to the note in NAGAZAWA Nobuhisa, trans., *Puraton: "Kokka"* (Tokyo: Tōkai University Press, 1970–1974), vol. 3, p. 1444, the phrase, "the plain of oblivion" (τὸ τηζ Ληθηζ πεδιον) is an antonym for "the plain of Truth" (πεδ ον Αληθειαζ); cf. *Phaedrus* 248b.

13 *SAWA* Ryūken, *Mikkyō bijitsuron* [Art of esoteric Buddhism] (Kyoto: Benri do, 1960), p. 71.

14 Ibid., p. 38.

15 YUASA Yasuo, *Kamigami no tanjō* [Birth of the *kami*] (Tokyo: Ibunsha, 1972), pp. 217ff.

16 Jung, *Psychologie und Alchemie,* in *Werke,* Bd. 12, S. 118 *usw.; Psychology and Alchemy,* in *CW,* vol. 12, pp. 92f; IKEDA Kōichi and KAMADA Michio, trans., *Shinrigaku to renkinjutsu* (Kyoto: Jimbun shoin, 1976), pp. 138ff.

17 MIYASAKI Yushō and UMEHARA Takeshi, *Seimei no umi: Kūkai* [Oceanic life: Kūkai], in *Bukkyō no shisō* [Buddhist thought], vol. 9 (Tokyo: Kadokawa shoten, 1968), pp. 79ff. For a detailed explanation of mandala, see chap. 3 of KANAOKA Shūyū, *Mikkyō no tetsugaku* [Philosophy of esoteric Buddhism] (Kyoto: Heirakuji shoten, 1973).

18 IYANAGA Nobumi, *Nihon mikkyō no mandala ni tsuite* [Mandala of Japanese esoteric Buddhism], vol. 2 [Osaka: Tōyō shisō kenkyūkai, 1977]. This explanation follows the interpretation of Professor Stan, of the College de France, Paris.

19 Jung, *Werke,* Bd. 12, S. 152; *CW,* vol. 12, p. 121; *Shinrigaku,* p. 174.

20 AKIYAMA, Satoko, *Seinaru jigen* [The sacred dimension] (Tokyo: Shisakusha, 1976), p. 56.

21 Kūkai, *Gobu darani mondō gesan shūhiron* [The secret poems of the dialogue on the Five Dhāraṇīs] in *Chosaku zenshū,* vol. 2, p. 552.

22 Arthur Avalon [Sir John Woodruff], *The Serpent Power,* 6th ed. (London and Madras: Ganesh and Co., 1958).

23 See YUASA Yasuo, trans., "Seiteki enerugi no henkan to shōka" ["Transmutation and sublimation of sexual energies"] by Robert Assagioli, in *Shūkyō shinri kenkyū,* vol. 7 (Tokyo: Institute for Religious Psychology, 1963).

24 Kūkai, *Himitsumandara kyōhōfuden* [Origin and history of the secret mandala teachings] in *Chosaku zenshū,* vol. 2, p. 77, p. 89.

25 Kūkai, *Goshōrai mokuroku,* in *Chosaku zenshū,* vol. 2, p. 31.

26 Kūkai, "Kanshouenshu ōhōsha zōhōmon," vol. 9 of *Seireishū* [Essays and Letters of Kūkai] in *Chosaku zenshū,* vol. 3, p. 390.

27 Kūkai, *Sokushinjōbutsugi* [Meaning of becoming a Buddha in this very body] in *Chosaku zenshū,* vol. 1, p. 44.

28 Kūkai, *Nenji shingonrikan keihakumon* [For the cultivation of Shingon meditation] in *Chosaku zenshū,* vol. 2, p. 519.

29 Kūkai, *Sokushinjōbutsugi,* p. 52.

30 Ibid., p. 55.

31 Kūkai, *Dainichikyō kaidai* [Introduction to the Mahāvairocana Sūtra] in *Chosaku zenshū,* vol. 2, p. 190.

32 Kūkai, *Hizōhōyaku* [Jeweled key to the secret treasury] in *Chosaku zenshū,* vol. 1, p. 167.

33 Kūkai, "Shodai-ji dasshin mon" [Prayers for the dead at Shōdai Temple], vol. 8 of *Seireishū* in *Chosaku zenshū,* vol. 3, p. 328.

34 KATSUMATA Shunkyō, *Mikkyō no nihonteki tenkai* [Japanese development of tantric Buddhism] (Tokyo: Shunjūsha, 1977), pp. 151, 162.

35 *Dōgen I,* in *Nihon shisō taikei,* vol. 12 (Tokyo: Iwanami shoten, 1970), p. 11.
36 According to ETŌ Sokuō, *Shōbōgenzō josetsu* [Preface to *Shōbōgenzō*] (Tokyo: Iwanami shoten, 1968), p. 67, this idea in Dōgen is influenced by Esoteric Buddhism.
37 Kūkai, *Unji gi* [Meaning of the letter *hūṃ*] in *Chosaku zenshū,* vol. 1, p. 99.
38 Kūkai, *Sokushinjōbutsugi,* pp. 55f.

Chapter 8: Contemporary Philosophical Mind-Body Theories

1 Henry Bergson, *Matière et mémoire,* 92nd ed. (Paris: Presses Universitaires de France, 1968), p. 169. In addition, Bergson frequently uses such expressions as *"systèmes sensori-moteurs"* and *"processus sensori-moteurs".*
2 Bergson, pp. 145–146.
3 Ibid., p. 147.
4 Ibid., pp. 121, 135, etc.
5 Ibid., pp. 99–107.
6 Ibid., p. 101.
7 Regarding this point, see NITTA Yoshihiro, *Genshōgaku towa nanika* [What is phenomenology?] (Tokyo: Kinokuniya, 1968), pp. 63ff.
8 Maurice Merleau-Ponty, *Phénoménologie de la perception* (Paris: Librairie Gallimard, 1945), p. 93 n2.
9 Ibid., p. 102.
10 Ibid., p. 114.
11 TAKEUCHI Yoshirō and OKONOGI Keigo, trans., *Chikaku no Genshōgaku* [*Phenomenology of Perception*], (Tokyo: Misuzu shobō, 1967), vol. 1, p. 340n. Regarding Head's "intrinsic receptive perception", see Hirai et al., trans., *Seirishinrigaku nyūmon* (Tokyo: Seishin shobō, 1973), p. 174. This is a translation of Robert L. Isaacson et al., *A Primer of Physiological Psychology* (N.Y.: Harper & Row, 1971).
12 Merleau-Ponty, p. 158.
13 Bergson, p. 11.
14 See TOKIZANE Toshihiko, ed., *Nō no seirigaku* [Physiology of the brain], 8th ed. (Tokyo: Asakura shoten, 1971), p. 168.
15 TAKIURA Shizuo and KIDA Gen, trans., *Me to seishin* [*L'Oeil et l'esprit,* Paris, Gallimard, 1953] by Maurice Merleau-Ponty (Tokyo: Misuzu shobō, 1966), p. 257.
16 Ibid., p. 259.
17 Merleau-Ponty, *Phénoménologie,* p. 281.
18 Ibid., p. 114.
19 Ibid., p. 142.
20 Ibid., pp. 119ff.
21 Ibid., p. 132. ("*Zeigen*" on p. 132 is assumed to be a mistake for "*Greifen*")
22 Ibid., pp. 182ff.

23 See NISHIMARU Yomo and TAKAHASHI Yoshio, trans., *Igakuteki shinrigaku* [*Medizinische Psychologie,* Stuttgart, Georg Thieme, 1950] by Ernst Kretschmer (Tokyo: Misuzu shobō, 1955), vol. 1, p. 66.

24 HIRAI Keishi and TAKEUCHI Yoshirō, trans., *Tetsugaku rombonshū* [Philosophical essays] by Jean-Paul Sartre, (Kyoto: Jimbunshoin, 1968), pp. 303ff.

25 IKEMI Yūjirō, ed., *Seishin shintai igaku no riron to jisai: sōronhen* [Theory and practice of psychosomatic medicine: general introduction] (Tokyo: Igaku shoin, 1971), p. 110.

26 Hirai, *Seirishinrigaku nyūmon,* pp. 274ff.

27 See MASUDA Keizaburo, trans., *Shūkyōteki keiken no shosō* [*Varieties of Religious Experience*] by William James (Tokyo: Nihon kyobunsha, 1962), chap. 1.

Chapter 9: Dual Structure of the Mind-Body Relationship

1 The limbic system of the cerebrum is divided into two different parts: the archi-cortex and the paleo-cortex. They are both often simply called the "old cortex," since their physiological functions are not fully known.

2 Kyōto Daigaku Soviet Igaku Kenkyū Kai, trans., *Daino hishitsu to naizō kikan* [Cerebral cortex and internal organs] by K. M. Bykov, (Kyoto: Eitokusha, 1955), pp. 381ff.

3 Sensory impulses, including the sensations of the internal organs, go through the sensory nerve's pathway through the outer side of brain stem and reach into the neocortex, causing sensation there. Also, this sensory nerve has some connections with the brain stem, through which it sends stimuli into the reticular system there. New kinds of impulses are caused in this way and sent into the cortex in some diffuse form via the thalamus. This impulse, however, does not cause epicritic sensation, but only vivifies the activity of cortex, as discovered by Magoun. Tokizane discovered that Magoun's vivifying system has to do with the sensations vivifying the neocortex and that there exists another vivifying system of the hypothalamus that vivifies the limbic system. This impulse is sent from receptors of protopathic sensation. Cf. Ikemi, pp. 116ff.

4 This centripetal impulse, coming from the internal organs' nerves, reaches only to the thalamus through the spinal code. See Tokizane, p. 267.

5 Ikemi, p. 114.

6 Concerning Selyé's discovery and its significance, see OMODAKA Hisataka, *Igaku gairon* [Outline of medicine] (Tokyo: Seishin shobō, 1960), vol. 3, pp. 91ff.

7 Bykov, a disciple of Pavlov, demonstrated this. (See note 2, Chapter 9, above)

8 Bykov, p. 96.

9 Ikemi, ed., trans. *Jiritsu kunren hō* [*Autogenic Therapy,* N.Y.: Grune & Stratton, Inc., 1969] ed. W. Luthe, 6 vols. (Tokyo: Seishin shobō, 1971). Concerning the relation with Yoga, see Jung, *Yoga and the West,* in *CW,* vol. 11.

10 New clinical areas called Neuro-internist or Psychotherapeutic Internist Departments have recently been organized in many hospitals in Japan. Of course, this is because of the increase in psychogenic diseases, like imbalances in the autonomic nervous system, as well as psychosomatic diseases. The previously mentioned development of psychosomatic medicine is important here as the theoretical background for such new medical areas.

11 "There are no diseases; there are only sick people," a phrase by Alan Gregg, is the fundamental idea of psychosomatic medicine.

12 NODA Matao, ed., *Descartes* in *Sekai no meicho* (Tokyo: Chuō kōronsha, 1967), pp. 461ff.

13 Tokizane, p. 237.

14 Concerning Penfield's view, see the following books: TSUKADA Yūzō and YAMAKAWA Hiroshi, trans., *Nō to kokoro no shōtai* [*The Mystery of Mind*, Princeton, 1975] by W. Penfield (Tokyo: Bunka Hōsō Development Center, 1977); TAKAGI Sadataka, *Kioku no mekanizumu* [Mechanisms of memory] (Tokyo: Iwanami shoten, 1976); Ikemi, pp. 111ff.

15 Hirai, p. 224.

16 Tokizane, *No no hanashi* [Story of the brain] (Tokyo: Iwanani shoten, 1962), pp. 32ff.

17 SHIMOYAMA Tokuji and ŌNO Mitsuko, trans., *Toyo no eichi to seiō no shinri ryōhō* [*Indianfahrt eines Psychiaters*], by Medard Boss (Tokyo: Misuzu shobō, 1973), pp. 143ff.

Chapter 10: Eastern Meditation

1 Ikemi, p. 22.

2 The temporary conjunction system caused by the conditioned reflex is supposed to occur either through the nerves themselves or through the neural fluid connected with the endocrine gland. Russian researchers used to think that the conjunction occurs between the sensory center and the part of the brain related to the particular organ, both of which are in the cortex. Recent studies, however, suggest that the conditioned reflex mechanism might be located at the reticular system of the brain stem beneath the cortex.

3 Jung, *Psychologie und Alchemie*, in *Werke*, Bd. 12, S. 68.

4 Ibid., pp. 78–83.

5 Erich Fromm, D.T. Suzuki, and Richard DeMartino, *Zen Buddhism and Psychoanalysis* (N.Y.: Harper & Row, 1960), p. 85.

6 YUASA Yasuo, trans., *Yungo to seishin tōgō* [*Jung and Psychosynthesis*] by Robert Assagioli, *Shūkyō shinri kenkyū*, vol. 10 (Tokyo: Institute for Religious Psychology, 1968), pp. 81ff.

7 Cf. NAKAMURA Hajime, *Bukkyōgo daijiten* [Dictionary of Buddhist terms], 3 vols. (Tokyo: Tōkyō shoseki, 1975).

8 The basic text of Yoga is Patanjali's *Yoga Sutra*, which was written in about the fifth century A.D. See SAHODA Tsuruji, trans. and intro., *Yoga konpon kyōten* [Fundamental scriptures of yoga] (Tokyo: Hirakawa shuppan, 1973).

9   Ibid., p. 150.
10 Ibid., p. 162.
11 Ernest Wood, *Yoga Dictionary* (N.Y.: Philosophical Library, 1956), p. 124.
12 HAYASHI Takashi, *Jōken hansha* [Conditioned reflex] (Tokyo: Iwanami shoten, 1964), pp. 190ff.
13 Motoyama, p. 109. Also, there is an interesting report by a group of Indian medical doctors. They measured three yogis who claimed to be able to stop their heart beats. According to this report, although the ECG is normal during concentration, the sound of the pulse disappeared. Using Roentgen fluoroscopy, they observed the heart transformed into a tubular shape. They hypothesized that the blood flow thereby becomes extremely small, causing the sound of the pulse to disappear. See "Investigation on Yogis Claiming to Stop Their Heartbeats," *Indian Journal of Medical Research,* vol. 49, Jan. 1961, pp. 90–94). The author observed the same phenomenon at Dr. Motoyama's laboratory in Tokyo, when we measured an Indian yogi some years ago.
14 UONO Kimiyoshi, *Jiritsu shinkei shitchōshō* [Autonomic nervous imbalance] (Tokyo: Bunken shuppan, 1975), p. 119.
15 Jung, *Psychologic,* S. 542.
16 Sahoda, p. 193.
17 NAGAHAMA Yoshio, *Shinkyū no igaku* [Medicine of acupuncture], in *Sōgen igaku shinsho* (Osaka: Sōgensha, 1970), p. 159.
18 Jung, *Yoga and the West,* in *CW,* vol. 11, p. 535.
19 Cf. TAMAKI Kōshirō, *Nihon Bukkyō shisōron* [Japanese Buddhist thought], (Kyoto: Heirakuji shoten), vol. 1, chap. 1.
20 Cf. Jung, *Psychological Types,* in *CW,* vol. 6. Also see KAWAI Hayao, *Yungu shinrigaku nyūmon* [Introduction to Jung's psychology] (Tokyo: Baifūkan, 1967), chap. 3.
21 Jung, *The Tavistock Lectures* (1935), in *CW,* vol. 18, pp. 13ff.
22 Jung, *Psychologie und Alchemie,* S. 140.
23 Jung, *The Tavistock Lectures,* p. 138.
24 Jung, *Psychological Types,* p. 453, definition 35.
25 Jung, *Tavistock Lectures,* p. 15.
26 Miyoshi et al., trans., *Yume—sono gensonzai bunseki* [*Der Traum und seine Auslegung,* Hans Hüber, Bern, 1953] by Medard Boss (Tokyo: Misuzu shobō, 1970), chap. 15.
27 KAWAI Hayao et al., trans., *Yungu jiden* [*Memories, dreams, reflections,* ed. Aniela Jaffé, Pantheon Books, N.Y., 1963] by C. G. Jung (Tokyo: Misuzu shobo, 1972), vol. 1, p. 224. See also the letters of Jung and Freud in Appendix I (vol. 2).
28 Jung, *Synchronicity: An Acausal Connecting Principle,* in *CW,* vol. 8. Also see A. Jaffé, "C. G. Jung and Parapsychology," in *Science and ESP,* ed. Smythies (N.Y.: Kegan Paul, 1967).
29 J. B. Rhine and Pratt, *Parapsychology* (Springfield, Ill.: Charles C. Thomas, 1957).
30 MOTOYAMA Hiroshi, *Shūkyō to igaku* [Religion and medicine] (Tokyo: Institute for Religious Psychology, 1975); and *Shinshin sōkan ni kansuru igakushin-*

rigakuteki kenkyū [Medical-psychological study of the mind-body correlation], *Shūkyō Shinri Kenkyū,* vol. 5 (Tokyo: Institute for Religious Psychology, 1962).

31 Motoyama, "The Mechanism by Which Psi-Ability Manifests Itself," *Impact of Science on Society,* vol. 24, No. 4, 1974. Also see Motoyama's book in English, with Rande Brown: *Science and the Evolution of Consciousness: Chakra, Ki and Psi.*

32 Sahoda, pp. 94ff, 147, 188.

Conclusion to the English Edition

1 Edmund Husserl, *The Crisis of European Sciences and Transcendental Phenomenology* (Evanston, Ill.: Northwestern University Press, 1970), Part II.

2 Ludwig Wittgenstein, *Tractatus Logico-Philosophicus* (London: Routledge & Kegan Paul), 4.111.

3 Ibid., 5.1316, 6.36311ff.

4 Ernest Jones, ed. & abridged by Lionel Trilling and Steven Marcus, *The Life and Work of Sigmund Freud* (N.Y.: Basic Books Publishing Co., 1961), p. 191. Concerning Jones' following account, see pp. 466–467.

5 Jung, *Freud and Jung: A Contrast,* in *CW,* vol. 4, p. 338.

Index

Acting intuition, 50-52, 65-72, 178-79; in Dōgen, 122-23; physiology of, 199-201; in Zeami, 108-109. *See also* NISHIDA Kitarō

Anātman. See Self, Buddhist views of

Animal spirit, 193

Apodicticity, 64-65

ARAMAKI Noritoshi, 132

Artistry (*geidō*), 27, 99-109

Assagioli, Robert, 146-48

Augustine, Saint, 42-43

Basho, 22, 38*n*, 56-65, 122-23; and Dōgen, 122-23; and Kūkai, 155; and Nō, 108; self as, 57-58, 68-72, 199-201. *See also* NISHIDA Kitarō

Bergson, Henri, 162-167; and Merleau-Ponty, 168-69, 170; and Nishida, 21; and physiological psychology, 193-96

Betweenness, 38-41, 53

Body: as Buddha, 148-53, 156; habitual, 169-70; as motor-scheme, 162-67; as quasi-body, 220-23; *See also* Physiological psychology; medicine; Psychosomatic medicine

Body-Mind. *See* Mind-body

Boss, Medard, 76

Brain. *See* Physiological psychology

Buddhism, 85-97. *See also* Esoteric Buddhism; Tendai (T'ien-t'ai) Buddhism; Zen Buddhism

Bykov, K. M., 189-90

Cakra, 145-46

Cannon, W. B., 187-88

Canons, Buddhist. *See Kairitsu*

Cessation and discernment. *See Shikan*

Chien-chên, 96

Chih-i, 126-27

Chinese Medicine. *See* Medicine, Chinese

Christianity, 42-43, 98, 204. *See also* God

Chu Hsi, 79

Climates, Watsuji on, 46-47

Confucianism, 26, 92, 128-29

Cogito: bright, 43-44, 62, 122, 193; dark, 122, 193

Consciousness: bright and dark, 4-6, 60-63, 65, 223; ego, 61; in general, 59-61; self, 39-41

Contemplation, Christian, 98

Cultivation (*shugyō*), 7-8, 25-27, 85-98; physiology of, 212-14; and psychotherapy, 207-10. *See also* Discipline (*keiko*)

Demons, 215

DENGYŌ Daishi. *See* Saichō

Depth psychology. *See* Psychoanalysis

Descartes, 43-44, 192-93

Dharmakāya, as expounding *dharma*, 133

Dhāranī, 101-4

Dharmas, and self, 114-17

Discipline (*keiko*), 27, 100-109, 208

Doctrinal interpretation systems (*p'an-chiao*), 126-27

DŌGEN Kigen, 83, 90, 111-23; and Kūkai, 154-55; and Nishida, 122-23

Sokushinjōbutsu, 148–53, 156
Spatiality, 37–46, 162–63, 172–74
Spiritual cultivation. *See* Cultivation
Subject, *shukan* and *shutai* distinction in, 38*n*. *See also* Object
Supranormality (*Leben mehr als*), 92, 98, 200–201; and psychotherapy 208–210. *See also* Self, as *basho*
SUZUKI, D. T., 21, 73

Taiken. See Experience
TAMAKI Kōshirō, 116, 118–19, 133, 153
TANABE Hajime, 72
Tantra, 137
Taoism, 26, 221–22
Temporality, 39, 41–46, 163
Ten stages of mind. *See under* Kūkai
Tendai (T'ien-t'ai) Buddhism, 91, 94–95, 114, 126–27. *See also* Shikan
Thomas Aquinas, Saint, 66
Three mysteries, 150–51
Thrownness, 52–55, 175
Time. *See* Temporality
Transmigration, 135–36

Unconscious, 185–87. *See also* Psychoanalysis; *Cogito,* dark

Vajraśekhara Sūtra, 134–35
Vidyā-rāja, 137–43, 145–46
Vinaya. See Kairitsu

Waka, 99–104
Wang Yang-ming, 92
WATSUJI Tetsurō, 22–24, 37–48, 86, 93
Weber, Max, 87, 96
Will, 4, 9–11
Wittgenstein, Ludwig, 234–35

Yin and *yang. See* Medicine, Chinese
Yoga, 26, 145–46, 211–15, 219

Zazen. See Seated meditation
Zeami, 104–109
Zen Buddhism, 65, 203, 105–106; monastic rules in, 90–91; and Nishida, 73. *See also* DŌGEN Kigen; Seated meditation (*zazen*)
Zen sickness, 215